CLARENDON ARI[...]

General Editor: J. L. ACKRILL

CLARENDON ARISTOTLE SERIES

ARISTOTLE'S
METAPHYSICS

BOOKS *M* and *N*

Translated
with Introduction and Notes
by
JULIA ANNAS
Fellow of St. Hugh's College
Oxford

CLARENDON PRESS · OXFORD

Oxford University Press, Walton Street, Oxford OX2 6DP

Oxford New York Toronto
Delhi Bombay Calcutta Madras Karachi
Petaling Jaya Singapore Hong Kong Tokyo
Nairobi Dar es Salaam Cape Town
Melbourne Auckland

and associated companies in
Beirut Berlin Ibadan Nicosia

Oxford is a trade mark of Oxford University Press

Published in the United States
by Oxford University Press, New York

ISBN 0-19-872085-8
ISBN 0-19-872133-1 (pbk.)

Printed in Great Britain by
Biddles Ltd., Guildford and King's Lynn

PREFACE

I am very grateful to Professor J.L. Ackrill, the editor of this series, who read drafts of the book with great care and made many valuable suggestions. In particular he saved the translation from numerous infelicities and barbarisms. I owe him many thanks for our discussions, which not only resulted in a greatly improved book, but were most enjoyable and illuminating about various aspects of Aristotle's philosophy.

My interest in *M-N* arose out of my Harvard doctoral thesis on Aristotle's criticism of Plato's theory of number. I owe a great debt to my supervisor, Professor G.E.L. Owen, whose sharp and sensitive approach to Aristotle encouraged and greatly improved my own work.

I would also like to thank Jonathan Barnes, who read the typescript through and from whose suggestions I have greatly benefited. James Dybikowski made many helpful criticisms of one draft. Michael Morgan did his best to make me see Plato's side of the argument, especially over non-combinable units; he will probably feel that I am still too impressed by Aristotle's arguments. I also owe thanks for helpful comments and discussions to Richard Sorabji and Malcolm Schofield.

I am grateful to the President and Fellows of Harvard University for appointing me James C. Loeb Fellow in Classical Philosophy for the fall semester of 1972-3, and to my College for giving me special leave of absence to take up the appointment. During this time the book began to take shape, and I would like to thank Professor Owen for many stimulating discussions during that period.

Finally I would like to thank Graeme Segal for his patience and understanding, without which this book would never have been finished.

St. Hugh's College, Oxford   JULIA ANNAS
January 1975

CONTENTS

INTRODUCTION

Books *M* and *N* of the *Metaphysics* have had a bad press. They embarrass students of Plato because the ideas of Plato's that they discuss seem strange and are different from anything in the dialogues. They embarrass students of Aristotle because they argue so minutely about apparently baffling topics. These dissatisfactions are often combined in the complaint that the books are tedious and scholastic.

The only way to show that something is not boring is to arouse interest in it. This is the aim of the present work. I believe that *M-N* is not nearly as difficult and mysterious as is usually thought, and that it is not a pettifogging discussion of mystical nonsense, but an acute treatment of philosophically live problems.

M-N criticizes Plato and the Academy, and presents Aristotle's own views, on topics which we should now call part of the philosophy of mathematics and of logic. We find discussed theories such as that numbers are 'separate', 'non-sensible' entities, and that they have 'elements' or 'principles' which are more ultimate than they are and which in some way explain them. Clearly these ideas have some affinity with modern questions about the nature and status of mathematical entities. Do numbers exist? If they do, what sort of entities are they? Can number-terms be analysed into terms of logic alone, plus definitions, and, if so, in what sense is this a 'reduction' of number to something more ultimate? From *M-N* we can see that Plato and Aristotle were concerned with this type of question, both in its own right and as having a bearing on the theory of Forms.

Since the problems in *M-N* often have modern analogues, it is sometimes only when we approach Aristotle with an orientation from modern problems that the text becomes philosophically rewarding. In some cases we can say that Plato and Aristotle were struggling with the same problem as ours although we would formulate it very differently. But it should be remembered that these similarities exist at a fairly high level of generality. It is misleading to think of Aristotle as discussing less technical versions of present-day theories. The problems of Frege and Russell cannot be detached from a particular theory and its terminology and compared with a context as different

1

as *M-N*. In particular, both Plato and Aristotle have a theory of number that is irredeemably pre-Fregean in approach; despite the fact that Aristotle makes statements suggestively like some of Frege's, he completely lacks the precise notions necessary for a definition like Frege's. Further, drawing specious modern parallels can lead (and has led) to presenting Plato with highly technical theories without, or even against, good evidence. Hence, while I have made use of modern ideas to elucidate what is going on in *M-N*, I have tried to avoid tempting but unsound parallels and misleading comparisons in detail.

In *M-N* Aristotle discusses Plato's ideas at length, but he has in mind not the dialogues but teaching and discussion in the Academy. He is attacking theories with which his lecture audience was familiar, but which are no longer directly available to us. In order to understand what Aristotle is getting at in *M-N* it is therefore necessary to have some reconstruction of those of Plato's theories that are discussed in *M-N*. I shall now go on to present such a reconstruction, together with an account of Aristotle's own position and, more briefly, those of other Academy members. Any such attempt takes us into well-mined fields of speculation.[1] In the case of Plato and the Academy the problems are complicated by the fact that our chief source is Aristotle, who not only criticizes Plato but has to some extent recast Plato's thought in his own terms in so doing. This has led to blanket dismissal of Aristotle's reports as biased and worthless,[2] and also to underestimation of the importance of *M-N*; there has been surprisingly little serious attempt to examine Aristotle's own ideas and the basis of his criticism of Plato. It is clear from *M-N*, however, that there was lively controversy in the Academy

---

[1] Our evidence for the unwritten doctrines is fragmentary and confusing, and has formed the basis of contradictory and extreme theories. According to Cherniss ((1), (2)), Plato did not have systematic philosophical teaching in the Academy, but merely gave one unsuccessful lecture. According to recent German scholars, the unwritten doctrines are the true heart of Plato's philosophy, and the dialogues can only be fully understood as imperfect reflections of them. See Krämer (1), (2), (3), Gaiser (1), (2), Gadamer and Schadewaldt, Wippern; and cf. also Findlay.

[2] Cherniss's extreme position, that Aristotle's reports of 'unwritten doctrines' are simply misunderstood or polemical projections from the ideas in Plato's dialogues, has been attacked by Krämer, ch. 4 and Findlay, Appendix II.

on these topics and that Aristotle regards himself as having success-fully criticized Plato's philosophy of mathematics and replaced it with a better.

To introduce the reader to *M-N* I shall therefore compare and contrast Plato's and Aristotle's philosophies of number and of geometry. In both cases I shall begin from the written works that we do possess and show that in them we can find a consistent over-all position. The evidence from the 'unwritten' doctrines will be dis-cussed in the light of these positions.

It emerges that Plato and Aristotle hold systematically opposed views, and this is relevant to the next section, which discusses the Academy's theories of the foundations of mathematics. For we can evaluate Aristotle's criticisms better if we are aware of their grounds, and do not have to ascribe them to hostility or stupidity. This is important where we lack independent checks on Aristotle's reports about the Academy's theories of 'first principles'.

Even if the reader is unconvinced by my reconstruction, in general or in some details, he or she will at any rate have gained some idea of the topics which Aristotle presumed to be familiar to his hearers when he gave the lecture course which we now possess as *M-N*.

1. Plato's philosophy of mathematics

A. Number[3]

The dialogues

It is clear from the dialogues, though nowhere explicitly stated in them, that Plato is a platonist in the sense current in the philosophy of mathematics. (To avoid confusion I shall use 'platonism' for this position, and 'Platonism' for the actual views of Plato and his follow-ers.) In modern philosophy of mathematics platonism is usually taken to be a type of realism, amounting to the belief that mathe-matical objects such as numbers literally exist, independent of us and our thoughts about them.[4] Numbers are not, of course, in the

---

[3] In treating number first and more fully compared with geometry I am reversing the usual emphasis; the justification of this can only be the plausi-bility of my account as a whole.

[4] Cf. Quine (1), the end of 'On What there Is'. Frege is the clearest and most forceful defender of modern platonism. Cf. also Russell's early works, and P. Bernays, 'On Platonism in Mathematics', in Benacerraf and Putnam.

world around us; they do not exist in space and time. But they exist none the less; they are there to be discovered before we think of the means of describing them. Russell in an early essay of 1901 says, 'Arithmetic must be discovered in just the same sense in which Columbus discovered the West Indians, and we no more create numbers than he created the Indians . . .'

Modern mathematical platonism is usually expressed as a theory about the truth of mathematical propositions. Plato, however, is more concerned about the existence of mathematical objects. There are two kinds of reason for this. Firstly, there is the somewhat naive conception of the subject-matter of mathematics which Plato shared with his contemporaries. As Lasserre puts it (pp.12-13), 'Mathematics has been regarded as the science of the relations uniting certain so-called "mathematical entities" '; he calls this a 'conception inherited from antiquity' and says also (p. 45), 'Whereas modern arithmetic has developed above all the art of computation . . . ancient arithmeticians set out to "know numbers".' The second reason why platonism appears in Plato as a belief in the existence of certain entities is his tendency, from which he never fully emancipates himself, to assimilate all knowledge to the model of knowledge by acquaintance, a relation between knowing subject and known object.

In the dialogues Plato sometimes uses idioms suggesting that when we know about numbers this is because the numbers are things that are there already to be known about (*Theaetetus* 198a-b, cf. *Alcibiades* I, 126c) and in two passages he makes an interesting contrast. There is on the one hand knowledge of numbers of physical objects, which are themselves spoken of as physical numbers (this shows that Plato's conception of a *number* does not distinguish it sharply from a *numbered group*, and this is worth remembering when we come to the more ambitious developments). But there is also knowledge of a different kind of number, not physical numbers but 'the numbers themselves', grasped by thought alone 'in the intellect'. These are numbers conceived platonistically: they are separate from the things we count, they exist and are accessible to our reason. (*Republic* 525c-d, *Theaetetus* 195d—196b. *Epinomis* 990c6 is not by Plato but clearly derives from him in thought and expression.) Plato's emphasis that these numbers are 'in the intellect'

4

is not a claim that numbers are creatures of our thought, rather the reverse. His point is like Frege's ((1), 115e): 'in arithmetic we are . . . concerned . . . with the objects given directly to our reason and, as its nearest kin, utterly transparent to it. And yet, or rather for that reason, these objects are not subjective fantasies. There is nothing more objective than the laws of arithmetic.'

At *Euthydemus* 290b-c platonism could be said to surface. There it is said that 'geometers and astronomers and calculators' contrast with philosophers in the way quail-hunters contrast with cooks: the former make real catches or discoveries and are not merely concerned with their diagrams, but they can make no good use of them and have to hand them over. Since this is the nearest that Plato gets to explicitness, it is possible that Aristotle has this passage in mind when he discusses platonism in *M-N* at 1077^{b}30 ff. and 1078^{a}28 ff. But the remark is rather a throw-away one in its context, and gives no substance to Plato's platonism.

In the dialogues, then, there is no explicit commitment to a platonist theory of number, but there is evidence that Plato found it natural to think of numbers platonistically. At *Sophist* 238a10-11 the Eleatic Stranger says in the course of an argument, 'Well, we take all number, at any rate, to be among the things that exist', and this elicits the comment, 'Yes, indeed, if anything is to be taken to exist.' To Plato it is just obvious that numbers exist. Moreover, if we consider his metaphysics in general, we have every reason to believe that he would not have rejected, but on the contrary would have welcomed, an explicit formulation of this readiness to accept the existence of abstract objects.

Further aspects of Plato's implicit platonism are indicated in the dialogues, though unemphatically. One is the way he draws the distinctions between two kinds of study of numbers, *arithmētikē* and *logistikē*.

Traditionally, the distinction between *arithmētikē* and *logistikē* in Plato has been thought to be that between on the one hand theoretical study of number (or arithmetic) and on the other hand practical calculation. This view is widespread, indeed the standard account. It is mistaken, however, for it has been conclusively shown by Klein and de Strycker that the opposition is not that of studying pure numbers versus ready reckoning, but that of counting versus calculating. *Logistikē* is certainly to be rendered as 'calculating'; *arithmētikē* can mean 'arithmetic', but is etymologically close to the words for 'number' and 'counting'.[5]

Counting and calculating do not look like generically different activities; there are numerous passages where Plato casually conflates them[6] and one (*Theaetetus* 204b-c) where he makes the natural assumption that they presuppose each other. (He never considers the possibilities of counting groups separately without being able to calculate, or of calculating formalistically without being able to count.) These are all, however, passages where Plato is *using* the notions of counting and calculating, and making natural assumptions about them. He does make an interesting distinction in passages where he is talking *about* them, *Gorgias* 451a-c with 453e, and *Philebus* 56d–57a with 57d-e.

In the *Gorgias* passage *arithmētikē* and *logistikē* are distinguished by their subject-matter. That of the former is 'the even and the odd, how much they happen to be in each case'. The latter studies not only how much each happens to be but their relations to one another. Klein points out (pp. 18 ff.) that the distinction made here is that between studying numbers, and studying numbers and their possible interrelations, and that this distinction holds not only on a practical but also on a theoretical level (where it was taken up and developed by the Neoplatonists).

The distinction between theoretical and practical levels is itself made in the *Philebus* passage at 56d:

Arithmetic is of two kinds, one of which is popular, and the other philosophical.

How would you distinguish between them?

There is a wide difference between them, Protarchus; some arithmeticians reckon unequal units; as for example, two armies or two oxen, two very large things or two very small things. The party who are opposed to them insist that every unit in ten thousand must

---

[5] Klein, pp. 18-19. 'Number' is *arithmos*, 'to count', *arithmein*. (But *arithmētikē* can mean 'arithmetic', and *arithmētikos* always means 'arithmetician'.)

[6] *Hippias Minor* 366-8, *Hippias Major* 285b-c, *Protagoras* 356e-357a, *Euthyphro* 7b-c, *Phaedrus* 274c-d, *Republic* 522c, 522e, 525a, 603a, *Laws* 817e, *Politicus* 259e. Cf. Klein, p. 39.

be the same as every other unit.

Undoubtedly there is, as you say, a great difference among the votaries of the science; and there may be reasonably supposed to be two sorts of arithmetic. (Jowett's translation)

The same is said to hold for *logistikē* and for *metrētikē* (the art of measuring), and at 57d-e Plato emphasizes the gulf between the 'two arithmetics and measurings and the rest', saying that they share a common name and nothing else. He spells out the difference only in the case of *arithmētikē*, but the others are clearly meant to be parallel to it.

Thus Plato is committed to a distinction between theoretical *arithmētikē* and theoretical *logistikē*: knowing how to count numbers, knowing what numbers are, is taken to be different from knowing the various relationships numbers stand in, the ways in which they are related by addition, multiplication, and so on. Plato is thus put firmly on one side of a controversy in the philosophy of mathematics. One side maintains, with Quine ((2), pp. 44-5), that 'arithmetic . . . is all there is to number: there is no saying absolutely what the numbers are; there is only arithmetic.' What could there be to knowing what numbers are, other than knowing what can be done with numbers, knowing the laws of arithmetic? The other side (cf. Russell ch. 1) maintains that knowing what numbers are *is* distinct from knowing how they can be manipulated; otherwise our ability to count would be unexplained. Plato, for whom platonism is a matter of the existence of certain objects, sees this distinction as being between numbers themselves on the one hand and their interrelations on the other. This suggests that numbers as the objects of *arithmētikē* can be identified independently of arithmetic; and this seems to have no possible basis but a platonist picture of numbers as already 'given' independent of our activities. Plato is prepared to accept this, and the consequence that there will be a study of numbers that is not arithmetic.

The *Philebus* passage shows how Plato thinks of units. His argument reveals a confusion which recurs in ever more sophisticated form in his later elaborations of the idea. He argues: the plain man thinks that a pair of shoes, for example, is two, each shoe being a one or unit. But there are two ways in which this is unsatisfactory (it is not clear which the *Philebus* indicates). Two objects can be brought under the same unit-concept to be counted and be very dissimilar in size, say. And one can count a pair of things that come under different unit-concepts, e.g. one ox and one army. In both these ways the plain man's units are very heterogeneous. The philosopher is to insist that when he counts a two, what he counts is just two, two units that are exactly the same and not dissimilar in any way at all. His unit, what he counts as one, is to be just one, not divisible in any way at all. This is said at *Republic* 525 and still insisted on in the later *Sophist* at 245a-b.

Plato's move here is significant in two ways. Firstly, it assimilates intransitive counting to transitive,[7] the reciting of the numeral-sequence to the use of numerals to measure sets. The way it is done reveals platonist assumptions: if one sort of counting is unsatisfactory, this must be because its subject-matter is unsatisfactory, and so a satisfactory type of counting is ensured by manufacturing a satisfactory type of subject-matter for it. No account is taken of the peculiar nature of this subject-matter, pure units, until trouble turns up later. Secondly, Plato takes it as obvious that a number is a number *of* something; the plain man's number is a number of shoes, so the philosopher's number must be a number of pure units. Once more it seems that numbers are not being distinguished carefully enough from numbered groups.

Plato is not very informative in the dialogues about what he takes to be the possible extension of 'number', but it is interesting that he frequently uses 'even and odd' interchangeably with 'number'.[8] At *Politicus* 262d-e he recommends division into even and odd as the appropriate way to divide number. There are also two passages[9] where the treatment of even and odd may foreshadow later developments.

---

[7] In intransitive counting ('one', 'two' . . .) we are reciting the numeral sequence, for whatever reason; in transitive counting ('one potato, two potatoes . . .') we are using numerals to measure sets. Cf. Ellis, p. 154, and Benacerraf. Aristotle's theory of number emphasizes the notion of this kind of measuring.

[8] e.g. *Charmides* 166a, *Protagoras* 356-7, *Gorgias* 451 and 453. (But cf. *Theaetetus* 185c-d where 'one and the rest of number' is mentioned separately from 'even and odd'.)

[9] *Euthyphro* 12d (cf. de Strycker.) Even and odd are characterized as isoceles and scalene. This is defective as a division into even and odd number (cf.

This attitude to even and odd has the (seldom noticed) consequence that 'number' for Plato seems naturally to have the force of 'natural number', what Frege called *Anzahl*—or, to be more precise, 'positive whole number' (excluding 0 and with unclarity over 1). This is important, for it is commonly assumed that Plato's concept of number marks a revolutionary breakthrough in being extensible beyond the natural numbers to cover rational and real numbers. For some scholars this is almost a *datum*, yet it rests on no evidence in Plato. It is rendered unlikely by Plato's use of 'even and odd' for 'numbers', and by his confusion of number and numbered group. (It is rendered even more unlikely by much of the 'unwritten doctrines'.) All the evidence in Plato's writings suggests that for Plato number meant *Anzahl*, the answer to the question, 'How many?' The only apparent exception is *Epinomis* 990d-e, a famous passage where the author says that what is 'absurdly' called geometry is really a means of studying in plane figures the assimilation of numbers which are themselves dissimilar. This is clearly a reference to the geometrical representation of incommensurable relations which cannot be expressed in whole numbers, and the passage has been hailed as a claim that 'number' can properly cover not only whole numbers but irrational numbers. But even if this is in fact the upshot of the passage, as is not certain,[10] it cannot count against the evidence of the dialogues, since even in antiquity the *Epinomis* was thought not to be by Plato.

Many scholars have none the less claimed that Plato's conception of number is 'geometrical', and that it was explicitly designed to cover rational and real numbers as well as integers. This claim is not evidentially based and is essentially *a priori*: since Plato was inter-

---

Heath (1), vol.i, p. 292). The terms have a wider application than to number (cf. *Laws* 895e) but are not derived from a geometrical use (cf. de Strycker). At *Phaedo* 103-5 the confusion of 'one' with 'unit' is interesting (see below); most translators shift from 'unity' as a translation of *monas* at 101c to 'a unit' at 103-4.

[10] Wedberg (pp. 24-5) explains it without including irrationals as properly being numbers. 'Two numbers, say a and b, are "similar" if a is a product $a'.a''$ and b a product $b'.b''$ and $a'/a'' = b'/b''$. In this sense, e.g., the numbers 1 and 2 are "in themselves dissimilar". But they can be "assimilated by reference to surfaces" in the sense that there exist two similar surfaces, e.g. squares, whose volumes are related as 1 to 2.'

ested in the geometry of his time, he must have been aware of the significance of his friend Theaetetus' work on degrees of irrationality, to which there is a reference in the *Theaetetus*.[11] In fact, however, it follows neither that Plato had a geometrical conception of number not that he should have had. (Even in the *Theaetetus* passage 'number' applies only to positive integers.) Too often conclusions about Plato's concept of number have been drawn from premises concerning geometry, on the grounds that he did not radically separate the two, which begs the question at issue. Plato's conception of number in the dialogues owes nothing to geometry.

A large element in the desire to ascribe a geometrical concept of number to Plato is the conviction that it is more 'advanced' than an arithmetical one; but this is not clearly true, as is pointed out by Frege.[12] Even if a geometrical concept of number can avoid the circularity of defining identity of ratios, etc. between lengths in terms of equimultiples, the exercise would still be futile: 'we should still remain in doubt as to how the number defined geometrically . . . is related to the number of ordinary life, which would then be entirely cut off from science. Yet surely we are entitled to demand of arithmetic that its numbers should be adapted for use in every application made of number.' Moreover, a geometrical concept will not suffice for arithmetic: it is not adequate for, e.g., the number of roots of an equation, whereas counting number or *Anzahl* 'can answer among other things how many units are contained in a length'.

Any *a priori* grounds for attributing the geometrical concept to Plato are not, then, adequate to outweigh the lack of evidential support. This is important, since it affects interpretation of the

[11] Cf. Milhaud (1), p. 362. Several of the passages in Gaiser's *testimonia* show that Plato was interested in mathematical problems, but there is no evidence that he had any special mathematical competence (see Cherniss (4)).

[12] Frege (1), §19. (Frege later went back on this, but not for reasons relevant to the present discussion.) He also points out that although the concept is wider than and includes the integers, it presupposes magnitude and relation in respect of magnitude. This would be a serious problem for Plato, for whom (as we shall see) numbers were importantly prior to, and presupposed by, magnitudes. (This is pointed out by Ilting (1); it is not enough to say, as does Gaiser ((1), 2nd ed. p. 580), that the problem is merely one of exposition.)

'unwritten doctrines' about number.

Plato is not, in fact, any further away from the ordinary Greek concept of number than Aristotle, though they are often sharply contrasted in this respect by scholars. This is illustrated by the way that they both have the same problem over 1. Is 1 a number? If number is thought of as *Anzahl* there is a temptation to say no, since 1 does not measure any plurality. (*Arithmos*, number, and *arithmein*, to count, seem to have a closer conceptual tie than the English words to the ability to give the tale of a given group, i.e. plurality). But on the other hand we do *use* 1 as a number, along with 2, 3, and the rest. Plato reflects this indecision. Sometimes he writes as though the first number were 1, sometimes as though it were 2. 1 is the first number at *Laws* 818c and *Sophist* 238b, whereas *Republic* 524d talks of 'number and one', and at *Phaedo* 103-5 1 is apparently not part of the number series but its basis.[13]

On the other hand, we shall find that in his explicit theory of number Plato does bring out what is latent in the everyday Greek concept, namely that number measures plurality and that the first number is 2. Both Plato and Aristotle in their theories (though not their usage) make 1 not a number but the basis or origin of number; their attempts are, of course, very different.

We can thus see that Plato is a platonist about numbers from some indications in the dialogues, mainly a readiness to use certain suggestive idioms and to accept lines of thought with platonist presuppositions. But it could be claimed that there is a more direct proof; for Plato is a realist about the existence of Forms independently of us and of our spatio-temporal world, and there seems to be evidence at *Phaedo* 103-6 that Plato accepted numbers as Forms. And Aristotle says twice[14] that for Plato numbers were Forms.

This is too swift, however. It ignores the problem of 'intermediates', which we will shortly come to. Further, it can be questioned whether

[13] The author of the *Epinomis* is even worse; at 977c he speaks of number as going, '2, 3 . . .' but a few pages later at 978b-c we find that counting goes, '1, 2, 3 . . .'

[14] 1090ª4-6; frag. 4 (Ross) of *On the Forms*.

the *Phaedo* passage in question is dealing with Forms.[15] The position can be supported by claiming that Plato recognized a Form for every general term, so that numbers would automatically come in; but Plato does not consistently subscribe to this as a Form-producing principle.[16] All we can say is that Plato did not regard number-terms as differing significantly in their logic from other general terms; this is shown by passages like *Theaetetus* 185c-d, *Republic* 523d ff., and the whole second half of the *Parmenides*. We are not entitled to bring in the theory of Forms as ontological backing for numbers.

Even the above more modest claim has been threatened by some interpretations of *Hippias Major* 301d–302b. Hippias there maintains that if each of two things has a certain property then they must both have it, and vice versa. Socrates refutes this by pointing out that they are each one, but as a pair not one but two; and that while together they are two, they are not both two, for each is one. It is tempting to take this as an anticipation of Frege's point that, 'whereas we can combine "Solon was wise" and "Thales was wise" into "Solon and Thales were wise", we cannot say "Solon and Thales were one"' ((1), 40e). But Plato is merely refuting Hippias' fatuous claim, and this is not his only example; he is not making a point about number in particular.[17] It does not justify us in the idea that Plato was aware that numbers are not at all like properties of things, and that a proper theory of number must recognize this, as Frege points out. In the dialogues, Plato appears as fairly naive and unreflecting about the logic of number-terms. At *Phaedo* 101 things are said to 'participate' in Oneness and Twoness in exactly the way in

[15] If this passage is about Forms, it overdraws considerably on the arguments for Forms earlier in the dialogue, as well as producing undesirable Forms like Death and Soul (yet Forms are said to be like souls). Cf. Owen (2), p. 112 n. 2, Nehamas, 'Predication and Forms of Opposites in the *Phaedo*' *Review of Metaphysics* 1973.

[16] *Republic* 596a seems to presuppose some such principle, but if so it is at any rate repudiated at *Politicus* 262-3. Many of Plato's arguments for Forms (e.g. *Republic* 523-5) are restricted to certain types of predicate; and if Plato had relied on this principle there could not have been the subsequent unclarity over which terms did and did not stand for Forms (*Parmenides* 130-1, *On the Forms* fr. 3 Ross).

[17] Plato at once adds an example using a geometrical term *arrhētos* (irrational), so the point of the passage cannot be one concerning number in particular.

which they elsewhere participate in any ϕness, where ϕ is a Form. Further, an argument at *Theaetetus* 204d-e shows that Plato learnt no Fregean lessons from the *Hippias Major* passage; for the argument in the *Theaetetus* involves the assumption that the number of a set of things is no different from the collection of all the things in the set.

Plato, then, says nothing that openly commits him either to asserting or to denying that numbers are Forms. He appears as prepared to think of numbers as genuine but non-perceptible existents, and he is at any rate half-way prepared to think of them as Forms.

The unwritten doctrines

The reports of Plato's 'unwritten doctrines' about number show clearly that the position of the dialogues underwent considerable development. (For present purposes it does not matter whether this took place after the writing of the dialogues or as a background to them.) The most important change is that according to Aristotle Plato recognized *two* kinds of number as having real mind-independent existence—Form numbers and intermediate numbers. These require separate consideration.

(a) *The Form numbers*   As we have seen, while Plato does not say that numbers are Forms, he expresses the relation between a 'pure' number and its instances in terms of 'participation', the relation between a Form and its instances (*Phaedo* 101). This suggests that a number is thought of as a numerical property, and that what earthly pairs participate in is Twoness. But the question, 'What does "two" stand for?' is more likely to be answered by mentioning not a property but an object, the number two, in Frege's words 'a definite and unique object of scientific study'. And in the *Phaedo* passage the Greek words for 'twoness' and 'threeness' are used interchangeably with those for 'two' and 'three'. In the dialogues Plato shows no awareness that these are very different ways of regarding numbers. But there is a tension between them, and it leads Plato into an elaborately misguided theory.

This tension can arise quite naturally when we consider number-terms, apart from the theory of Forms. But it arises with peculiar force because of a problem proprietary to Forms, one which surfaces in the problems of *Parmenides* part 1. Plato often tends to think of Forms in such a way that a Form can be taken to be both a characteristic and a perfect example of that characteristic. The Form of Beauty in the *Symposium*, for example, seems to be both what makes all beautiful things beautiful, and also itself a supremely beautiful object. The conflation of 'twoness' and 'two' suggests that the number two was similarly taken by Plato to be not only the property characteristic of all pairs but as being itself a perfect pair.[18] Here the tendency to think of Forms as standards plays a part: Twoness would be thought of as being also the paradigm set of two things for counting.[19] This way of taking the Form numbers is also supported by a natural way of thinking about numbers, mentioned by Wedberg (p. 83):

'The definition of the number N as a certain designated set containing N elements is a reasonable alternative to a definition which makes the number N a property predicable of any set containing N elements . . . . A definition that identifies the numbers with such sets also seems to do perfect justice to the use of numbers in statements such as, 'Socrates and Gorgias are 2 men'. Instead of interpreting this statement as meaning: 'The set whose elements are the men Socrates and Gorgias has the property 2', we may understand it to signify: 'The set whose elements are the men Socrates and Gorgias can be correlated one-to-one with the set which is the number 2'. Numbers thus come to be thought of rather like canonized sets which function like the Standard Yard.

But with numbers we get a consequence which we do not get with other Forms—we have to answer the question, 'What is the number 2 a standard set *of*?' *What* is being correlated one-to-one with Socrates and Gorgias?

The answer is, 'units'. We have seen that the *Philebus* already

---

[18] Cf. some remarks by Gödel (in Benacerraf and Putnam: '. . . the following definition of the number two: "Two is the notion under which fall all pairs and nothing else." . . . "There is certainly more than one notion in the constructivist sense satisfying this condition, but there might be one common 'form' or 'nature' of all pairs.'

[19] Cf. Ellis, p. 156: 'It is conceivable that we should use groups of stones or marbles as numerical standards, and that they should be kept in special museums to protect them from destruction. All number determination would then be done by matching the group whose number is to be determined with one of the standards.'

contains the requisite notion of units as the pure items that pure numbers are numbers of, by comparison with the objects that 'physical numbers' are numbers of. In earlier works Plato does not seem to have distinguished carefully between *one* and *unit*: they are confused in the *Phaedo*, and at *Republic* 525-6 Plato in talking about 'one' shifts disconcertingly between singular and plural. But in the *Philebus* Plato is equipped with a (perhaps new) word for 'unit', and they appear, in the plural, as the satisfactory things we count when we count pure numbers.

This concept of numbers as paradigmatic sets of pure units is referred to by Aristotle as *monadikos arithmos*,[20] and he ascribes it both to Plato and to other members of the Academy, who had a similar and similarly platonist theory of number, differing only in not taking numbers to be Forms. Plato took Form numbers to be *monadikoi arithmoi*, but, as we have seen, it is possible to come to the concept of *monadikos arithmos* independently of the theory of Forms.

The reader should be warned at this point that it is somewhat heterodox to hold that this *was* in fact Plato's conception of number. The traditional view, still widely held, is that Plato's concept of number was not that of discrete units making up an arithmetical number (i.e. number as used in counting), but rather a geometrical concept of ratios between magnitudes or distances, and that this was not tied to counting, but was capable of extension to cover rational and irrational numbers. As I have said, I think that there is no good evidence that Plato held this view, and good evidence that he did not. The non-Aristotelian evidence will be considered in due course, in the section on the foundations of mathematics; here I shall just say that I do not think it is at all adequate to support a 'geometrical interpretation' when set against the counter-indications in Plato, and the fact that Aristotle in *M-N* consistently and specifically attacks

---

[20] 1092^{b}20, where units are contrasted with things counted; 1080^{b}19, 1080^{b}30, 1083^{b}17, all concerned with the Pythagoreans, where Aristotle claims that their numbers are not *monadikoi* because their units have magnitude; *Nicomachean Ethics* 1131^{a}30 ff.; *de Anima* 409^{a}20, where Xenocrates' muddle of units and points is called a 'unit-point', *stigmē monadikē*, a kind of category mistake. *Monadikos arithmos* thus clearly means 'number made up of abstract units', not just of units.

the arithmetical conception as being Plato's. To hold that Plato did not have such an arithmetical conception of number, one must also hold that all Aristotle's criticisms are either massively misguided or completely unfair, gratuitously presenting Plato with a position totally unlike any of his actual views, merely in order to refute it. This has been maintained, but any plausibility it might have can hardly survive a serious reading of the arguments in *M-N*. They are detailed, technical, patient, and incisive; it is not likely that the person capable of producing them either stupidly aimed them all at the wrong theory, or indulged in the pointless (and easily detectable) ruse of falsely attributing to Plato the position they did refute. Scholars have thought Aristotle capable of one or other of these, because often they have thought him incompetent at mathematics and therefore incapable of intelligent thought about mathematics, but there are no good grounds for this.

Aristotle has several arguments of a general nature against Plato's conception of Form numbers, most of them in *M-N*. He argues that this conception raises problems with the Platonist account of the derivation of numbers (1083^b23-36, 1085^b4-34); that it produces absurdities given the way we naturally think of numbers and of units (1084^a21-5); and that it rests on a confusion about the logic of 'one' ($1084^b2-1085^a7$). But he also attacks the idea at its roots. There is a passage in *A* 9 which there is good reason to believe was replaced by *M-N* as a whole.[21] Among the arguments there, five concern units,[22] and of these two are very important, in spite of their brief and elliptical nature. At $991^b31-992^a1$ Aristotle remarks that, 'the units in two must each come from a prior two; but this is impossible'.[23] And the next sentence asks, 'Why is a number, when taken all together, one?' In combination, these arguments present Plato, for whom numbers are unique Forms, with a real difficulty. If *any*

[21] See section 4. The *M* arguments about combinable units are much more developed than those in *A* 9, so much so that the passage in *A* 9 (991^b23-6) is usually interpreted in the light of *M*.

[22] 991^b21-7; $991^b31-992^a1$; 992^a1-2; 992^a2-10; 992^b9-13.

[23] Commentators assume here that the 'prior two' must be a reference to the indefinite two, which produces numbers (see section 3). But there is nothing in the context to make this likely, and Aristotle does not usually miss out the important qualification 'indefinite' unless the context makes it quite clear that it is to be understood.

two units could make up the number two, then there would be many twos and not just one. If the number two is to be unique, it must be made up of units that make up *two* and only that number. On the other hand, we cannot elucidate the nature of two by saying that it is made up of *two* units, or that it is a perfect *pair*. For, as the first argument indicates, there is a circularity in saying that two is made up of two units. We find here the same vicious circularity that threatens, in the Third Man argument (*Parmenides* 132a-b, 132d—133a), Forms conceived of as paradigms, a Form being both a characteristic and a perfect instance of that characteristic. If two is *both* Twoness *and* a perfect pair, then we need another Twoness, by participating in which the first two is a pair; but if *this* Twoness is also a pair, we have an infinite regress. Further, Aristotle has already (991^{b}26) pointed out that the difference between the units cannot be a qualitative one; units have no qualities.

In these brief remarks all the moves are made that are necessary for a refutation of Plato's concept of Form numbers as sets of units. The 'pure' units cannot after all be undifferentiated, since then the numbers would no longer be unique; but no intelligible account can be given of how they differ. They cannot be qualitatively different; but they cannot differ in *number*, or we get an infinite regress. (Admittedly Aristotle does not say this explicitly, but it is hard to see why it is impossible for two to come from a prior two, unless two is unique; and this would give an argument parallel in structure to the Third Man.)

It is my hypothesis that it was to meet this challenge that Plato developed a theory of units that are 'combinable' (*sumblētoi*). The evidence for ascribing this theory to Plato is all indirect; it is the theory that has to be understood as the target of Aristotle's criticisms in a long, elaborate, and brilliant section of *M* (1080^{a}11—1083^{b}23). The traditional view which takes Aristotle's criticisms to be basically beside the point has given no adequate account of this passage.

'Combinability' will be explained in more detail in the notes to that passage, but the main point will be sketched here. Units are combinable in a number if they can be 'combined' or grouped to make up that number and no other. The units in 2, for example, are differentiated by the fact that they cannot be combined together to make up any other number. The notion of (non-)combinability seems to have been transferred to the units in Form numbers from the Form numbers themselves. Form numbers are not combinable in two ways. They cannot be added (or have other mathematical operations performed on them), since there is only one of each, so that '2 × 2 = 4' cannot make reference to the Form number 2. And each is unique of its kind, so that each number is specifically different, and they are not items of the same kind. The second point is what Aristotle means when he says that the Platonists recognized no Form of number.[24] Numbers are not instances of any common kind: being a number is not some common property shared by all numbers, but is constituted by membership in the number-series. Thus for Plato Form numbers are specifically different (this being a fact about the number-series and not about Forms as such) as well as not being addible. So for the Form numbers non-combinability comes down to non-addibility and difference in kind. This feature is transferred by Plato from the Form numbers to the units in them in an attempt to avoid the problem which Aristotle points out as being latent in a conception of numbers as sets of units and at the same time unique Forms.

Another problem is also met, namely that of making Forms compound. Plato often stresses the simple and indivisible nature of Forms, and even in his later dialogues calls them 'ones' or 'units' (*Philebus* 15a-b). Yet surely if a Form number is made up of units its own unity is thereby destroyed? The theory of combinable units offers a way out here. The 'combinable' units in a Form number are not to be thought of as independently characterizable as so many units into which the number might be divided; so the unity of the number is not threatened.

We have this theory only in Aristotle's criticism of it, and this is in some ways unfortunate, since, as is brought out in the notes on the passage, it is not certain whether Aristotle is quite consistent in his understanding of what it is for units, as opposed to numbers,

---

[24] 999a6-10; 1080b11, 1086a11; *Nicomachean Ethics* 1096a17. Cf. Cherniss (1), Appendix 6. Cf. Frege (1), p. 15e: there are no properties common to all numbers which they possess already, without having to be proved common (this of course being useless to a platonist).

to be combinable or non-combinable. But it is certain that Aristotle's arguments demolish the theory beyond hope of resuscitation by re-formulation, and that the original problem re-emerges. The fact that Plato's ideas did not pass into the philosophical tradition is no doubt due to this effective refutation.

(b) *The intermediates* According to Aristotle, Plato believed in two sorts of numbers, Form numbers and intermediates. There has been vehement controversy and considerable literature on the problem of whether Plato did or did not believe in intermediates.[25] Aristotle's statements on the one hand are matched against the evidence of the dialogues on the other, and the two are often held to conflict. Their relationship, however, seems to be more subtle.

Aristotle often says quite unmistakably that Plato accepted intermediate numbers distinct both from Forms and from physical objects.[26] The majority of his references are not very helpful as to the nature of the intermediates, but in two passages (991^a4, 1028^b 18-21) he calls them 'many but eternal', and at 987^b14-18 gives his fullest account of them: 'Further, besides sensible things and Forms, [Plato] says that there are the objects of mathematics, which occupy an intermediate position, differing from sensible things in being eternal and unchangeable, from Forms in that there are many alike, while the Form itself is in each case unique.' Intermediates are thought of as 'between' Forms and physical objects, because they share some of the properties of both sets of items.

The line of thought Aristotle presents here is very simple (and the present exposition lays no claim to novelty). Each Form number is unique of its kind. There is only one Form number 2. But what are arithmetical statements, like '$2 + 2 = 4$' true of? Not Forms. But not physical objects either, for they are not held to be true or false in virtue of facts about physical objects. So it looks as though these statements are about a third kind of number: mathematical number

---

[25] I argue fully the view sketched here in 'On the intermediates', *Archiv für Geschichte der Philosophie* 1975.

[26] Plato is mentioned by name at 987^b14-18, 1028^b18-21. Cf. 987^b16, $^b29$, 991^b29, 992^b16, 995^b17, 997^b2, $^b13$, 998^a7, 1002^b13, $^b21$, 1059^b6, 1077^a11, 1090^b35.

or the number we do mathematics with. The intermediates are regarded by Aristotle as Plato's answer to what we might call the 'Uniqueness Problem': arithmetical statements do not describe the world around us, but they cannot be about Forms either, each Form being unique of its kind.

Aristotle frequently criticizes the attempt to introduce intermediates as a third set of objects, like Forms and physical objects but distinct from both. Many of these criticisms occur in *M-N*. Aristotle objects to the ontological extravagance involved (1090^a 2-15, $^b31$ ff.); to the assumption that the truth of arithmetical statements requires the existence of distinct objects for them to be true of (1077^a9-14); and to the conflict with Plato's own theory of the derivation of numbers (1090^b32–1091^a5).

Do Aristotle's reports and criticisms refer to an idea that Plato actually held? Many attempts have been made to discover the intermediates in the dialogues, the most thorough being Wedberg's (Appendix D). None of the purported references in the dialogues, however, touch on what Aristotle sees as being the point of intermediates. There are many odd mentions of number which could if pressed fit the intermediates, but which are quite unspecific. *Phaedo* 101b-d, *Theaetetus* 198a-d, and *Cratylus* 432a-b all distinguish pure numbers from numbers of objects, and these numbers, although separate from physical objects, have features that cannot be true of Form numbers, like availability for computations. But there is nothing to suggest that Plato has explicitly thought about and accepted intermediates; the impression is rather that Plato has not yet reflected on the points that were to lead him to distinguish two sorts of pure numbers.

There are only two passages in the dialogues where we seem to have an explicit argument for intermediates, *Republic* 509d–511a and *Philebus* 56c–59d (with 61d–62b). But in neither passage is there any recognition of the Uniqueness Problem. The *Republic* passage is concerned with distinguishing stages of intellectual achievement, and it can be so read as to distinguish two stages by different subject-matter, intermediates and Forms, though the interpretation is not forced on us by the text. The *Philebus* passage tries to deal with the supposedly unsatisfactory nature of everyday counting.

Neither of them is recognizably about Aristotle's concern. Further, the concept of pure numbers as sets of units was accepted not only by Plato but by Speusippus, who rejected Forms and so could not have thought of this *Philebus* argument as a sufficient argument for items intermediate between Forms and physical things.

We find, then, that Aristotle assumes that the intermediates are presented as a solution to the Uniqueness Problem, whereas this line of thought does not turn up in the dialogues. Aristotle may be 'rationalizing' Plato, presenting him with a single argument making sense of all his statements. Or it may be that Plato did at some time formulate the Uniqueness Problem for himself and explicitly accept intermediates as an answer to it.

B. Geometry

The dialogues

References to geometry bulk larger in the dialogues than references to number, and the examples tend to be more integrated into the argument. Plato shows more interest in it than in arithmetic, both in its own right and in development of the theory of Forms. This is in keeping with the fact that it was in geometry that the greatest mathematical advances were made in Plato's lifetime, many by friends of his or members of the Academy. (Theaetetus and Eudoxus were both associated with Plato.) Plato was interested in the actual results, but even more so in the great strides made by geometers in methodological self-consciousness. He is himself credited with inventing the method of analysis, though this is not certain.[27] Axiomatization of geometry, and rigour in the presentation of proofs, were undoubtedly developed in the Academy; Euclid's *Elements* goes back in parts to earlier *Elements* produced by members of the Academy.[28] Plato was impressed by the way geometry had left behind empirical rules of thumb for land-

[27] Testimonium 18 in Gaiser. But cf. Cherniss (4). Plato is rather suspiciously said to have invented the method but handed it over to Leodamas, who made use of it.

[28] Proclus in his commentary on the first book of Euclid (66.4 ff.) tells us that prior to Euclid *Elements* were composed by Hippocrates, Leon, and Theudius; the last was a member of the Academy. The Academy was also the scene of a dispute about the nature of mathematical truth between Speusippus and Menaechmus.

measuring and the like, and had become a fully organized science. There was nothing comparably impressive in the case of arithmetic. In the central books of the *Republic* geometry is the model for the projected science of dialectic, the philosophical super-science, which is envisaged as reaching an 'unhypothetical first principle' from which will flow the first principles of all the subordinate sciences. What is in mind is a system of theorems deduced rigorously from axioms whose truth is self-evident, and geometry is clearly the model.

It is thus methodologically that geometry interests Plato most and proves most fruitful. (I leave out of present account the geometrical interest at the basis of the *Timaeus* cosmology.) Aristotle's response to this is itself interesting, but takes us too far from present concerns. In *M-N* he is concerned solely with Plato's ideas about geometry itself, and in particular about the nature of its subject-matter. Here Plato's views are quite straightforward, and close to his ideas about the subject-matter of arithmetic. In both fields he is a platonist in the modern sense—he is 'realist' in taking geometry to be concerned with objects which genuinely exist, but not in the spatio-temporal world around us.

Geometrical examples figure in two very important passages concerning 'recollection'—*Meno* 81a–86a and *Phaedo* 73a–77a. In the first passage a solution to a geometrical problem is put forward as the clearest sort of case to show us that we can acquire knowledge without appeal to our empirical acquaintance with the world around us. Knowledge of geometrical propositions can be obtained by pure thought (and hence is held to support the thesis that the soul acquired such knowledge before contact with our world). For Plato geometry is a striking example of a branch of knowledge whose subject-matter can be known non-empirically. The *Meno* is more concerned to establish this fact than to discuss the nature of the geometer's subject-matter.

Republic 527a-b takes us a little further. Plato there complains about the current language of geometers, who talk of 'squaring', 'extending', and the like, as though their subject-matter were items made or constructed by the geometer's activity. Plato claims that such language is inappropriate: there is no constructing involved; geometry is concerned solely with pure knowledge about timeless entities. Plato here runs together two different complaints about the geometers' way of speaking. Their use of tensed language might tempt the unwary into thinking that the objects they describe are created in the course of the proof, whereas for Plato the proof is merely a tracing on our part of relations that hold eternally. And their use of words like 'applying' and the like might suggest that geometry is essentially concerned with what we do, whereas our actions are completely irrelevant; what the geometer is concerned with is knowledge, and any applications of it are quite another matter.

Plato's platonism about the objects of geometry derives, then, clearly from a conviction about the truth of geometrical statements. The argument underlying his ideas is clearly an 'argument from objectivity': geometry is true, but it does not truly describe the relations of things in the spatio-temporal world; therefore it truly describes the relations of existing but non-spatio-temporal things. The argument from objectivity is much more to the surface than it is in the case of number, and Aristotle's systematic anti-platonist arguments in chapter 2 of *M* correspondingly concentrate on it.

The prominence of this argument no doubt owes something to the intuitive nature of geometry, especially the geometry of Plato's time, which was to develop into that of Euclid and can therefore not unfairly be called 'Euclidean'. Euclidean geometry was thought of as describing relationships of objects in Euclidean space, and the assumption that space has to be Euclidean was a very natural one, and compatible with the belief that we never come across any perfectly Euclidean objects. The axioms of 'Euclidean' geometry appeared to Plato as self-evident and therefore privileged truths, but still as true statements. He is far removed from the modern conception of geometrical axioms as axiom-schemata containing variables that can be interpreted in different ways.

Given the idea that the propositions of geometry are true by virtue of corresponding to relations actually holding between objects, and a conviction that these objects are not to be found in the spatio-temporal world, platonism about the objects of geometry has a kind of obviousness, and in his references to the subject-matter of geometry Plato does not often feel it necessary to stress the point that these objects *exist*; it is their *ideality* that is emphatically contrasted with the deficiencies of physical objects as supposed alternatives. In the *Seventh Letter* this is forcefully stressed (343a): by contrast with the ideal circle, circles drawn in exercises or turned on the lathe are said to be 'everywhere in contact with the straight'. The *Letter* is probably not genuine; but similar morals can be drawn from the *Republic*. It is only the inexplicit *Euthydemus* passage that stresses existence.

The unwritten doctrines

In contrast to his thought about numbers, Plato's ideas about the subject-matter of geometry do not seem to have undergone much development. We find, however, the same distinction made as is drawn in the case of number: there are the geometrical Forms and then intermediate objects of geometry, which are what the geometer actually studies. All Aristotle's arguments indicate that the argument for intermediates was applied to geometry and arithmetic in exactly parallel fashion.

But whereas the Form numbers are prominent in the unwritten doctrines that Aristotle criticizes, the geometrical Forms fade out. This is clearly because the number Forms are identified with the series of natural numbers, whereas there is no such role for the geometrical Forms, and so the intermediate geometrical objects, the object of the geometer's study, receive more emphasis. So Aristotle even comes to lump *all* Plato's ideal geometrical objects together as 'the things after the numbers'.[29] The arguments throughout *M-N* however, clearly indicate that the objects of geometry were Forms and intermediates, even though the former were inconspicuous.

The resulting unclarity as to whether Forms or intermediates are meant in any given case as the ideal objects of geometry can be traced back to some signs in the dialogues. At *Philebus* 56-9, 61-2,

[29] 992^{b}13-18, 1080^{b}23-9, 1085^{a}7-9. The second passage discusses differences of opinion in the Academy, some people distinguishing intermediate geometricals from 'the ones after the Forms', others collapsing the distinction. Intermediates would normally be contrasted with Forms. Clearly all geometrical objects, whatever their status, were felt to come after Forms (including numbers).

Plato talks about geometry and arithmetic as completely parallel. Although this passage does not contain an argument for intermediates, the numbers that are indicated as the object of philosophers' study have features of the intermediates. But the subject-matter of geometry seems to be Forms, 'the circle and divine sphere themselves' (62a7-8). At *Timaeus* 50c items are involved which seem like geometrical intermediates, but their status is unclear. At *Phaedo* 74b-c there is the odd phrase 'the equals themselves', which has been much discussed, but seems to reflect merely a felt difficulty with Forms rather than a choice of alternative.

The real argument for geometrical intermediates is, again, the Uniqueness Problem. A theorem mentions two circles intersecting. What is referred to cannot be the circles drawn in the diagram (cf. the *Euthydemus* passage), for these may fail to give the needed result through careless drawing or the like. But nor can it be the Form of Circle suggested (carelessly) in the *Philebus*, for that is unique. So geometrical intermediates are required as adequate ideal subject-matter for geometry.

Aristotle's criticisms point up two complications with the geometrical objects. In some passages the 'things after the numbers' are said to be 'lines, planes, and solids', and points are omitted. At 992ª19-24 Aristotle says that Plato battled against points as being 'a geometers' dogma', and frequently laid down instead that indivisible lines, and not points, were the principle of the line. Unfortunately we do not know the reasoning behind this surprising declaration. In the Aristotelian Corpus there is a small work, 'On Indivisible Lines', which gives reasons (very bad ones) why people have believed in indivisible lines, and several arguments against them (some very bad, but some effective). However, scholarly opinion assumes that this work is not by Aristotle but by a later follower, and that it attacks not Plato but Xenocrates. We also lack any information on how if at all Plato reconciled what seems like a denial of the existence of points with his uncompromising platonism about other geometrical objects. What criteria are we to appeal to in order to test which supposed mathematical objects really exist and which are mere 'geometers' dogmas'? We shall see that in his derivation of mathematical objects from simpler principles Plato runs into trouble with points.

Aristotle puts his finger on a second difficulty when he complains at 1090ᵇ20-30 that the geometrical entities are not properly accounted for in Plato's scheme of derivation, since they have to form a distinct 'fourth class' (being neither Forms, numbers, nor physical objects). Why is this? The general argument for intermediates suggests the following scheme: mathematical Forms (Form numbers and geometrical Forms); intermediate numbers and geometrical intermediates; physical instances. Why do the geometrical entities not fit in? The answer is indicated by Aristotle's complaint at 1092ᵃ17 ff. that it is absurd to produce space along with the ideal solids. Lines, planes, and solids demand an ideal *space*;[30] and this puts them in a different category from the unextended ideal numbers, of whatever kind. Worse: the space of ideal geometricals is presumably ideal space; what relation does it bear to our space? The transition from numbers to spatial objects will be another difficulty for Plato's unified derivation of numbers and magnitudes from the same principles.

2. Aristotle's philosophy of mathematics

Aristotle does not present anywhere in his work a sustained and dialectical attempt to deal with the problems of the philosophy of mathematics (as he does for time, place, etc. in the *Physics*). The positive ideas of his own that are presented in *M-N* occur in the course of a mainly polemical treatment, and so it is helpful to supplement them with some account of his views scattered elsewhere, especially as the latter sometimes represent a different and often improved line of thought from the one suggested in *M-N*.

Aristotle's attitude is best characterized as 'anti-platonism'. His hostility to platonism in mathematics is clear and unwavering, and hence brings him into sharp conflict with Plato (indeed, his interest in the subject, as shown in *M-N*, seems to have grown out of his criticisms of platonist ideas in the context of an attack on Plato's philosophy as a whole, in *A* 9). He is rather like some moderns who have declared, 'We do not believe in abstract entities'; what divides

---

[30] Aristotle mentions only solids here, presumably because he is thinking in his own terms of planes as defined in terms of solids and lines in terms of planes; but clearly the spatiality requirement holds even if one begins with lines.

him from Plato is the question whether mathematical objects exist. This seems so clear from the arguments in *M-N* that I have used 'exist' to translate the Greek verb *einai*, which elsewhere in Aristotle is often better translated 'be'.

So although Aristotle introduces the topic (1076^{a}36) by saying that the problem is not whether but how the objects of mathematics exist, it would be wrong to take this as a concession to Plato. Aristotle is firmly of the opinion that what the platonists say is, if interpreted plainly and literally, false. Aristotle distinguishes various senses of 'exist' (or 'be') and in none of them is it literally true that numbers exist. In similar fashion he often, in the course of *M-N*, distinguishes various ways in which a particular platonist saying can be clearly understood, and concludes that in none of them is it true. The platonist can always complain that what he says should not be taken so baldly, that its content is not exhausted by Aristotle's literal interpretation. Aristotle's response is unsympathetic; he regards this as resort to mere metaphor or mystical unclarity.

At one point Aristotle seems to have thought that the platonists' sayings were actually meaningless or unintelligible, that *no* sense could be given to them. Syrianus in his commentary on the *Metaphysics* (159.33–160.5) preserves a fragment of Aristotle's lost work *On Philosophy*, which goes, 'Thus, if the Ideas are a different sort of number, not mathematical number, we can have no understanding of it; for of the majority of us, at all events, who comprehends any other number?' Syrianus says crossly that Aristotle is here playing down to the ignorant multitude and merely revealing his failure to understand Plato's 'divine' thought; but the lack of understanding that concerns Aristotle here is more like the kind professed by positivists who declare metaphysics 'meaningless'.[31] But if this idea is taken seriously it would seem impossible for there to be any argument, whereas in fact Aristotle devotes large amounts of time and effort to interpreting what Plato says.

More often, and more defensibly, Aristotle argues on the assumption, not that what Plato says is unintelligible, but that if interpreted literally it has implications which are false or absurd. A large

[31] Aristotle is impatient with those who find assertion of the existence of number unproblematical; cf. *Posterior Analytics* 76^{b}17-18, and 1090^{a}2-15.

27

proportion of the arguments in *M-N* have the form of reductions to absurdity. This strategy, which is very common in *M-N*, is quite common in Aristotle and is very characteristic of him. He interprets what the opponent says in literal terms and goes on to show that this leads to falsity or absurdity. It is always open to the opponent to specify a (non-metaphorical) sense for his words in which they avoid these objections, but if he fails to do so Aristotle regards this as an admission that what has been said is either hopelessly unclear, or clear but false. This strategy has the disadvantage of laying Aristotle open to unjustified charges of being a naive and simple-minded interpreter, and even of failing to grasp Plato's intentions. The same approach, however, would show that in his criticisms of his predecessors Frege was naive. In fact Aristotle's arguments are extremely effective and at times reminiscent of Frege's attacks on current theories of number in the *Foundations of Arithmetic*.

If, however, the platonist's statements lead to absurdity as literally understood, how *are* we to understand them? Aristotle never answers this question in so many words, but it seems clear that his theory of mathematical objects is rather like his theories of time, place, and the infinite. Aristotle wants to say that time, place, etc. do not exist in their own right, but are dependent for their existence on the existence of individual Aristotelian substances—physical objects and in particular living things. His treatment of time, place, etc. is reductionist in that he does not say that they exist in a different sense from the sense in which substances exist (as he does with qualities, for example, which are likewise dependent on substances). He wants to analyse what is said about time, for example, by reference merely to events that are timed and familiar activities like counting. His treatment of mathematical objects is on the same lines; their existence is to be 'explained away' like that of time and place, rather than taken to answer to a distinct legitimate sense of the verb, as is the existence of qualities.

It is thus misleading to characterize Aristotle's position in modern positive terms like 'constructivism'. He does at 1051^a21-32 make interesting remarks which suggest that he has the rather modern thought that a proof of a given geometrical construction can be said to exist just to the extent that the successive steps are actually carried out by the geometer. 'It is by an activity also that geometrical constructions are discovered, for we find them by dividing. If the figures had already been divided, the constructions would have been obvious; but as it is they are present only potentially . . . Obviously, therefore, the potentially existing constructions are discovered by being brought to actuality; the reason is that the geometer's thinking is an actuality . . .' (Oxford translation). However, whatever his words here may suggest, it is not Aristotle's considered view that for a mathematical proof to exist is just for it to be worked out, for at *de Caelo* 279^{b}32–280^{a}10 Aristotle rests an argument on the claim that a geometrical construction cannot be regarded as a process taking time. Moreover, there is no indication that he was even tempted by the idea in application to areas of mathematics other than geometry.

Aristotle's own positive views get their longest and most explicit formulation in *M* 3, which is rather a pity; *M* 3 is sketchy and vague, and objections can be brought against it which do not hold against his better (though unsystematic) insights elsewhere.

Aristotle begins from the necessity of reconciling two beliefs both of which he firmly holds: mathematics does not directly describe physical objects, for these may fail to instantiate the relevant properties (997^{b}3–998^{a}6, 1059^{b}10-12)—but neither does it deal with a separate supersensible range of subject-matter. He resolves the problem by the solution that the mathematician does deal with physical objects, but not directly as the natural scientist does (*Physics* 193^{b}24–194^{a}7). Mathematics is distinguished from science and from everyday investigation not by its subject-matter but by its method. The mathematician abstracts certain properties of physical objects and studies them. The word 'abstraction' does not occur in *M* 3, but it turns up frequently in other works in this connection.

M 3 is more a promissory note than a full account, and it presents the mathematician's task in two ways: he studies the physical but not *qua* physical, and he studies only the properties essential for his interests. He will study a man, for example, as being extended if he is a geometer, as countable if he is an arithmetician; in either case he will ignore the properties possessed by the man in virtue of being a physical object, a compound of flesh and bones, etc. Both these characterizations are somewhat vague, and while they make the point that the nature of mathematics is elucidated by its method and not by its subject-matter, they are not very informative as to the nature of the method. (We shall see shortly that this is eked out with a psychological account, but *M* 3 is independent of this.) The theory of abstraction is characterized more by what it avoids (commitment to abstract objects) than by any positive programme. Aristotle has not given it the thorough, dialectically argued treatment that he gives to time, place, etc., and incoherencies are latent in it in its application both to geometry and to arithmetic.

Mueller in his valuable article points out a problem in Aristotle's conception of geometrical objects which springs from an ambiguity in 'abstraction'. What is it that is abstracted? Sometimes it seems to be matter (e.g. the bronze of the bronze sphere). This will lead to thinking that geometry studies *properties* like roundness. Sometimes, however, what seem to be abstracted are properties (e.g. the isosceles nature of a particular triangle). This leads to thinking of the geometer as studying *objects*, and this is the view uppermost in *M* 3. The conception of geometrical objects as properties fits better Aristotle's ideal of a science that can be demonstratively displayed as a series of necessary connections between universals (not particular objects). But it conflicts with his rejection of ontological commitment to universals, and also with the spatially intuitive nature of Greek geometry. Mueller explores a conception of geometrical objects as individuals whose matter is intelligible matter, conceived of as extension. He concludes that, 'there are two sorts of geometrical object in Aristotle. First, there are the basic objects: points, lines, planes, solids. The last three are conceived of as indeterminate extension and, therefore, as matter on which geometric properties are imposed. The imposition of these properties produces the ordinary geometrical figures, straight or curved lines, triangles, cubes, etc.'[32] Mueller's reconstruction is attractive, and does give Aristotle a systematic and well-thought-out account. But it is a reconstruction, and depends fairly heavily on the later Greek commentators; Aristotle's comments·

[32] Mueller connects his distinction with that in the *Posterior Analytics* (76^{a}31-6, ^{b}11-16) between (i) common axioms, (ii) the genus, the things whose meaning and also existence is assumed (Aristotle's examples are units, points, lines, magnitudes), and (iii) the properties whose meaning only is assumed (Aristotle's examples are odd, even, square, cube, straight, triangle, incommensurable, inclination, deflection).

are fragmentary and desultory, and it is dubious whether we should give him the credit for a coherent scheme.

As applied to number, abstraction runs into really disastrous difficulties, well brought out by Frege ((3), pp. 123-7, cf. (2), pp. 84-5):

'If through [abstraction] the counting blocks become identical, then we now have only one counting block; counting will not proceed beyond 'one'. Whoever cannot distinguish between things he is supposed to count, cannot count them either . . . On the other hand, if the word 'equal' is not supposed to designate identity, then the objects that are the same will therefore differ with respect to some properties and will agree with respect to others. But to know this, we don't first have to abstract from their differences.

Number involves counting something—units of some kind; but the units have to be differentiable, so abstracting from the objects to be counted is either futile or disastrous.

Moreover, it is a prominent conceptual fact about number that we can count anything, no matter of what sort—cows or concepts. Number is type-promiscuous. But this tells against the idea that it is abstracted from physical things, as Frege points out ((1), 31e): 'It would indeed be remarkable if a property abstracted from external things could be transferred without any change of sense to events, to ideas and to concepts. The effect would be just like speaking of fusible events, or blue ideas, or salty concepts or tough judgements.' The doctrine might be saved if one demanded that number-terms change their sense with the different types of thing that they were applied to—a drastic idea, but one which has found supporters.[33] Aristotle once puts the idea forward (*Physics* 248^{b}19-21), but it is not developed, and in any case probably derives not from his theory of number as such but from the doctrine that 'one' is like 'is' in having not a single sense but different senses in different categories.

In any case there is lack of correspondence in the application of abstraction to geometry and to number. In *M* 3 what seem to be abstracted are geometrical *objects*, but numerical *properties*, and

---

[33] Cf. Whitehead: 'the number "three" as applied to entities of one type has a different meaning to the number "three" as applied to entities of another type.' Whitehead, however, draws this conclusion from Russell's theory of types, which is a precise way of avoiding a specifiable paradox, whereas Aristotle is at most informally avoiding intuitive nonsense.

geometrical objects could have numerical properties. Aristotle does not attempt to deal with this. There is an odd passage at *Physics* 207ᵇ7-10 where it is said that '2', '3', and all other number-terms are 'paronymous'; this seems to mean that their use as nouns is logically derivative from their use as adjectives. But this passage is isolated and does not fit the *Categories* account of paronymy;[34] in any case paronymy is a limited logical notion, incapable of solving such a major difficulty.

Some of the problems latent in abstraction may have escaped Aristotle because he did have a psychological theory of how we abstract. Sextus Empiricus (*Adv. Math.* 3.57) reports that 'Aristotle . . . says . . . that the length without breadth of which the geometers speak is not unintelligible, but that we can without any difficulty arrive at the thought of it. He rests his argument on a rather clear and indeed a manifest illustration of it. We grasp the length of a wall, he says, without attending also to its breadth, so that it must be possible to conceive of the length without breadth of which geometers speak.' Abstraction thus comes down to (deliberate) lack of attention. This is clear also from a passage in the *de Memoria*;[35] the mathematician has before his eyes something with a determinate size, but thinks of it simply as having size.

No doubt we can do what Aristotle describes, but does this show that abstraction gives an adequate account of mathematical objects as being the results of abstraction? Without any defensive moves, Aristotle is wide open to the kind of objection raised by Frege to the nineteenth-century abstractionists: if we try to identify the object purely as the result of abstraction, we run into incoherence:

[34] *Categories* 1ᵃ12 ff., 6ᵇ13, 10ᵃ27-ᵇ11. In the *Categories* it is the adjective (e.g. 'brave') which is derived from the noun (e.g. 'bravery') by inflection. In the *Physics* passage, on the other hand, the use of '2', '3', etc. as nouns seems to be derived from their use as adjectives, thus reversing the priority.

[35] '[In drawing a diagram] though we do not make any use of the fact that the size of the triangle is determinate, we nonetheless draw it with a determinate size. And similarly someone who is thinking, even if he is not thinking of something with a size, places something with a size before his eyes, but thinks of it not as having a size. If its nature is that of things which have a size, but not a determinate one, he places before his eyes something with a determinate size, but thinks of it simply as having size' (translation by R. Sorabji in his edition of the *de Memoria, Aristotle on Memory*).

'Inattention is a very strong lye; it must not be applied at too great a concentration, so that everything does not dissolve, and likewise not too dilute, so that it effects a sufficient change in the things . . . Suppose there are a black and a white cat sitting side by side before us. We stop attending to their colour, and they become colourless, but are still sitting side by side. We stop attending to their posture, and they are no longer sitting (though they have not assumed another posture), but each one is still in its place. We stop attending to position; they cease to have place, but still remain different . . . Finally we thus obtain from each object a *something* wholly deprived of content; but the *something* obtained from one object is different from the *something* obtained from another object—though it is not easy to say how . . .' ((2), p. 85).

It is easy to show that abstraction leads to incoherence when the result of abstraction is to be something *countable*; it is probably no accident that Aristotle's examples come from geometry, where abstraction seems more plausible because of the intuitive nature of the subject-matter. (It is worth noting how at 1061ª28-ᵇ3 Aristotle begins by talking about the *mathematician's* use of abstraction, and slides without noticing it into talking about the subject as *geometry*). So to the extent that abstraction as a psychological theory is at all plausible, it is inadequate as a theory of all mathematical objects. However, the appeal to psychology forms no part of the theory sketched in *M* 3, and is apparently an independent strand of thought.

One oddity in Aristotle's thought, the concept of intelligible matter, may be partly explained by the problems raised by abstraction. If abstraction is thought of as abstracting from the matter of physical objects, then the properties studied are pure properties of forms, and this comes dangerously close to Plato. Perhaps it is worry about this that leads Aristotle to say at 1036ª9-12: 'Some matter is perceptible and some intelligible, perceptible matter being for instance bronze and wood and all matter that is changeable, and intelligible matter being that which is present in perceptible things not *qua* perceptible, i.e. the objects of mathematics' (Ross's translation; cf. 1037ª4-5, 1045ª33-5). But the matter of mathematical objects is an obscure notion, and never clarified (though at 1059ᵇ 14-21 Aristotle says that it is philosophy that should study it). Aristotle's notion of matter is primarily framed to cope with the explanation of change, and few of its applications make sense in the

33

case of unchanging mathematical objects. The relation of bronze to a statue does not helpfully elucidate the problem of what it is that the mathematician is studying if he is studying neither physical objects as such nor pure forms. The distinction between the two kinds of matter might be taken to make a useful distinction between body and extension, but in *M* 2 Aristotle reveals that he is capable of confusing a three-dimensional geometrical object with a three-dimensional physical object. Later (e.g. in Proclus' Prologue (part 2) to his commentary on Euclid Bk 1) intelligible matter acquires other functions. It is presented as what makes mathematical objects accessible to the imagination, which has to picture them as extended, divisible, and repeatable, unlike pure forms. But this idea is not to be found in Aristotle himself either. In any case if intelligible matter is thought of as extension it has no application to number. Aristotle sometimes applies the form/matter distinction to numbers (e.g. $1084^b 28$-9), but he is not appealing to the special notion of intelligible matter, merely to the idea that units are the matter of numbers because they have merely potential existence.

Is there anything to Aristotle's philosophy of mathematics apart from the theory of abstraction? Because of the scattered nature of the other passages, *M* 3 has been taken as Aristotle's last word on the subject. But *M* 3 is not the last word even on abstraction. Aristotle's views on geometrical objects can be developed in some such way as that suggested by Mueller; and his views on number can also be developed from statements elsewhere.

Aristotle is often credited (or discredited) with a theory of number rather like Plato's. He does sometimes distinguish between 'two senses' of number:[36] what we count and what we count with. This, together with the theory of abstraction, suggests that Aristotle thinks of pure numbers as abstractions from groups, made up of pure units which are abstraction from physical objects—ghosts of departed quantities, in Berkeley's phrase. Aristotle does sometimes characterize units as 'points without position';[37] and this is a doctrine

---

[36] *Physics* $219^b 5$-7 (with Ross's note), and cf. $1092^b 19$-20, which suggests that he thinks of 'concrete numbers' as having the characteristics of things themselves.

[37] $1084^b 26$, $1069^a 12$, *Physics* $227^a 27$-32, *de Caelo* $300^a 18$, *Posterior Analytics* $87^a 36$, $88^a 33$.

open to all Frege's criticisms. So Aristotle does sometimes seem to think of numbers this way, as reached by abstraction from groups; and he struggles with a resulting problem: when you have ten sheep and ten dogs you have (by abstraction) the same number, but you don't have the same ten. He offers the dubious solution of making tens species of the genus number.[38]

However, Aristotle has a better view of number, though it is to be found not in his pronouncements on number but in his long discussion of 'one'. Unlike the above view, it represents a real advance on Plato's theory, and thus gives him a defensible basis for his criticisms of Plato, which would otherwise have come down to the single point of difference that Plato believes that numbers really exist whereas Aristotle takes them to be mere abstractions.

There are a few passages where Aristotle indicates that the logic of 'number' is different from that of terms for objects of any kind, that number-terms are essentially dependent or relative in some way. He says that a number is always a number *of* something (1092^b19), and that 'number' is a relative term presupposing a substance or independent object to which it is relative (990^b17-22; *On the Forms* fr. 4 Ross; 1057^a2-7). In some places also he renders misleading idioms about number harmless. He disinfects the idiom 'to be in number' from its suggestion that numbers are already there for things to be in;[39] and he points out that the idiom of 'parts of number' is not to be taken literally: numbers contain parts or units in a different sense from that in which the words apply to ordinary objects.[40]

---

[38] *Physics* 224^a2-15. Ross in his note criticizes the idea, but it is defended by Wieland in his comments on the passage in *Die aristotelische Physik*.

[39] *Physics* 221^a9-17 and 221^b14-16. 'In number' might suggest to the logically naive that numbers were there for things to be in, prior to any counting being done. Aristotle insists that 'in number' means only, of a term, that its definition presupposes mention of number, and of a thing, that 'its being is measured by the number that it is in'. A triptych would be 'in' the number 1 and its panels 'in' the number 3: what we are talking about when we say that there is one is the triptych, but when we say that there are three we are talking about the panels.

[40] *Categories* 5^a15-38: a number has parts only in the sense that we increase numbers by adding one more each time. 1023^b12-17, 1034^b33-5: numbers have parts in a different sense from the sense in which objects have parts. 1024^a11-19: when units are substracted from a number it is not there-

Aristotle's most extended discussion is in the first two chapters of Book *I* of the *Metaphysics*. The relativity of number to what is numbered is there explained by saying that the unit (whatever is counted as *one*), is the *measure* of the number. This means that one is not a number but the measure of number; this is not just a consequence of the ordinary Greek concept of number, as we have seen, but a conscious stipulation to produce a general theory. Aristotle wants to stress the analogy of the unit of counting to the unit of measurement. We cannot just measure an object—we first have to determine a unit of measurement, like an inch or an ounce or a degree on some scale. Then we can say that the thing is 2 inches long, or weighs 5 pounds, or is 60°F; the measurement in each case is relative to the unit chosen. Aristotle extends this to counting: in order to count objects, we first have to pick out something to count as our unit—we cannot count until we know what it is that we are to mark out as we count, whether chairs, colours, or what. 'In colours the one is a colour, e.g. white . . . Therefore, if all existent things were colours, existent things would have been a number, indeed, but of what? Clearly of colours; and the 'one' would have been a particular colour, e.g. white. And similarly if all existing things were tunes, they would have been a number, but a number of quarter-tones . . .' (1056^{b}28 ff., cf. 1011^{b}7-8). At 1052^{b}18 ff. Aristotle explicitly puts together the unit of measurement and the unit in counting as both being a choice of measure. He insists on the parallelism also at 1053^{a}24-30, which brings out a further point:

'The measure is always homogeneous with the thing measured . . . that of length is a length . . . that of weight is a weight, that of units a unit. (For we must state the matter so, and not say that the measure of numbers is a number; we ought indeed to say this if we were to use the corresponding form of words, but the claim does not really correspond—it is as if one claimed that the measure of units is units, and not a unit; number is plurality of *units*). (Ross's translation).

A stick ten inches long is measureable in inches; and if I count ten then that ten is countable in units of some kind (chairs, or whatever

---

by 'mutilated'. 1039^{a}11-14: number is a 'collection' only of potential units, not of actually existing ones.

I am counting).

This theory succeeds in taking the mystery out of counting, and thus solves a philosophical puzzle, as do so many of Aristotle's analyses, like those of time and place and the infinite. We have had the concept explained and thereby a temptation is removed to adopt an extravagant solution like that of reifying numbers and units as abstract objects. The indivisibility of the unit is also explained. The unit of measurement is what is taken as indivisible for the purposes of measurement, and similarly the unit in arithmetic is what is taken to be indivisible for the purposes of counting or computation. Thus the problem of the indivisibility of the mathematicians' unit is solved without Plato's postulation of perfect pure and indivisible units. The mathematicians' unit is just an ordinary physical object *regarded as* indivisible for counting; it is not a different sort of object altogether. This characterization of 'unit' appears elsewhere in Aristotle,[41] and when he says that mathematicians posit the unit as in every way indivisible ($1052^{b}35-1053^{a}2$) he is making a great advance on the 'point without position' characterization. The former account shows how mathematical truths are *held to be* true even when empirical facts fail to measure up, whereas abstraction would seem to have the consequence that anomalies in the behaviour of physical objects might in time come to provide counter-examples to mathematical truths. (Aristotle never considers this problem, nor the related problem of mathematical objects that cannot be abstracted from properties found in nature.)

Aristotle's account of number is quite penetrating, and at points suggestive of Frege (though the comparison cannot be pressed, as we shall see shortly). Scholars have frequently complained that it is naive and archaic, but this seems to come from noticing only that he calls number 'plurality of units'[42] without attending to the account he gives of how this is to be understood.

---

[41] *Physics* $206^{b}3$; $1089^{b}35$ (with Ross's note), $1016^{b}17$ ff. (where it is not very successfully brought into connexion with the first characterization).

[42] $1020^{a}13$, $1053^{a}30$, $1039^{a}12$; cf. *Physics* $226^{b}34-227^{a}5$ for units in numbers as discrete. Cf. Ross's note on *Posterior Analytics* $76^{a}2$-5 listing passages showing that in that work arithmetic is said to posit the existence of numbers or of units indifferently. Cf. also *Topics* $141^{b}5$, where it is said that the unit is more 'intelligible' than number.

One caution which should be entered to prevent hasty assimil-ation of Aristotle's ideas to modern ideas (and in particular to Frege's) is that although in *I* Aristotle achieves a remarkable analysis of what it is to be one in number, he never clearly distinguishes it from another problem about *one*, namely, what it is to be *unitary*. Both in *I* and in Δ 6 (the entry for 'one' in Aristotle's philosophical lexicon) the two problems are discussed together, and being one in number is not clearly set apart from being one in genus or in kind. To some extent Aristotle is the victim here of the Greek language, since the single word *hen* covered ground that we parcel out between 'one', 'unit', and 'unity'; it is indeed impressive that Aristotle succeeds in making the distinctions that he does make. Still, a passage like 1077ª20-4 shows clearly that Aristotle does not succeed in holding apart a thing's unitariness and its being one of something. This considerably restricts his achievement, and means that it cannot be compared at all closely with Frege's ideas. Perhaps this may go some way towards explaining why Aristotle does not put the *I* analysis to work in areas to which it seems relevant, like that of individuation. He might have formulated his problems rather differently if he had come to see that problems about units are quite distinct from problems about unity. Apart from the discussion of time in *Physics* book IV Δ,[43] the *I* analysis remains disappointingly unintegrated into Aristotle's meta-physical discussions. It is not even integrated into what he says about mathematical objects in *M*, although it is presupposed in ch. 1 of *N*.

In the above sketch I have assumed that Aristotle's theory of number is to be sought in the discussion of 'one' in *I*. Elsewhere Aristotle appears to give different characterizations of 'numerically one', which have nothing to do with *I*. Thus at 999ᵇ33–1000ª1 he says that it makes no difference whether you say 'numerically one' or 'individual', for by 'individual' we mean precisely 'numerically one'; at 1016ᵇ32-3 he says that things are numerically one whose matter is one; and at 1040ᵇ17 we learn that things are one if their reality (*ousia*) is one. Aristotle is not, however, offering a spate of unreconciled alternative analyses of what it is to be one in number. He is, I think, assuming that we know what it is for something to be

---

[43] *Physics* Δ book IV chs. 10-14. Time is called a kind of number, and there are several passages which recall the *I* account.

numerically one, and drawing links between this and his own meta-physical concepts of matter and reality.

Aristotle's concept of number, in making number relative to what is numbered, ties number firmly to counting, making it analytic that number is what we count with. This is a suitably anti-platonist theory: numbers do not exist independently of us and our activities of counting. (Cf. *Physics* 223ᵃ16-29 where Aristotle concludes that there would be no time—which for him is a kind of number—if there were no conscious beings to count). But it could be said that Aristotle has merely crystallized the everyday Greek concept of number and made it a conceptual truth that nothing is a number that is not used for counting. It is not quite fair, however, to complain that Aristotle has just hardened our ordinary intuitions. His theory demands that 0 and 1 should not be numbers. Since the Greeks had no notation for 0, this is not surprising;[44] but 1 is more complicated. Aristotle, like Plato, *uses* 1 as a number,[45] and one of his criticisms of Plato's production of the number series is that it does not proceed by adding 1 every time; Aristotle regards this as essential to any account of the number series. So when, in giving his own theoretical account and mentioning, rather than using, 1, he says that 1 is not a number and that the first number is 2 (1056ᵇ25, 1085ᵇ10, *Physics* 220ᵃ27-32), he is consciously innovating. His analysis explains away something ordinarily accepted (that 1 is a number) in order to give an account of number and counting which is general and accounts for the fact without platonist solutions.

So Aristotle's concept of number is not an unthinking reflection of ordinary usage. But it can still be criticized as not allowing for advance. Aristotle does in fact exclude rational numbers and states firmly that a ratio of numbers is not a number.[46] So rationals would

[44] At *Physics* 215ᵇ12-18 Aristotle says that 'nothing' (*to mēden*) does not stand in any relation to a number; but it is wrong to translate this (as Ross does) as, 'zero is in no relation to a number'; talk of 'nothing' does not amount to talk of zero in the absence of a proper notation for zero. The platonism of Frege, who recognizes '0' as just as good an answer to the 'How many?' questions as '2' goes a long way beyond everyday intuitions ((2), 84).

[45] 1082ᵇ35, 1080ᵃ24; cf. *Physics* 220ᵃ32; also 1080ᵃ25 for criticism of Plato for not producing numbers by adding 1.

[46] 1013ᵃ27-9 *may* include *logoi* (ratios) of numbers as being themselves numbers, but is more likely to be saying that number in general explains ratios. 991ᵇ9-21 argues firmly that a ratio of numbers is not itself a number.

presumably be for him not numbers but items dependent on numbers. This is presumably because of the close tie he finds between number and counting: we can count halves and so would intuitively be happy to say that ½ was a number, but we can hardly count with 17/102. More serious is the fact that Aristotle excludes irrationals from being numbers (though the passage is difficult[47]) on the ground that number cannot apply to what is not commensurable. This is a consequence of his assimilation of counting to measuring: he treats incommensurability as though it were simply a case of measuring things by two different measures on two different scales—'the diagonal of the square and its sides are measured by two quantities' (1053^a16-17). But this is not an adequate account. The problem of what to do about $\sqrt{2}$ is not solved, but merely shelved, by comparing it to the case where two things do not have a common measure because they are measured by different units, and thus on different scales.[48]

This problem forces on our attention a general problem in Aristotle's account. Choosing a unit to measure by involves choice of a scale by reference to which the measurement is made. '2 lbs.' measures a thing in weight; '2 feet' measures it in length. But when '2' 'measures things in number' there is no corresponding scale. If the analogy were perfect, '2 men' would measure a pair in men, '2 human beings' would measure it in human beings, and so on. But choice of a concept under which to count things as units is in many ways unlike choosing a scale of measurement. All that is necessary for a counting concept is that there be criteria for identification and reidentification, but more is necessary for there to be a scale: things must be comparable in respect of it. Further, the concepts suited for counting typically do *not* allow for comparative judge-

---

[47] 1021^a5-6: ' "number is not predicated of that which is not commensurate." But Ross's text is disputed (cf. Stenzel, *Kleine Schriften*, pp. 210-12, who argues that the point here is that the ratio specified at lines 3-4 is said with respect to number, but not any numbers that are commensurable, since both terms of the ratio are unspecified). See Gaiser ((1), pp. 507-8) for a discussion.

[48] In this he is no worse off than Plato, who at *Parmenides* 140b-d (especially c2-4) explains incommensurability in terms of measures in a similarly unsatisfactory way. If A and B are commensurable, A is bigger (smaller) than B if it is of more (less) measures; if they are not commensurable, A is 'of smaller or bigger measures' than B.

ments of degree, as is possible with a scale (one is not more or less a man, for example). In this respect also Aristotle is far from Frege. And there is another problem (pointed out by Ellis, pp. 155-9): while a unit of measurement can be defined arbitrarily, a unit for counting cannot be. I can say, 'let this be 1 minch long', since I am defining my scale along with my unit of measurement. But I cannot say, 'Let this be 1 clong', since I am not likewise defining what it is to be a clong. I cannot define a 'clong-scale' unless I already know what a clong is, but to know that is to be able to tell when there is one clong and when two; but if I can individuate clongs, then it is *already* true or false that there is 1 clong, and I have not done any *defining* at all.

Aristotle would no doubt claim that the analogy of counting and measuring was not meant to be perfect, but problems like the above suggest that it needs more thorough treatment than he devotes to it.

3. Plato, the Academy, and Aristotle on the foundations of mathematics

Plato's theories about the foundations of mathematics, the derivation of numbers and (later) of geometrical objects do not figure in the dialogues. They have to be recovered from indirect sources. It is clear, however, from the preceding two sections, that we have good independent grounds for ascribing to Plato and to Aristotle consistent and opposed conceptions of the nature of mathematics, and this gives us a basis from which to evaluate the sources and distinguish Aristotle's criticisms. This is a difficult area, and the problems have been increased rather than diminished by the many competing hypotheses that undertake to explain the fragmentary but suggestive evidence.

The different contributions of the Academy members are even more difficult to determine, since when Aristotle discusses various ideas in *M-N* he seldom mentions names. The theories of Speusippus and Xenocrates are the only ones dealt with in *M-N* that can be reconstructed with any degree of confidence, and since they clearly derive from Plato's theory the latter is the point from which to begin.

Plato

(a) *Analysis of number: one and the indefinite two*   Aristotle says at 987^{b}21-2, 29-35, that Plato derived the numbers from two 'elements' or 'principles', one and the indefinite two.[49] *M-N* frequently presupposes this or comments on it. At 987^b one and the indefinite two figure as principles of number; in other passages they figure also as the principles of geometrical objects, and the derivation of numbers appears as part of a larger theory. But it can be doubted whether the derivation of numbers was always conceived of merely as part of a wider scheme. There are persistent difficulties in fitting it into the wider scheme, and while we have relatively specific information about the derivation of numbers, the derivation of magnitudes is known only from a few indications of a different and very general kind. This suggests that the production of numbers from one and the indefinite two was originally a separate idea. In any case, it aids clarity to consider it on its own first.

The idea of deriving numbers from elements of number at once suggests modern analogues in the work of Frege and of Russell and Whitehead, the logicist attempt to derive arithmetic from logic alone and to show that all statements or arithmetic are reducible to statements of logic plus definitions.[50] This parallel has been a help in suggesting a point to what had hitherto often been dismissed as ludicrous nonsense, but in spite of this valuable service it should not be pressed too hard in explaining Plato's ideas. The logicists invented and used powerful new formal systems, and Frege in particular revolutionized logic; whereas we have only a few untechnical hints from Plato. Secondly, the logicists were clear that they were doing meta-

---

[49] I use 'indefinite two' and not the traditional 'indefinite dyad' since the word translated, *duas*, is the ordinary Greek word for 'two' and suggests nothing as grandiose as 'dyad'. I use 'one' rather than the traditional 'the one' since the English 'the one' is again more laden with pretension than the Greek *to hen*, which is regularly used for 'one' or 'oneness'.

[50] The logicist programme is not, of course, capable of realization as originally intended. 'Logic' for Frege included set theory, and the discovery of Russell's paradox necessitated various *ad hoc* adjustments. Modern axiom-sets for set theory make no claim to be intuitively self-evident in the way traditionally demanded of the laws of logic.

mathematics, whereas Plato is not so clear about the difference between using the number series and giving a theoretical account of it. (In this respect Plato is nearer to the neo-intuitionist Brouwer, who says that the 'intuition of two-oneness gives rise to the numbers one and two, and other numbers by repetition'; it is not clear whether Brouwer is talking about conceptual features of counting, or about the existence of particular numbers.[51]) Thirdly, the logicists were clear that 'deriving arithmetic from logic' was a matter of deriving propositions from other propositions, whereas both Plato and Aristotle use *'archai'* ('first principles') not only for propositions but also (and sometimes with confusion) for objects, interchangeably with 'elements'. This is not simply a matter of trivial reformulation of what can be expressed in terms of propositions, as is clearly the case with Frege ((3), p. 143) when he talks about the 'purely logical building blocks' of arithmetic. That it goes beyond this is clear from the fact that Plato was tempted into the use of temporal and indeed biological language in his account of the relation of numbers to one and the indefinite two. Aristotle reports that Plato had a 'generation' of the numbers, and though sometimes the language is vague (1080^a 14-16, $1085^b 7$), there are many explicit uses of the verb for 'come into being' ($987^b 22$-35, $1082^b 30$, $1087^b 7$, $1091^a 4$-5). Once ($988^a 1$ ff.) Aristotle relies on it to make a joke about the parenthood of numbers. Aristotle in fact argues that Plato is committed by his language to the view that the production of numbers is a temporal and not merely a logical process ($1091^a 23$-8); his grounds, however, seem weak. All we can justifiably say is that Plato was led to say many things which are potentially and perhaps actually misleading, and that he could not have said them if he had spoken only of deriving propositions from other propositions.

If we bear these warnings in mind, however, the logicist programme is a helpful analogue: there is the same impulse to unify and render transparently intelligible a wide and disparate field by 'reducing' it to a few simpler ultimate principles.

One and the indefinite two are analogous to the two principles

---

[51] 'This intuition of two-oneness, the basal intuition of mathematics, creates not only the numbers one and two, but also all finite ordinal numbers . . .' 'Intuitionism and Formalism', p. 69 in Benacerraf and Putnam.

of Limit and Unlimitedness of the Pythagoreans. And in the *Philebus* (16-18) Limit and Unlimitedness appear prominently, with evident awareness of their provenance. It is therefore often assumed that one and the indefinite two were already developed as principles by Pythagoreans in Plato's day, and also that they are to be explained at once by reference to the *Philebus*, and to those of the unwritten doctrines that obviously refer to it. Both assumptions, however, are over-hasty. It is dangerous to stress too much the Pythagorean nature of the principles, because our sources for the Pythagoreans are extremely uncertain, and it may be the case that these ideas were in fact read back into fictional early Pythagoreanism by Neo-Pythagoreans building on Plato.[52] It is also unsound to lay too much weight on analogies with Limit and Unlimitedness even as they figure in Plato's own *Philebus*, since we can see from Aristotle's complaints in ch. 1 of *N* that there were many different ways of describing the two principles, all going with slight variations in theory.[53] If we confine ourselves for the present to their role in the derivation of numbers, it is best to begin from Aristotle's clear statement that what Plato introduced was the notion of making the principle opposed to one, a two, or principle of duality (987^b25-7). This turns out to give a useful clue for reconstructing an account of how the principles worked. There has been dispute over whether use of the phrase 'the indefinite two' should be ascribed to Plato, or merely to Xenocrates, but detailed examination of texts has led to the conclusion that there is no reason not to ascribe it to Plato (see Ross on 1081^a14, and Robin, pp. 641-54).

When we try to reconstruct the generation of numbers, we have to start from Aristotle's commentators, but the idea suggested there

[52] Cf. Burkert and Philip. In Sextus Empiricus, *Adv. Math.* X.248-83, an indefinite two is ascribed to Pythagoras, although we know from Aristotle (987^b25-7) that this was recognized as Plato's special contribution.

[53] The alternative specifications of the indefinite two are discussed by Robin, pp. 654-60. The one Aristotle uses most frequently is 'the great and small' (or 'the great and the small', presumably out of reluctance to let one subject have contradictory characteristics). The other variants are listed by him at 1087^b4 ff. It is interesting to note that the one variant that never occurs is 'the infinite two' (*he apeiros duas*), though this turns up in later writers (e.g. Plutarch, *Quaest. Plat.* 1001f–1002a. See Merlan ((1), pp. 115-16). This suggests that Plato's original indefinite two should not be connected too hastily with the *apeiron* ('unlimitedness') of the *Philebus*.

is amply confirmed in Aristotle's many criticisms of the principles (mostly contained in *M-N*).

Our best source is Alexander, the only one of Aristotle's Greek commentators to have access to important lost works in which he expounded and criticized Plato. He comments on the puzzling passage from *A* 6 already mentioned, in which Aristotle says that Plato made one of his principles a two because all the numbers (with a puzzling exception) could be produced from it, and adds, 'as if it were an *ekmageion*'. This word is often translated 'plastic material', as if the indefinite two were matter on which form is imposed. But Alexander takes it to mean a mould, and understands the analogy to be with the way moulds or matrices make everything poured into them come out the same. So the numbers produced from the indefinite two are produced by the application of a single repeatable operation. It is clear from another of Alexander's comments[54] that this was some kind of doubling: 'He [Aristotle, in reporting Plato] thinks the dyad divided everything to which it is applied; that is why he called it duplicative. For, by making into two each of the things to which it is applied, it in a sense divides it, not allowing it to remain what it was; which division is the genesis of numbers' (Ross's translation). Alexander adds that only the even numbers were produced in this way.

The way in which doubling was connected with dividing is illustrated by a passage of the Neoplatonist Porphyry reported by a later commentator Simplicius.[55] Plato used the example of halving a cubit length. If this is halved, half of it again halved, half of that again halved, and so on, the process goes on for ever. This division 'doubles' in the sense of dividing into two halves at every stage; and the steps of this infinite process can be regarded as marking off the

---

[54] *On the Good* fr. 2 Ross. A caveat should be entered: this part of Alexander's commentary comes after he has concluded his exposition of arguments from *On the Good* by name, and may be his own comment; indeed, shortly afterwards he appears to make a mistake (see below).

[55] Simplicius, *in Phys.* 453.25–454.19. Simplicius warns us that Porphyry was trying to 'put into articulate shape' the ideas in *On the Good* and to reconcile them with the *Philebus* (a road that many have tried to travel), so the passage cannot be trusted very far as a report on Plato. But we know that Porphyry was using Aristotle's version of the lecture, and it is very unlikely that he actually fabricated the example.

numbers in an infinite series, each division marking off another number, without appeal to the idea of adding 1 to the number before.

This is not, however, very helpful as to what exactly could be meant by doubling. Alexander takes the indefinite two to produce even numbers by a process of simple multiplication by two:[56] 'For when applied to 1 it makes 2 (for twice 1 is 2), when applied to 2 it makes 4 (for twice 2 is 4), when applied to 3 it makes 6 (for twice 3 is 6) and so on too in every other case' (Ross's translation). And this is supported by a remark of Aristotle's (1091^a23-4) that suggests that the indefinite two produced all the even numbers. But this is not satisfactory. Where have the odd numbers (1,3) in Alexander come from? And the process envisaged does not seem like that suggested by Plato's example of the cubit, where the point was that the process applied in each case to what it had produced at the stage before.

Many of Aristotle's references to the indefinite two in *M-N* suggests something different, namely, production of the powers of two, i.e. the sequence 2,4,8 . . . numbers of the form 2^n. At 1081^b 17-22 he says that, 'number cannot be generated as they generate it from the two and one . . . <for them> what came from the first two and the indefinite two is four—two twos other than the original two. . . And two, also, will result from the original One and another one. . .' There are also the passages at 1082^a13-15: 'the indefinite two, so they say, took the definite two and made two twos, since it was a duplicator of what was taken', and 1082^a28–32: 'suppose the twos in four come into being simultaneously; they are still prior to those in eight, and just as two generated them they generated the fours in the original eight.' This idea appears in other passages also.[57] Most explicit is the complaint at 1091^a9-12 that Plato's principles of number cry out as though manhandled—all they are capable of producing is the series of powers of 2.

These complaints are all very specific, and it is more likely that Alexander has gone wrong here than that Aristotle has. What Aris-

[56] *On the Good* fr. 2 Ross. Elsewhere (54.3-7) he also appeals to the standard Greek definition of even number as divisible by two.

[57] 1083^b35-6: the job of the indefinite two was to *double* (so it cannot produce a one or unit); 1024^b34-6: in a sense 8 can be called 'double', because of the '*logos* (here, definition) of the two'.

totle tells us is that the indefinite two produced the powers of two only; and this would fit the model of halving the cubit. Alexander probably takes it to be simply multiplication by two because he includes odd numbers as material for the indefinite two. But this is probably a mistake; odd numbers are associated with the other principle, one. Alexander's reconstruction gives us the indefinite two already working on the products of the other principle; Aristotle, however, is concerned with what the indefinite two does on its own.

If the indefinite two produces only the powers of two, what connection has this with evenness?

One of the Greek categories of number now unfamiliar to us is that of the 'evenly times even'. There are two ways in which this is defined. Euclid (def. 8) defines such numbers as even multiples of an even number. But there are also definitions in later writers which define them as powers of 2: 'The evenly times even is then the number which has its halves even, the halves of the halves even, and so on, until unity is reached. In short, the evenly times even number is always of the form 2^n. . .'[58] Heath regards these definitions as 'Pythagorean', and certainly they are less straightforwardly mathematical than Euclid's definition; what they stress is that *even* numbers only are concerned, and one of the authors, Iamblichus, faults Euclid's definition simply because it does not prevent an evenly times even number from also being evenly times odd.[59] The survival of these 'Pythagorean', mathematically somewhat futile definitions which insist on the connection of numbers of the form 2^n with pure evenness suggests that Plato may have thought that in producing the powers of two the indefinite two was producing numbers which were, as it were, the paradigmatically even numbers, namely the evenly times even numbers. (This is not yet to solve the problem of how the indefinite two could be taken (as by Alexander)

[58] Heath, ed. of Euclid, vol.ii, pp. 281-2. The definitions occur in Theon, ed. Hiller, 25.6 ff., Nicomachus, ed. Hoche, 15.4 ff., and Iamblichus, *in Nic.* ed. Pistelli, pp. 20-1.

[59] Iamblichus points out that a number can be both according to Euclid; this is meant as an objection, but Heath (p. 282) shows that Euclid meant his definition as stated, since he proves (IX. 32) that a number of form 2^n is evenly times even only.

to produce *all* the even numbers; we shall return to this after examining the working of the other principle, one.)

There are two passages in Plato's dialogues where ideas like the above seem to appear in embryo. We cannot say that in either one he has the indefinite two in mind, merely that the above reconstruction of the working of the indefinite two gains plausibility if we can find Plato already interested in elements of it.

At *Phaedo* 101c Plato claims that there is only one adequate explanation of a pair of things' being two, and that is 'participation in Twoness'; he rejects the proffered explanations of 'addition' and 'division', since what one explains the other will explain equally well, although they are opposites (97b). It is interesting that Plato regards dividing and not subtraction as the opposite of addition, and regards them both as equally good explanations (as far as they go) of participation in Twoness; later we find that the process associated with the indefinite two is regarded as a kind of doubling by division which adds on a number every time.

Parmenides 142b—144e is a passage often called 'the generation of numbers', though there has been much dispute as to what this means.[60] Two stages are distinguished, corresponding to two processes which, it is claimed, can be carried out if certain conditions hold for the subject of the hypothesis, the One. At the end of the description of the two processes the claim is made that 'we have all number'. Whatever is intended in the actual *Parmenides* passage, I believe that Stage 1 (142b5—143a2) has a process in mind which resembles the working of the indefinite two, and Stage 2 (143a4—144a5) indicates a process which is reminiscent of the way one works as a principle. At present I shall consider only Stage 1. The argument begins from the assumption that the subject, the One, is— *hen estin*. If the One is, then in saying so, we use two words, 'one' and 'is'; and since these are not interchangeable, they must refer to different 'parts' of the subject; but of these parts in turn we can go on to say the same—what is true of the one is true of each part so produced. The crudity of the argument is less important here than

[60] See most recently the articles by Allen and Schofield. It is quite misleading to regard it as anything like a modern proof of an infinite set or the infinity of the number series; Wedberg does so on p. 23, but he misrepresents the actual structure of the argument in the text.

its result: we have a process of infinite doubling which corresponds well to the way that numbers of the form 2^n are produced from 2. The process is thus akin to that of the production of the powers of 2 by the indefinite two. But it is thought of as producing the *even* numbers.[61]

The working of the indefinite two, then, can plausibly be regarded as a development of ideas already present in embryonic form in the dialogues; it functions as the producers of the powers of 2, but is also thought of as producing the even numbers. The powers of 2 are thought of as the even numbers *par excellence*. But even so there is an obvious gap between these two roles; we shall come back to this after taking a look at the way one functions.

In two passages in the *Metaphysics* Aristotle makes criticisms which suggest that Plato took one to be specially connected with odd numbers; it is thought of as what makes odd numbers odd. There seems to be a confusion with the additional unit which transforms an even-membered group into an odd-membered one. At 1084^a36 ff. Plato is said to have identified the odd with one because 'if [the odd] were in 3, how would 5 be odd?' The suggestion is that Plato identified the odd with one because it is always the presence of a *one* that makes an odd-membered group odd. Adding one to an even number is confused with adding an extra unit to an even-membered group. This confusion is additional evidence that Plato did not free the idea of *number* from that of *numbered group*. It is presupposed in the other passage also, 1083^b28 ff.: 'But what about the units in 3? For one of them is odd. Perhaps this is why they put 1 in the middle of the odd.' 'In the middle' suggests the Greek way of representing numbers by dots or pebbles: an odd number contains dots paired off in one-one correlation plus an extra one 'between' the two rows.

Aristotle's criticism of the principles of number at 987^b34-6 contains a difficult passage which probably also represents one as the producer of odd numbers. Aristotle says that the indefinite two

---

[61] At the end of the whole passage, where we have even and odd numbers, it may seem that both have been produced in Stage 2, via the numbers 2 and 3. But this would leave Stage 1 without any work of its own to do. Stage 2 needs to *re*introduce evenness to define oddness.

could produce all the numbers easily 'except the first ones' (*exō tōn prōtōn*). The 'first ones' here could mean the primes, but if so the criticism is incredibly compressed and unobvious. 'First' here has been taken as 'odd', but it cannot naturally mean this, and I incline to follow those scholars who have thought that *prōtōn* here should be emended to *perittōn* (odd).[62] Aristotle's criticism is then that Plato's grounds for making one of his principles a two, namely, the supposed easy production of the numbers, are not sound—for the indefinite two produces only the even numbers, odd numbers being left to the other principle.

There are traces in the dialogues also of the idea that oddness is connected with one, because of the confusion of adding one to an even number and adding an extra unit to an even-membered group. In both cases the passages go with the passages already cited as anticipations of the indefinite two.

At *Phaedo* 103-5 oneness is brought in as the explanation of oddness. As fire always participates in heat and snow in cold, so odd numbers always participate in *monas*; and *monas* must here mean 'a unit', although at 101c it meant 'oneness' or 'the number one'. (Translators usually render *monas* differently in the two cases.)

Stage 2 of the *Parmenides* argument begins by considering the One on its own and not as divisible as in the previous stage; taken as an indivisible unit (143a7) it is contrasted with its being, and in an amazing move the difference between them is brought in as a third item. Of these three items we can take pairs, and in every case there will be one item left over, which when added to the other two makes three. Three is odd, two even. So in this stage, which began

[62] The possible meanings of *exō tōn prōtōn* have been canvassed by Robin, n. 266, II) and n. 322, and by Ross in his note on 987^b34. The only four real candidates for *hoi prōtoi* are (a) the first numbers 1 and 2. But Aristotle regards 2 and, more doubtfully, 1 as numbers, and it is hard to see a reason for distinguishing between them and the other numbers. (b) The 'primary' Form numbers. But it is clear from many passages in *M-N* that it is the Form numbers if any which *are* produced from the principles. (c) The primes. (This is a natural meaning for *prōtoi* in Greek). But this is an odd omission to complain of, and does not fit with any other evidence. It is perhaps possible if we assume, with Allen, that for Plato 'the primes may have been classified as odd-times odd numbers'. (d) The odd numbers. This involves an emendation, but it does give a natural sense to the passage if the odd numbers, as suggested by other evidence, were produced by one alone.

by taking the One as an indivisible unit, we have reached the idea of adding a unit to an even-membered *group* and thereby producing an odd *number*. There is the same confusion of adding a unit with adding 1.

The *Parmenides* passage also provides an indication of the way in which one and the indefinite two were later thought of as the producers of number. Stage 2 concludes that once we have two and three, and so even and odd, we have even × even, odd × odd, even × odd and odd × even, and so we have all number. This is not a classification of number like Euclid's; if it were it would be both defective and redundant.[63] It seems rather to be a synonym for 'number, as studied in computations'; at *Charmides* 166a ff. and *Gorgias* 451a-c Plato defines the subject of *logistikē* as 'the even and the odd, how much they are to themselves and to each other', and the Neoplatonist scholiasts explain this phrase in the terms used in the *Parmenides*.[64] The *Parmenides* thus 'produces numbers' only in the sense of sketching the processes that generate even numbers and odd numbers respectively.

There remains, however, the problem noticed above: if one and the indefinite two produce odd and even numbers respectively, they produce numbers in a reasonably comprehensive way and one which finds echoes in the dialogues, and explains most of Aristotle's criticisms, and the attitude of the Greek commentatotrs like Alexander. But the two did *not* produce all even numbers, only the powers of two. Powers of two plus odd numbers do not add up to 'all number'.

[63] Defective because even and odd are omitted; redundant because even × odd is not interestingly different from odd × even. See Heath's edition of Euclid, vol.ii, pp. 282-4: 'odd × even' appears in the text as well as 'even × odd', but Heath omits it not only because it is 'pointless' but because it creates inconsistencies with the text elsewhere. In the *Parmenides* the combinations of 'even' and 'odd' do not answer exactly to the production of even and odd numbers in the text, suggesting that a general characterization of number is aimed at rather than a precise classification.

[64] Olympiodorus expands to this effect: Multiplication is always either by what is multiplied or by another thing. So the only possible ways of multiplying numbers, which are all odd or even, are: even × odd, odd × odd odd × even and even × odd—the very combinations turning up in the *Parmenides* passage. See Klein, p. 14 and n. 11; there is a corruption in the text, but Klein compares another (anon.) scholion to the same effect.

This is a standing puzzle with Plato's principles of number, and perhaps is not resolvable, but I think that a plausible suggestion can be made.

At $1083^b36-1084^a7$ Aristotle makes a remark about the generation of number, and although unfortunately he does not attribute it to anyone, the terminology suggests that it is an Academic theory. The passage goes: '. . . generation of numbers is always of an odd number or an even one. An odd number is generated when one applies to an even number; the numbers doubled from one [the powers of two] when the two applies; and the other even numbers when the odd numbers <apply>.' Number is thus produced by (i) adding 1 to an even number (ii) producing the powers of 2, and (iii) getting the other even numbers by some operation with odd numbers (it is not clear whether addition or multiplication is meant). It is striking here that (i) is what one does and (ii) is what the indefinite two does. (Oddly, (i) comes before (ii), although it seems to presuppose (ii); but this can be explained as a matter of exposition.[65]) But what is (iii)? It is simply the filling of the gap we have noticed— i.e. the provision of the even numbers that are not powers of two. This suggests the following: the indefinite two *on its own* produces the powers of two; given these, one produces the odd numbers; and *both* are also necessary to produce the remaining even numbers (since for these to be obtained odd numbers have to be available). This would explain why Aristotle sometimes speaks as though the indefinite two produces only the powers of two, and sometimes as though it produces all even numbers: even numbers are the province of the indefinite two, but *on its own* it can produce only the evenly times even numbers in the restricted sense of the powers of two.

It certainly seems from this passage that Plato produced some such solution, to enable one and the indefinite two to produce all numbers between them. It seems at first that (iii) introduces an entirely new process. However, the process envisaged was perhaps addition (or multiplication, which the Greeks regarded as abbrevi-

[65] Alexander (57.15-16) says (in a different context) that odd numbers usually are 'prior' to even; Speusippus (fr. 4) exploits this: the dekad must end with an even number (10), because every even number has to be preceded by an odd one (!).

ated addition[66]), which would be covered already by the process associated with one. If odd numbers are introduced by adding 1 this process can be extended to even numbers as well. This does have the disadvantage that it is one that really bears the responsibility for these even numbers, rather than the indefinite two. Moreover, this move reveals the weakness of the whole scheme, for (iii) simply amounts to 'fill in the gaps left by (i) and (ii)'; but how do we know that there *are* any gaps unless we already think of the numbers as forming a series each of which is 1 more than its predecessor? Once 'adding 1' can be used to produce even numbers as well as odd it becomes clear that this is *all* that is necessary, and that (ii), the working of the indefinite two, can simply be dispensed with. Certainly Aristotle always regards the indefinite two as a futile excrescence on any account of how to produce the numbers.

The above suggests that numbers were not produced in the right order, i.e. as a series increasing by one every time, and this seems to be supported by a passage (1081^b17-22) where Aristotle complains that for the Platonists each number will not be part of the one following. Other passages considered might also suggest that since numbers were produced as a result of three processes (or two, one with two applications), they came out in a bizarre order. This has been found the most intriguing feature of the Platonic generation of numbers, and much ingenuity has been spent on diagrammatic reconstructions of the possible deviant orders in which the numbers were supposedly produced.[67] However, what Aristotle says at 1081^a

[66] This indicates again that only the positive integers were thought of as numbers. See Euclid vii, def. 15 (Heath's ed. vol.ii, p. 287), and Wedberg, p. 69.

[67] A selection of the major attempts: Robin, pp. 442-68, esp. 449; Stenzel, pp. 30-53; Becker; Wilpert (3), pp. 202-21; Berti, pp. 291-7. Attempts to derive the Form numbers as ratios of some kind, i.e. in effect rational numbers rather than integers, include those of Taylor, Töplitz, van der Wielen (in Ross), Ross ch. 12 (in a very weak form), Gaiser (1), pp. 115-25. Gaiser ingeniously constructs the Form numbers as 'Schnittverhältnisse', ratios produced by sections through a triangle and tetrahedron; this produces also the harmonic intervals of octave, fourth, and fifth (see his figs. 30 and 31), which are put to ambitious use. Ilting (1) objects that since Aristotle tells us that the ideal magnitudes are 'after the numbers' they cannot be used to generate them. Gaiser's reply ((1), 2nd ed., p. 580), that this is just a matter of exposition, is not satisfactory: this problem threatens all attempts to give Plato a 'geometrical' view of number.

21-5 suggests that the Platonists did not think of the number series as having an unorthodox order (cf. 1082^{b}33-7). Plato is guilty not of the eccentricity of producing a wrongly ordered number series, but of producing numbers in a way that is totally unrelated to the way they are counted, and so of divorcing number from counting.

At *Phaedo* 104a7–b4 Plato talks about '3, 5, and the whole half of number' and then of 'the whole of the other column (*stichos*) of number'. Even and odd numbers are thought of as produced in two open-ended columns, which together make up all numbers. Plato is not, of course, taking this to have anything to do with the way we *count* numbers. This is a slight indication that Plato may have combined without discomfort the idea that numbers are counted in a certain order and the idea that numbers are produced by the separate and joint operations of one and the indefinite two. It may well have been dissatisfaction with this which prompted Aristotle in his own theory of number to tie number much more closely to counting.

Aristotle says three times that the Platonists generate number only as far as the *dekad* (the numbers up to and including 10). Aristotle's statements are so definite that they cannot be explained away, and we must accept that Plato did only give an account of the production of numbers as far as 10. This peculiar fact has given rise to extensive speculation, mainly on the lines that Plato must have assigned a special and exalted status to the numbers 1-10, and produced other numbers from them in a way different from the way they were themselves produced. Nothing supports this extravagant idea. A more reasonable suggestion is that Plato may have had some notion of a decimal system, but this is most unlikely in view of Greek number-notation, which would not suggest the idea. The most plausible solution seems to be to suppose that Plato just produced the numbers up to 10 and then stopped, apparently assuming that it was obvious that the process(es) could be continued *ad infinitum*. Aristotle's complaint at *Physics* 206^{b}27 ff. suggests this: 'though he makes the infinites two, he does not use them. For in the numbers the infinite in the direction of reduction is not present . . . nor . . . in the direction of increase, for the parts number only up to the decad.' Aristotle is attacking the fact that Plato has produced only a fragment of the number series, giving no indication either that it does not continue indefinitely downwards (it stops at 1, the Greeks having no notion of 0 and the negative numbers as numbers) or that it *does* continue indefinitely upwards (there being no last number). It is characteristic of Aristotle's tendency to take Plato at his word to say that Plato thought that there were only 10 numbers; but in fact it is not the upper bound 10 he objects to, but the fact that what has been done is not what has been claimed. Plato has not produced *number* by his methods, for it is essential to number that numbers go on for ever, whereas Plato has just produced a few numbers and stopped, without showing how they can go on for ever.

It is also true, however, that the number 10 had special significance for the Pythagoreans, and Plato may have been influenced by this in stopping at 10. We possess a long and strange fragment of Speusippus (fr. 4 Lang) which expatiates on the virtues of the number 10 and the 'completeness' of its nature. Speusippus claims that within it can be found exemplifications of all mathematically interesting properties of numbers. The Pythagoreans were also interested in the dekad because it can be expressed in the form of a 'tetraktys' or succession of the numbers 1-2-3-4, represented as dots or pebbles arranged in a triangle. This sequence is sometimes connected with the sequence of point—line—plane—solid. Interest in this sequence is shown in the way the principles were extended to derive magnitudes, and some modern scholars have connected it with the stopping of the number series at 10, taking them to be parts of a single unified theory of derivation of numbers and magnitudes. However, there is no real basis for such a conclusion. There were many different interpretations of the tetraktys, and we know nothing about their historical relationships. If we keep the derivation of numbers separate from any wider scheme of derivation it seems more plausible to explain the stopping at 10 in terms of considerations about number alone.

(b) *Derivation of magnitudes: the extension of the principles* So far we have seen that an account can be reconstructed of the way in which one and the indefinite two figured as the producers of numbers, an account in which their features as one (or unit) and as two (or duality) were utilized in the way suggested by the references to them by Aristotle and by his commentators. Nothing suggested that these same principles could also be principles of items other than numbers; indeed, their production of numbers as 'the even and the odd' would seem to tell against any extension of the principles to derive magnitudes. However, it is clear from *M-N* as well as other sources that Plato's two principles were thought of as producing geometrical magnitudes as well as numbers. The principles themselves are used more widely and acquire a wider scope; different terms were used for them in ways which show that their function underwent some reinterpretation. Aristotle in ch. 1 of *N* gives the best survey of the different terms used; it is clear from that passage that there were many different theories in the Academy, some of which do not turn up in the later tradition and no doubt never got beyond the stage of informal discussions. The indefinite two appears in several variations, as 'the great and small', the many and few', or more generally 'the exceeding and exceeded'. It also appears as 'plurality' (this was Speusippus' contribution), 'the unequal(s)', 'the other nature', 'the different'. The other principle, one, was sometimes reinterpreted to match as 'the equal or 'the same', but more often remains simply 'one' (or 'oneness').

It is certainly not the case that we always find the principles of number described as one and the indefinite two, while the other descriptions were reserved for the wider role. One and the indefinite two are sometimes claimed as principles of the whole scheme, numbers and magnitudes (e.g. by Theophrastus, *Metaphysics* 6ª15– ᵇ17); while numbers alone are sometimes said in *M-N* to be produced from the great and small. However, we have seen that the characters of one and the indefinite two, as unity and duality, play a role in the production of numbers which cannot be performed by 'the great and small' or 'the unequal', and this makes it legitimate to assume that the derivation of magnitudes proceeded by a generalization of the functions of two principles originally specialized to the production of numbers.

It is tempting to think of this as a chronological development in Plato's thought –first a derivation of number from two principles, then a generalization of the same kind of thing on a wider scale. In one of Aristotle's earliest works, *On the Forms*, one and the indefinite two appear as the principles of the Form numbers. In another lost work, *On the Good*, a report and criticism of Plato, one and the indefinite two appear as principles of a much wider scheme, along with ideas which seem to be later than those in *On the Forms*.[68] But no chronological schemes can claim firmness in this area. We can safely say at most that the derivation of the numbers was probably independent of its incorporation in the wider scheme, judging from its greater specificity compared with the vaguer way in which the derivation of all the magnitudes was comprehended.

The extension of the principles raises three new points. First, the opposition of 'equal/unequal' and 'same/other' which appears in some reinterpretations of the principles points to the 'Academy theory of categories'. From various later sources[69] we know that the Academy 'reduced' different types of terms to two logically basic types, *kath'hauto* terms and *pros ti* terms. *Kath'hauto* terms pick out items that are independent, and are in many ways akin to Aristotle's substance terms. *Pros ti* terms pick out items that are relative or dependent on *kath'hauto* items. There are some faint foreshadowings of this idea in the dialogues.[70]

Later reports tell us that *kath'hauto* terms were in some way 'reduced' to one and *pros ti* terms to the other principle, via the oppositions equal/unequal and same/different. Most modern reconstructions of *On the Good* present this 'kategoriale Reduktion' as part of the 'reduction to the principles' which Aristotle is criticizing in *M-N* and which appears in later reports. I am very doubtful about this. It seems to me much more likely that the 'theory of categories' and any reduction of them to two basic principles formed quite a different part of the Academy's ideas, and that they have nothing to do with the derivation of numbers and magnitudes from the principles. This cannot be argued here, but in any case it does not matter for discussion of *M-N* itself, for although Aristotle uses

[68] See my article, 'Forms and first principles', *Phronesis* 1975, where I try to show this in connection with the notion of 'natural priority'.

[69] Alexander, 83. 24-6 (*On the Forms* fr. 3 Ross); Xenocrates fr. 12 Heinze; *Divisiones Aristoteleae* 39-41 Mutschmann, Hermodorus, quoted by Simplicius *in Phys.* 247.30–248.15 (translated in de Vogel, and as 16 in App. I of Findlay).

[70] *Charmides* 166-8, *Republic* 438b-d, *Theaetetus* 160b, *Philebus* 51c, *Sophist* 255c-d. The matter is rather complicated, however; cf. n. 33 of the article mentioned in n. 68.

his own theory of categories in it, he never uses or discusses the Academy theory.

The second new idea imported by the reinterpretation of one and the indefinite two in wider terms, one which does appear in *M-N*, is the way the principles come to function in a way rather like Aristotle's principles of form and matter. (Since Aristotle was a member of the Academy, and there seems to have been much internal discussion, this similarity is not very surprising.) Aristotle says at one point (*On the Forms* fr. 4 Ross) that the Academy called their principles form and matter, but this need mean no more than that they used them as such. More telling is the fact that in *N* chs. 1-2 he argues at length on the assumption that the Platonist principles are meant to be doing the job of form and matter but fail to do so. The appropriateness of this criticism appears from the fact that the later ancient tradition took up interpretation of Plato's principles in terms of form and matter (though in this, of course, they may have been influenced by Aristotle).

So the derivation of magnitudes from the two principles does not involve a precise theory, rather the idea that lines, planes, etc. are the products of the imposition of form or definiteness on an indefinite material.[71] It is worth noticing in this context that Aristotle talks of reducing magnitudes to the principles as well as deriving them from them,[72] and the idea would certainly make better sense if thought of as a logical analysis into the formal elements of form and matter, rather than as a metaphysical generation of magnitudes from two omnicompetent principles. But Aristotle's criticisms in

[71] When the derivation of numbers appears in this context it is sometimes described in this vague way as well. Cf. Alexander, 55.20 ff. (*On the Good* fr. 2 Ross).

[72] Compare 992^{a}10-19 (reducing things to first principles) with 1085^{a}7-14 (producing things from first principles), where what is involved seems to be the same process. Aristotle quotes an oral dictum of Plato's (*Nicomachean Ethics* 1095^{a}30-^{b}2) to the effect that Plato thought it important to ask whether one was on the way to or the way from the principles; but this remark, in the context of an ethical discussion, cannot bear the weight put on it by recent reconstructions of the unwritten doctrines, which distinguish sharply between a 'Reduktion' of the world of phenomena to the principles, and a subsequent 'Deduktion'. It may be, of course, that *On the Good* contained something like the 'upward and downward path' of the *Republic*, but if so, we are not entitle to infer it from this remark.

M-N make it clear that the system could not be taken unequivocally as either logical analysis or as cosmology, and seemed to him an unclear blend of both. (Recent German reconstructions of the unwritten doctrines take Plato's ideas here more seriously, treating them as an 'Ableitungssystem'.)

The third new idea brought in by the extension of the principles is increased emphasis on the progression of dimensions, from length to breadth to depth. Interest in this is vestigially apparent in the dialogues (*Republic* 528a-b, *Sophist* 235d, *Politicus* 284e, *Timaeus* 53c, *Laws* 817e, 819d, 894a). From Aristotle (1017^b17-21, 1028^b 16-18, 1090^b5-7) we learn that the Academy were occupied with the special type of dependence that this sequence illustrates. Solids are bounded by planes and planes by lines; so there could be a plane without a solid but not a solid without a plane, and a line without a plane but not a plane without a line. This asymmetry was found interesting because it suggests that the simpler items are prior to the complex in a special sense (listed duly as 'natural priority' by Aristotle in his philosophical lexicon at 1019^a1-4). Aristotle regards this with contempt as an argument for *ontological* priority. None the less, it is suggestively similar to the search for the simpler principles of magnitudes, and turns up often in the same context. It does not fit the form/matter analysis very well, however. And it does not help the unified scheme of a derivation of numbers and magnitudes from the same principles, for properly the series should end with points, and there is no room for numbers, which cannot be obtained by any transition of the same kind. Late and scrappy reports deriving from the Academy project adopt different expedients to cover the gap at which the 'natural priority' argument ends and numbers have to be fitted in.[73] They disagree, however, and no consistent picture can be recovered. This suggests that Plato did not have a single and coherent account, and that the 'natural priority' of lines to planes and planes to solids was used to support, but was not well integrated into, the scheme of deriving magnitudes from the principles.

According to Aristotle, magnitudes were produced from different types of the great and small: lines were produced from the short and

[73] At this point Alexander's account (55.20 ff.) differs from Sextus (X259 ff.), and there is no way of harmonizing them. See de Vogel, pp. 283-5.

long, planes from the broad and narrow, solids from the deep and shallow. These are thought of as different types of indeterminate quantity, which have determinateness imposed on them by the formal principle. There is a vexed and at present perhaps insoluble problem about the formal principle. Either it was one in each case (Alexander, 228.10-28, specific on this very point), or it was 2 in the case of the line, 3 for the plane, and 4 for the solid.[74] (The latter view seems to be that of Xenocrates, and the question is whether it was that of Plato as well.)

All the sources are remarkably unspecific about the status of the magnitudes produced. They should be Forms if they are to correspond to the numbers produced by one and the indefinite two. But Forms are unique of their kind, whereas Aristotle often presupposes in his criticisms that the ideal geometrical objects are plural. It is perhaps best to regard them as Aristotle does, as forming a distinct class. The problem of Forms seems to have worried Plato remarkably little in the lecture *On the Good*, and he probably did not make a specific assertion or denial on this point.

The extension of the principles to cover the derivation of magnitudes involves Plato in two large problems. Firstly, the principles have to be reinterpreted in varying ways in different cases: the long and short, broad and narrow, etc. have to be different forms of the same material principle (the great and small). This raises a problem about the identity of this principle: in what sense is it the *same* principle that these are different forms of, and from which are produced the different magnitudes? Aristotle complains, with justification, that the types of great and small can be neither generically different nor species of one genus (992^a13-19, 1085^a7-20, $^a31$-1085^b4). Speusippus was to solve the problem by making them completely different principles. This brings out the unsatisfactoriness of explaining the series of dimensions in terms of form and matter. The Academy appear to have tried to meet such problems by various re-

---

[74] Pseudo-Alexander, 777.16-21. (Cherniss (3), p. 85, shows that this is derived from Syrianus, 154.9-13). Cf. 1090^b13-1091^a5, *de Anima* 404^b16-30 (see the recent discussion of both these passages in Gaiser (2)); and two passages where 2 is 'the number of the line' (1036^b12-17, 1043^a29-36). On the dispute whether Plato or just Xenocrates is referred to here, see Ross, pp. 208-11, Saffrey, and Cherniss (3).

interpretations of the two principles. Aristotle complains in *N* ch. 1 that this is merely verbal redefinition and gives no real content to the idea that it is the same two principles at work under all the different descriptions.

Secondly, the geometrical magnitudes presuppose space, as numbers do not. Aristotle's criticism on this point has already been noted. This difficulty surfaces in the impossibility of getting a clear and coherent account from the sources of how the transition from numbers to magnitudes was made, and whether and how it involved points. Modern German reconstructions assume, optimistically I think, that this move from the unextended to the extended was part of Plato's explicit plan, and part of the point of the whole derivation. I think it more likely that the transition to space-occupying items was not accompanied by much thought about the nature of this space. Perhaps partly because of this, and because of failure to distinguish clearly at this point between ideal space and actual space in which we live, Plato's ideas may have harked back to earlier and cruder Pythagorian cosmologies which 'created the world out of numbers'. It is even possible that archaic Pythagorean ideas like the importance of the *dekad* may have come to intrigue Plato when his derivation of magnitudes began to seem rather like the earlier ideas. Whatever his unclarity at this point about space, however, Plato did not confuse ideal magnitudes with magnitudes surrounding us; Aristotle stresses that the Academy were always distinguished from Pythagoreans by their separating of numbers and mathematical objects from objects in the spatio-temporal world. What brings Plato close to the Pythagoreans is his derivation of numbers and geometrical magnitudes from the same principles. No doubt this lies behind Aristotle's strict separation of these two realms and their principles.

The fact that Plato used the same principles to derive numbers and geometrical magnitudes has been used to support the idea that his concept of number was already a 'geometrical' one. I have tried to show that his actual views about the numbers so generated were quite different: they were thought of as sets of units. (Aristotle indeed brings out the tension between this fact about them and the way they are derived.) The unified derivation of numbers and magnitudes does not show (and is never regarded by Aristotle as showing) that Plato had a geometrical view of number; rather it reflects Plato's belief, visible in the central books of *Republic*, that the departmental sciences can be unified by deriving their special principles and axioms from principles more general and common to all of them.

(c) *The identification of Forms and numbers* The grand derivation of the objects of arithmetic and geometry from common principles suggests the claims made for dialectic as a mistress-science in the *Republic*; and just as the ultimate 'unhypothetical first principle' of that dialogue is the Form of the Good, so the lecture in which Plato presented his grand synthesis was titled *On the Good*. As far as we can determine the contents of the lecture, it was a sketch of the foundations of mathematics such as we have seen, unifying arithmetic and geometry to the extent of deriving numbers and magnitudes from the same principles, and with the relation of mathematics to the world left, perhaps conveniently, rather hazy. Recent German work, especially that of Krämer,[75] has interpreted the lecture as an ambitious ethical undertaking and found in it the theory of an ethical mean. Such an undertaking is, however, in large part pure speculation, and in order to get any support from the dialogues has to rely on a theory of the primacy of Plato's 'esoteric' teaching to his 'exoteric' dialogues. A more modest and plausible hypothesis would see *On the Good* as an attempt to carry out the sort of programme envisaged in the *Republic*;[76] the paucity of our evidence for it would be explained by Plato's probable revulsion, during the period of the later dialogues, from the kind of bold speculation apparent in both it and the *Republic*.

Inflationary views of *On the Good* take it to have been a total 'Ableitungssystem' of reality, and to have derived from the principles not only the world of the senses but all the items accepted by Plato at any time as belonging in the world of the intellect—in particular Forms.

[75] Krämer (1) has led the way here, and much recent work follows him. Earlier work on *On the Good* (Wilpert, Bröcker (in Wippern)), ignored this side apart from references to the Form of the Good in the *Republic*.
[76] Ilting (2) envisages it as something like this. It is interesting to compare Whitehead's attempt to do something like what he imagined the lecture to be.

One ground for this is the fact that Forms seem to appear in the derivation process as we hear about it from Alexander, the best witness for the contents of the lecture. But he was using Aristotle's version, and the appearance of Forms can, I think, be explained as due to Aristotle's polemic rather than a reflection of Plato's own teaching.[77] The appearance of Forms in later reports can be explained away as the result of later attempts to harmonize all possible aspects of Plato's ideas at any time. (This is particularly true of Sextus Empiricus X, 248-83, the passage which forms the basis for most modern reconstructions of the unwritten doctrines.)

The chief ground for holding that derivation from the principles did involve Forms is the fact that Aristotle in his criticisms, in several places throughout M-N, uses the expression 'Forms are numbers.' Some passages seem to claim that Plato identified all Forms with numbers and as such derived them from one and the indefinite two. The idea that Forms are numbers has been very variously interpreted, and particularly in recent German reconstructions has been made to bear a lot of (sometimes dubious) philosophical weight. However explained, it alters the way the target of M-N is conceived, making it no longer a matter of the existence of numbers where numbers are in question, but also of Forms. I take Aristotle (and Plato) to be concerned simply with numbers in passages outside M 4-5, and my interpretation therefore differs at almost every point from that of someone who accepts that Plato *did* identify Forms with numbers.

---

[77] The passage at Alexander, 55.26–56.7 (in *On the Good* fr. 2 Ross) seems to be an interpolation into the argument. It discusses and refers to Plato in a way unlike the rest of the passage; it uses Aristotelian terminology; and it renders the passage internally incoherent. First we were told that first principles must be primary and incomposite (these conditions being fulfilled by one and the indefinite two). But now we are suddenly told that Forms must be identical to numbers since both are primary, where by this is meant 'prior to individuals', a much weaker condition than the two already set out. Moreover, we get the conclusion that the first principles of both Forms and numbers must be the same—whereas Forms were introduced *as* first principles. It seems as though an argument by Aristotle, to the effect that Forms and numbers must be identified by the Academy, has got interpolated into the main stream of a different Platonic argument, with the result that the notion of 'first principle' has no over-all coherence in this argument. The 'Aristotelian' argument has affinities with other arguments (discussed below) whereby Aristotle sets out to prove that the Academy *must* have identified Forms with numbers.

But Aristotle does often *say* that Forms are numbers, so we have to see how this is to be taken.

There are many passages[78] where Aristotle ascribes to Plato or to the Platonists the idea that 'Forms are numbers' or 'the Forms are numbers', but not all these passages can have equal weight put on them, and some should be treated very differently from others. In two passages (1073^a17-22, 1090^a16-17) Aristotle casually mentions identification of Forms with numbers in the course of an argument about something else, and nothing is made of it, so little light is shed. Two other passages (1086^a11-13, 1080^b11-12) which are commonly discussed (and translated) as though identification were in question, in fact concern the difference between Form numbers and mathematical numbers, not all Forms. The expressions used in all these passages are not helpful in the search for the exact force of this supposed identification. The idioms vary, and so does use of singular and plural and of the definite article (compare 1073^a18-19, 1086^a11-12, 1090^a16-17). In the most famous passage where identification is imputed (987^b21-2) the expression is so uncertain that different scholars have responded by emending the text in different ways.[79]

We thus find that Aristotle's ways of referring to the theory that Forms are numbers are loose at best, and that to find out what is really meant we have to look at passages where the idea is unmistakably referred to in a context where it bears some weight: we have to look at the use to which it is put.[80]

---

[78] 987^b18-25; 991^b9-10; 992^b13-17; 1073^a17-22; 1080^b11-12; 1081^a5-17; 1082^b23-4; 1083^a17-20; 1086^a11-13; 1090^a16-17; 1091^b26 ff.; *On Philosophy* fr. 11.

[79] The Greek literally goes: 'from these (the great and the small) by participation in one the Forms are the numbers.' It is apparently grammatically anomalous to have both Forms and numbers. Some (e.g. Christ, Jaeger) cut out the numbers, others (e.g. Zeller, Ross, Tredennick) cut out the Forms. Stenzel keeps both and reads it as an apposition; Merlan (2) defends this reading on the grounds that Asclepius read it and that it is supported by a passage of Plotinus.

[80] I do not agree with de Vogel and Gaiser ((1), pp. 118, 125 ff.) that the problem is solved by Aristotle's statement at *Physics* 206^b32-3 that Plato produced only the numbers up to 10, whereas there are obviously more than 10 Forms. These isolated statements are more in need of an explanation in terms of a satisfactory theory about the 'identification of Forms and numbers'

Four of these passages can in fact be explained away; they impute no such idea as the identification of all Forms with numbers.

(i) Syrianus, *in Met.* 159.3-160. 5 (*On Philosophy* fr. 11 Ross). This passage has already been discussed above (p.27) in a way which makes it clear that it concerns the nature of the Form numbers. It is not plausible to take it, as has often been done, as a reference to the idea that all Forms are numbers; this is not how Syrianus understands it.

(ii) 991^{b}9-10. This comes at the point in *A* 9 where Aristotle turns from the original theory of Forms with the words, 'If the Forms are numbers . . .', and introduces a further collection of arguments. These however, have no reference to any identification theory, but concern either the number Forms and ideal magnitudes,[81] or the Academy theory of elements and principles. This whole section appears to have been worked up into the contents of our present *M-N*, since several arguments in the latter appear to be more developed versions of arguments in *A* 9.[82] Whatever Aristotle's words, what he actually goes on to talk about is the sort of problem with Academic theories of mathematics which fills the bulk of *M-N*, not any theory identifying all Forms with numbers. Identification has been found in the first argument because it begins with the words, 'If the Forms

---

than capable of providing it themselves. Moreover, while we are told at 1084^a 12-17 that the theory provides numbers only up to 10, we are also told at 1073^{a}17-22 that it sometimes treats them as going up to 10 but sometimes as infinite (*contra* de Vogel, this cannot mean, 'some say the one and some say the other'), which suggests that this is a difficulty in Plato's theory of number and not tied specially to Forms.

[81] Objections to the nature of the Form numbers run from 991^{b}9-992^{a}10. 992^{a}10-^{b}18 concerns the other mathematicals, and problems with mathematical platonism generally; 992^{b}18-993^{a}10 deals with the problem of first principles. It is worth noting that the problems about numbers and their derivation appear in a different discussion from the more general problems of the derivation of the ideal magnitudes.

[82] Even the order of discussion (first the ideal objects and problems with them and their derivation, then the principles from which they are derived) is preserved in *M-N*. Krämer ((1), pp. 433-4) objects that *M-N* cannot just be dealing with 'nur ideale Zahlen, nicht Ideen-Zahlen', since it would be disproportionate to spend so much time refuting the existence of one type of Form, when the general theory had been refuted. This is to assume that neither Plato nor Aristotle had anything of interest to say about numbers, apart from their being Forms; but this is clearly not true.

are numbers, how can they be causes?' But the genders here compel us to take 'they' as numbers, *not* as Forms. The argument is about the difficulty in taking *numbers*, not Forms, to be causes (cf. 1093ª 16-17). The argument concerns only the number Forms, and depends on the claim that ratios cannot be regarded as numbers.[83]

(iii) 1082ᵇ23-4; (iv) 1083ª17-20. These two passages occur in the course of a long and complicated passage; detailed discussion can be found in the Notes. The whole passage deals in technical detail with the question of how numbers can be Forms, given certain alternatives. Nothing remotely resembling an identification theory is in the offing; and in context the references to the idea that 'Forms are numbers' cannot mean what they appear to mean. Two such incidental references cannot overturn the sense of an extended passage of clearly directed criticism. It is possible that they are mistakes—either that Aristotle used the phrase 'Forms are numbers' as a scornful shorthand way of referring to Plato's idea about Forms and numbers in general (we shall see shortly that he has some justification), or that the phrases are due to a later editor arranging for publication lecture-notes on a subsequently neglected and ill-understood topic.

It is not impossible for Aristotle to refer to someone's ideas in an abbreviated and misleading way: he refers to the Atomists in a similar style (*de Caelo* 303ª3-10). But not all of his references can be so explained away. There are four passages (all from the *Metaphysics*) in which an argument is given that definitely identifies Forms with numbers, and does not just concern number Forms.

(a) 987ᵇ18-25. 'Since the Forms were the causes of all other things, [Plato] thought their elements were the elements of all things. As matter, the great and small were principles; as essential reality, the One; for from the great and small, by participation in the One, come the Numbers.' This is the Oxford translation, but there are grammatical troubles with the text here; see note 79.

---

[83] The argument is not (as Ross takes it) that ratios imply a substrate, implausible for Forms; rather the point is that if Forms are conceived of as numerical ratios of some kind this has no weight as showing them to be numbers, since ratios are not numbers. The argument is often misread because of Jaeger's unsupported insertion of 'Form' into the text at 1. 20, changing the argument from, 'a ratio will not be a number' to 'a Form will not be a number'.

(b) 992^b13-17. 'Nor can it be explained either how the lines and planes and solids that come after the numbers exist or can exist, or what significance they have; for these can neither be Forms (for they are not numbers), nor the intermediates (for these are the objects of mathematics), nor the perishable things' (Oxford translation).

(c) 1081^a17-17. 'But if Forms are not numbers, they cannot exist at — all. From what principles will Forms come? Number comes from one and the indefinite two, and the principles and elements <of things> are said to be <the principles and elements> of number; but Forms cannot be ranked either before numbers or after them.'

(d) 1091^b26 ff. 'Besides, if Forms are numbers, all Forms are kinds of good. But suppose there are Forms of anything one pleases. If there are Forms only of goods, Forms will not be real objects; but if there are Forms of real objects too, then all living creatures and plants and everything participating in Forms will be good.'

(c) and the elliptical (d) are discussed in the Notes. In all four passages there is a single structure of argument: the identification of Forms and numbers is not presented as a report of what Plato actually said but as the conclusion of an *argument*: Forms *must* be identical with numbers, because they both come from the same principles. Aristotle is relying on a general principle that if As and Bs come from the same principles (or elements) and are not explicitly differentiated, then they are the same type of thing. He is no doubt influenced by his conception of definition as proceding by genus and differentia; if no differentia is given there is no reason to believe that there is a genuinely different type. He employs the principle not only in the case of Forms and numbers, but also in the case of other products of the Academy principles; he uses it also to show that Form numbers and mathematical numbers must be the same, since they are produced from the same principles and are not explicitly differentiated. At one point (990^a29-32) Aristotle even accuses Plato of identifying physical objects, as well as their Forms, with numbers, because they are all derived ultimately from the same principles. Clearly in all these cases the conclusion is Aristotle's own. So, just as we do not conclude that according to Aristotle Plato identified Form numbers with mathematical numbers, nor physical objects with Forms and with numbers, there is no need either to conclude that Plato identified Forms with numbers.

There is therefore considerable force to Cherniss's claim ((2), p.59) that the identification of Forms and numbers was never a theory of Plato's but is merely the conclusion of Aristotle's polemic: 'If your opponent asserts a thesis which you undertake to refute, you do not begin by *proving* that he asserts it.' In (a)–(d) Aristotle *proves* that the identification must have been Plato's view, employing a principle which it is natural for him to have thought important, given his own concern with definition by employment of genus and differentiae.

We therefore do not have to assume that Plato ever identified all Forms with numbers, and *a fortiori* that he ever identified particular Forms with particular numbers. Aristotle sometimes puts forward such particular identifications, but he is clearly making up his own examples: within a few lines he identifies Man with both 3 and 2, and suggests that 4 may be identified with Horse or White (1081a 11, 1084a23, 25). This further suggests that there were no actual statements of Plato's that could be appealed to to show that Plato really thought that all Forms were numbers.

But it is not enough to explain away Aristotle's attribution to Plato of the identification of Forms and numbers as being merely the conclusion of his own argument; for why ever should Aristotle have thought it apt to suggest that Plato must be committed to such a theory? Aristotle is naturally impatient with the production of different items from the same principles without any attempt at adequate differentiation, but this alone would not explain the frequency of his allusions to 'Forms are numbers'. Surely there must have been something in what Plato actually said to give these remarks of Aristotle's a point. We still have to account not only for the passages where Aristotle is using 'Forms are numbers' to refer to *some* idea of Plato's, but also for the fact that Aristotle's very argument assumes that for Plato Forms as well as numbers were derived from the indefinite two. According to Cherniss the latter assumption also is not Plato's, but if so Aristotle is simply misrepresenting Plato, and this does not seem likely.

I think that we can in fact find traces indicating that Plato did at some time hold that Forms could be 'reduced' to numbers, and hence to the principles of numbers, one and the indefinite two. These ideas did not, I believe, figure in *On the Good*, and so are not directly relevant to Plato's ideas about the foundations of mathematics. But they explain why Aristotle can refer to Plato's theories about Forms and numbers as a confused notion that 'Forms are numbers', and why he can argue that to be consistent Plato *should* hold that Forms are the same sort of thing as numbers, since they are ultimately derived from the same principles. (Some of Aristotle's criticism has found its way into our accounts of *On the Good*, which derive from Aristotle's version of it, and make it seem as though identification of Forms with numbers did form a part of it; but I think that the original line of thought did not concern Forms at all. See n. 79.)

Plato's 'reduction' of Forms to numbers seems to have been of the sketchiest, and though it survives in the indirect tradition seems never to have been written down. Reconstruction of it must necessarily be speculative, and for present purposes I must be brief and dogmatic; but I believe that all the statements made here can be supported by a longer account.

In the later dialogues, Plato's characterization of Forms changes in important respects, one being the replacement of the earlier insistence on the singleness and simplicity of Forms, the Form F being such that not-F will not apply to it at all in any respect.[84] Plato now emphasizes the way Forms are interrelated: the *Sophist* shows brilliantly that Forms must combine if connected discourse is to be possible at all, and collection and division are recommended as the philosopher's tools for sorting and classifying Forms.[85] At

---

[84] *Phaedo* 66a2-3, *Protagoras* 330c-e, *Symposium* 211b1-4, *Hippias Major* 291d1-5. The point emerges clearly at *Parmenides* 128e-129e, where Socrates says that the theory of Forms removes the puzzle of how one thing can be like and unlike, or one and many, but that he would be amazed if anyone could show him not-F applying to the Form F in any way whatsoever. Some scholars, like Cherniss, believe that Plato never abandoned this conception ((1), p. 515, cf. (2), p. 54.)

[85] The middle-dialogues language of sight and showing use of dialectic gives way to that of sorting and classifying: 'collecting' and 'dividing' are the hallmark of the dialectician in the difficult passages *Phaedrus* 265d-266c, *Sophist* 253d5-e2. Interest in the making of divisions, apparent at *Cratylus* 424b ff., flowers in the *Phaedrus*, *Sophist*, and *Politicus*.

Philebus 14-18 Plato faces the fact that the problem of how one thing can be many turns up not only with things in the physical world, as was recognized in the *Parmenides*, but with the Forms themselves, as was not recognized there.[86] A Form is one in that it picks out a unity, classifies things that form one kind or sort, but it is also many, in that it implies a number of other Forms which it 'contains'. Plato suggests that this ceases to be a problem if we determine the *number* of Forms involved: we should search for two or three kinds within the kind we are concerned with, and continue subdividing 'until we come to see not merely that the one we started with is a one and an unlimited many, but also just how many it is' (16d).

Plato is here putting forward the idea that what a general term picks out is not only a unity but also divides into a plurality in the sense of being analysable into other Forms. The unity of a Form, the fact that it is a *one* over the many, is not questioned in the *Philebus*. What Plato now concentrates on is the plurality inherent in Forms, pointing out that this does not threaten the unity of a Form if we can analyse it into a definite *number* of sub-kinds.[87] Protarchus had objected that if pleasure is really a genuine single thing, then there cannot be different kinds of pleasure; all pleasures, however different, have in common the same single feature of being pleasure. Socrates insists that pleasures, like colours and shapes, can *differ* precisely in so far as they are pleasures. He extends the point more generally: it is unscientific merely to say that pleasure is a single thing and also that it turns up in unlimitedly many different individual instances. What we should do is narrow down the field and find out how many

[86] This depends on one interpretation of a disputed text. Three questions are put at 15b1-2, 2-4, 4-8. Some emendations of the grammatically peculiar text run the second and third together, reducing the question to that discussed in the *Parmenides*. But the genders indicate that the second question is, how can many units be one unit? And Striker (*Peras und Apeiron*, pp. 17-23) points out that the answer involves Limit and Unlimitedness in the nature of *Forms*, not of everything, so the question must concern Forms.

[87] Plato seems to concentrate on what look like genus-species analyses, but if this is all he has in mind, it would leave the position of the infima species rather obscure: it would be a unity as being a one over the many individuals, but would not be further analysable into sub-species, and so not a 'one' in the sense of 16d5. The 'pluralization' of Forms that Plato has in mind probably covers a wider field of analysis than division of genus into species.

different kinds are genuinely different forms of pleasure and not mere differences between individuals. Between unity and unlimited differentiation it is number that imposes the limit and produces intelligibility and the possibility of knowledge. So there is a sense in which knowledge of a Form involves knowledge of number, namely the number of the Forms into which it can be spelled out, and this is what supersedes the unhelpful information that the Form is one (being a unity) and unlimitedly many (turning up in infinitely many individuals). The *Philebus* thus says quite distinctly (though not, it must be admitted, very clearly or precisely) that a Form is not only one but many, and not simply an unanalysed many but a definite number. This is not just accidentally true of Forms but essential to their being what they are, since it is essential to their being objects of knowledge, and Forms are always (and emphatically in the *Philebus*) objects of knowledge.

These suggestive hints in the *Philebus* are not followed up in any of Plato's dialogues, but there are passages in later authors which suggest that Plato 'reduced Forms to numbers' in a way which has nothing to do with the ideas in *On the Good* and seems rather to be a development of what is in the *Philebus*. Theophrastus, at *Metaphysics* 6^a15-$^b17$, discusses Academic theories which derive things from principles like one and the indefinite two, but which stop at lines, planes, and solids, instead of dealing with physical objects, and adds that Plato did it differently: 'Now Plato in reducing things to the ruling principles might seem to be treating of the other things in linking them up with the Ideas, and these with the numbers, and in proceeding from the numbers to the ruling principles . . .' (Ross-- Fobes translation). Here we are told that Plato 'reduced' Forms to numbers, in the same way, presumably, as he 'reduced' things to Forms and 'reduced' numbers to one and the indefinite two. Theophrastus is uninformative on what this 'reduction' was; but however he envisaged it, it is clearly nothing to do with identification of Forms with numbers, such as Aristotle argues that Plato is committed to. (It is worth noting that at 1036^b12, $^b22$, 1044^a13 Aristotle refers briefly to the Academy 'reduction to numbers', and the context makes it clear that what is in mind is not identification of particular items with particular numbers, but something more like the

71

transformation of a defining expression into a statement of numerical ratio.)

We get more information from Sextus Empiricus, *Adv. Math.* X.258, where Plato's Forms are cited as examples of immaterial principles which turn out to have principles themselves. '[The Forms] are not principles of existing things, since each Idea taken separately is said to be a unit, but two or three or four when taken in conjunction with one or more others, so that there is something which transcends their substance, namely number, by participation in which the terms one or two or three or a still higher number than these is predicated of them' (Bury's translation). Each Form is a unity, but also plural when considered in relation to other Forms, and this 'pluralization' does not destroy its unity. So Sextus is probably right when he says (in anachronistic terminology) that number 'transcends the substance' of the Forms. What is envisaged is something fairly simple, a development, as in the *Philebus*, of the idea that a general term 'contains' other general terms. This seems to have little connection with the theories of *On the Good*, and the extremely elaborate modern suggestions for interpreting the thesis that 'Forms are numbers'.

If this is the sense in which Forms were 'reduced' to numbers, the sense in which Forms were 'reduced' to one and the indefinite two, the principles of numbers, was a fairly remote one (this is suggested by the Theophrastus passage, where the two stages are separate). This is supported by a set of arguments brought against Plato by Aristotle in *On the Forms*, where Forms as being first principles come into conflict with one and the indefinite two as principles of number, and their claim to be first principles.[88]

To sum up this more speculative section: we have seen some rather vague though suggestive ideas in Plato which might well be summarized by saying that number is more ultimate than Forms, that there is thus a sense in which Forms can be 'reduced' to numbers as first principles. So the principles of numbers have to be regarded as also prior to Forms. Aristotle, perhaps in irritation at the vagueness of such ideas, tends to make dismissive references to the idea

[88] The twelve arguments at Alexander, 85.21–88.2 (*On the Forms* fr. 4 Ross). See the article mentioned in n. 68.

that 'Forms are numbers', and sometimes produces the argument that since according to Plato both numbers and Forms are produced from one and the indefinite two, and are not explicitly differentiated as products of these principles, they must be the same sort of thing. One such argument has found its way into the tradition of *On the Good*, and has helped to suggest that Plato's theories about mathematical objects (the background of *M-N*) involved some such identification of Forms with numbers. But in fact there is no such identification, and the idea that Aristotle has in mind when he argues that Plato is so committed arises from problems specific to Forms, and is not particularly germane to the subject-matter of *M-N*.

Speusippus

Throughout *M-N* we often find several alternative theories distinguished, but irritatingly we often lack information about the holders of different views, and the only theories we can identify with any confidence are those of Plato's two successors, the first being his nephew Speusippus.[89] His theories are clearly derivative from Plato's, in spite of what seem at first like major differences. He rejected the existence of Forms, but this does not take him as far from Plato as might appear, since he maintained that numbers exist (fr. 42a-e), and did so as the result of a consistent platonism (frs. 30, 46, 47). (His rejection of Forms probably had little to do with the concerns of *M-N*, being concerned rather with his interest in divisions and classification of kinds by reference to their interrelations; he produced works on 'Resemblances'.) Aristotle, from his anti-platonist position, cannot understand how anyone can believe in the existence of numbers unless committed to it already by a prior theory like the theory of Forms (fr. 43, ·1090ª3 ff.).

Speusippus retained Plato's two principles which produce numbers,[90] but rejected the way they were stretched to function more widely; he avoided the problems attending Plato's extended principles

[89] References to fragments are to the collection of Lang. See also the article by Stenzel in Pauly–Wissowa–Kroll, *Realenenkyklopädie* III A 1636-69 (esp. 1661-6).

[90] It is rather disturbing that the commentators (e.g. ps.-Alexander, 782.31) sometimes attribute what Aristotle calls the three different views about Forms and mathematicals differently. See Zeller, *Die Philosophie der Griechen*, 2.1, pp. 1003 n. 1 and 1015 n. 2; also Ross, pp. 151-3.

by replacing them by a set of different principles for different functions. For him the principles of number are not one and the indefinite
two but one and plurality (frs. 35 a-c, 48 a-c). This suggests that he gave
up Plato's idiosyncratic derivation of 'the even and the odd' and
replaced it by something vaguer in terms of a formal and a material
principle. The principles of geometrical objects are the point and
plurality (fr. 49). We know very little about the details of this, but
a charge repeatedly made about him is that he took the different
realms that Plato had united by derivation from common principles
to be distinct, and derived from different principles (frs. 33a-e, 42g,
49, 51). It is a frequent gibe of Aristotle's that his account of the
world is like a bad tragedy (fr. 51); he means a series of unconnected
episodes. This is perhaps ungenerous of Aristotle, since he too had
reacted against Plato's unified scheme of philosophy and science by
insisting on the autonomy of the different sciences and the distinctness of their principles. But he may well have thought that his own
enterprise represented a complete rethinking of the subject, whereas
Speusippus had merely tinkered unsuccessfully with Plato's basic
idea. We do not really have enough evidence to judge.

Speusippus rejected Plato's conception of the principles themselves as well as of their scope. One is no longer the hero of the
whole drama; it is sharply distinguished from being (fr. 34e) and
goodness (34a-d, 35d, 37a). This is interestingly reminiscent of
Aristotle's early interest in 'is', 'one', and 'good', but again our testi-
monies are sketchy in the extreme. We know little about his treatment of the other principle, but we do know that he found implicit
reference to the indefinite two in the *Parmenides* passage discussed
above,[91] and so agreed to some extent with the interpretation of
the indefinite two given there; it is not clear what made him drop
the specificity of the indefinite two in favour of the vaguer 'plurality'.

Speusippus seems to have tended to the obscurantist: his long
fr. 4 on the virtues of the dekad shows regression into Pythagorean
number-mysticism of an unappealing kind. We are told (fr. 40) that
he identified soul with the form of the all-extended, and while it is
hard to know what to make of this, it is in line with some of Xen-

[91] A new fragment in Proclus' commentary on the *Parmenides* (in Latin),
ed. Klibansky, Labowsky, 1953, p. 86.

ocrates' ideas about identification of soul with mathematical objects; the Academy seems here to have embarked on a course which modern analytic philosophy can only follow with great difficulty (Merlan (1), ch. 2, is an attempt in a different tradition to understand the idea sympathetically).

When Aristotle is criticizing Speusippus in *M-N*, his chief grounds of complaint are the latter's platonism about mathematical objects, and the lack of connection in his derivations of the different types of object; he criticizes a few details of his system, but not as copiously as Plato's. In general, one gets the impression that he does not think Speusippus worth criticizing in his own right, merely as representing unsuccessful modifications to Plato's position. This may not be quite fair; some of Speusippus' reactions to Plato appear to have been fairly similar to Aristotle's own, as pointed out, and Aristotle knew, for example, that Speusippus defined time in a way interestingly like his own ('the quantity in change', fr. 53). It may be that our picture of Speusippus in *M-N* is distorted because of the prominence given to Plato's position. Aristotle is most probably right, however, in regarding Speusippus as a basically unoriginal mind and treating his views as dependent on Plato's.

Xenocrates

Aristotle's tone towards Xenocrates in *M-N* is contemptuous; Jaeger ((2), pp. 190-1) attributes this to the fact that Xenocrates was running a rival school (he was head of the Academy after Speusippus), but the contempt is directed to those of his ideas under consideration in *M-N*, and need not imply a similar attitude to the whole of Xenocrates' work.

Xenocrates retained Plato's two principles (frs. 28,33),[92] but developed further their relation as form and matter. He used them in fanciful cosmological speculations, with a good deal of peculiar theology (Stobaeus, *Ecl.* i, 62 ff., frs. 23, 26, 24). Aristotle does not consider these ideas in *M-N*; he confines himself to Xenocrates' contributions to the philosophy of mathematics. Xenocrates regarded this as an important field (fr. 2, ps.-Iamblichus, *Theol. Arith.* 61 g E), and wrote voluminously in it. His main contribution was to retain

---

[92] Fragments are given as in the collection of Heinze.

Forms (fr. 30) but to identify them with their corresponding mathematical objects—Form numbers with mathematical numbers (fr. 34), geometrical Forms with ideal magnitudes (frs. 37, 38). We know annoyingly little about what this amounted to, or the grounds on which it was maintained, though it may have been connected with his peculiar epistemology (fr. 5) and his ideas about indivisible lines (frs. 41-9), attacked in *On Indivisible Lines*, by Aristotle or one of his followers). It is possible that Xenocrates was led to this idea simply because he was confused about the nature of mathematical truths, as Aristotle several times implies in *M-N*. It is also, however, possible that Xenocrates' identification of Forms with mathematicals may have had something to do with Aristotle's arguments to the effect that Plato *ought* to identify Forms with mathematicals, since they come from the same principles. Xenocrates may have accepted this argument for the mathematical Forms at least. Speusippus' abandonment of Forms *may* also have had something to do with this emphasis on principles and arguments concerning them. Xenocrates may have accepted Aristotle's arguments to some extent (as Plato apparently never did), whereas Speusippus would have rejected the dilemma by abandoning Forms.[93] The peculiarity of identifying mathematical Forms with mathematical objects makes it likely that Xenocrates was driven to it by difficulties with the principles rather than attracted by it in its own right.

Xenocrates followed Speusippus into peculiar number-mysticism, and 'defined' the soul as a 'self-moving number' (fr. 60); he also interpreted the creation of the soul in the *Timaeus* as the 'generation of number' (Plutarch, *The Creation of the Soul in the Timaeus*). Aristotle regards ideas like this as aberrations about the nature of psychology, and attacks them in *de Anima* book 1; he does not think of them as relevant to the concerns of *M-N*.

Aristotle

Aristotle is the only truly original member of the Academy. He shows no traces of any Academic theory about the foundations of

---

[93] This is not the whole story, however, since Speusippus certainly had other reasons for abandoning Forms not connected with problems over numbers: cf. Cherniss (1), ch. 1.

mathematics.[94] Indeed, it is in some ways a pity that he did not attempt a more systematic exposition of his thoughts about number and geometry than the sketchy and scattered indications that we have. Perhaps Aristotle reacted in this from over-schematic and dogmatic Academy theorizing. This reaction was, however, in itself valuable, for it produced the *Posterior Analytics*, his own investigation into the structure of a science, which has proved to be a philosophically fruitful work, as the grand unifying schemes of the *Republic*, *On the Good*, Speusippus, and Xenocrates have not.

Aristotle's main contribution to the Academy debates is a negative one: exposing and clearing up muddle, and laying the foundations of a sounder view, without actually producing a systematic alternative. When Plato gave his lecture *On the Good* Aristotle, Speusippus, and Xenocrates all took notes, but Aristotle was the only one who reacted to them in a creative way; instead of producing yet another system derivative from Plato's he rejected the whole framework, and produced *M-N*.

Aristotle is often at his philosophical best when he is being polemical. This is not often enough acknowledged, since attention is too frequently diverted to the question whether he is being 'fair' to his opponents. No doubt there are many points in *M-N* where Plato's position is stated in a form in which Plato would not wish to hold it. But this is not the unfairness of malice, or lack of insight. (Aristotle does sometimes have lapses, but they are clearly recognizable, and often understandable.) Aristotle is interested in the truth, and his polemic comes from a desire to see the argument through. Because of this, parts of his argument, particularly *M* 6-8, challenge comparison with the critical parts of Frege's *Foundations of Arithmetic*. It is no accident that the argument is similar in one or two places; both are patient, precise, and ruthless dissections of muddle and pretension. Of course Aristotle has nothing to compare with Frege's positive achievement. But *M-N* shows that even if Aristotle lacked the Academy's passion for mathematics, he leaves them far behind in his contribution to the philosophy of mathematics.

[94] Unless we are to count some rather odd remarks in *Metaphysics* Γ as a survival of interest in the 'reduction' of types of term to one principle (1003 ^{b}35–1004^{a}2, 1004^{b}27–1005^{a}13). Cf. Merlan, (1), ch. VII.

4. The structure of *M-N*

M-N falls roughly into the following sections:

M

(a) 1076ᵃ8-37 (ch. 1). Aristotle proposes to discuss platonist theories of Forms and numbers; theories are classified according to whether they accept the existence of either or both. Mathematical objects will be treated first; then, briefly, Forms; the third inquiry is whether numbers and Forms are the principles and realities of existing things.

(b) 1076ᵃ37–1077ᵇ17 (ch. 2). Criticisms of the platonist conception of mathematical objects.

(c) 1077ᵇ17–1078ᵇ6 (ch. 3). Aristotle's own alternative account.

(d) 1078ᵇ7–1080ᵃ11 (chs. 4-5). Criticism of Forms (taken over, with minor alterations, from *A* 6 and *A* 9).

(e) 1080ᵃ12–1083ᵇ23 (chs. 6, 7, 8). Refutation of the theory that Form numbers are made up of combinable units. This is imperfectly worked into a framework of argument against all platonist theories of number.

(f) 1083ᵇ23–1086ᵃ21 (chs. 8-9). An unconnected series of arguments pointing out various difficulties and confusions in Plato's theory of Form numbers and Speusippus' theory.

(g) 1086ᵃ21–1086ᵇ13 (ch. 9) A section resuming the theme of (a), i.e. platonist theories that Forms and/or numbers exist and that 'their elements are the elements and principles of existing things'. A short analysis of the intellectual origins of the theory of Forms, clearly referring back to *M* 4 (= *A* 9).

(h) 1086ᵇ14–1087ᵃ25 (ch. 10). Discussion of a problem about principles not proprietary to Platonists. Aristotle offers a solution, referring back to the problem's formulation in *B* (1003ᵃ5-17).

N

(i) 1087ᵃ29–1088ᵇ14 (ch. 1). Criticism of the two Academy principles and the various ways they are described.

(j) 1088ᵇ14–1090ᵃ2 (ch. 2). Criticism of having principles of eternal things, and of treating the two principles as principles of being and not-being.

(k) $1090^a2-1091^a29$ (chs. 2-4). A string of arguments against the assumptions that numbers exist and that they are 'causes'.

(l) $1091^a29-1092^a17$ (chs. 4-5). Difficulties in relating the Platonist principles to the good.

(m) $1092^a17-1092^b8$ (ch. 5). A brief section of problems about the Academy principles.

(n) $1092^b8-1093^b29$ (chs. 5-6). A string of arguments against the supposed 'causal' role of numbers.

This breakdown shows clearly that M-N is not a firmly planned unity; on any interpretation, different sets of notes seem to have been worked up into a whole. But though there is no strongly marked linear plan throughout, this puts M-N in no worse case than many lecture-courses and works built from them. M and N hang together; they share topics treated in no other (published) work of Aristotle. There are also a few indications in the text that they were given together as a whole course.[95]

M-N does as a whole carry out the programme announced in M 1, though with complications. In M 1 Aristotle proposes to discuss platonist theories under three headings: (i) mathematical objects, (ii) Forms, (iii) the question whether Forms and numbers are causes and elements of things.

(i) is done neatly in chs. 2-3, and (ii) in 4-5. But then we get complications. The long section $1080^a12-1086^a21$ appears to be a digression. In fact it is an attack on platonist theories of number, but aimed at specific versions and not against the general presuppositions of any such theory, as ch. 2 was. (The section $1080^a12-1083^b23$ seems to be an early broadside worked into a more general framework.) Chs. 6-9 are at first glance an untidy mess, yet there is a unifying aim—the arguments are all applied forms of Aristotle's general objection to platonism. None of these arguments deal with

---

[95] M 9 refers back to M 4 (though this is not conclusive, since the reference *could* be to the same material in A 6). Λ, which contains copious parallels and references to N (see notes at beginning of N) contains one reference also to M (1076^a19-22, the classification of theories of number, which Λ seems to pick up at 1069^a33-6.) In N ch. 2 (1090^a13-15) there is a clear reference to Aristotle's theory of mathematical objects, which is expounded in M ch. 3, and nowhere else explicitly. And the last sentence of N sums up the discussion of M-N as a whole, and not just N.

numbers and Forms as causes[96] (except the arguments in *M* 5 against Forms as causes, and their presence is clearly due to the fact that the whole passage *M* 4-5 has been lifted bodily out of *A* 9 and not much rewritten).

At 1086ᵃ21 a halt is called to all these minor arguments, and we are returned to the theme of *M* 1: we are to move on to the third topic. This confirms the impression that Aristotle regards everything up to 1086ᵃ21 as concerned with the first two topics of *M* 1: problems with the existence of Forms and of numbers. We are now told that we must discuss principles and causes, and theories that numbers and Forms are such things. Those who make numbers causes are put off (they recur in *N*, 1090ᵃ2 ff.), and there is a brief analysis of the essential error of the theory of Forms. We thus expect now to begin on topic (iii) of *M* 1.

M ch. 10 then discusses a problem faced by *any* theory of principles; this appears as a prologue to the discussion of principles in *N*, and is clearly relevant to the topic, but equally clearly is self-contained as it stands and written separately. In a modern book it would appear as a footnote.

N discusses principles and elements as causes, but not in the way we expect from the formulations of *M* 1 and *M* 9. Sections (i), (j), (l), and (m) are separate discussions of different types of inadequacy found in the Academy principles. (The first three are quite long and may have been written as independent essays.) Only the two sections (k) and (n) discuss the inadequacies of numbers themselves as causes; and these are among the least finished parts of *N*, consisting of long strings of arguments presented in a linear way. So *N* does not distinguish the question asked in *M* 1 and *M* 9, 'Can numbers (and/or Forms) be causes (explain things adequately)?' and the question, 'Can the principles of numbers (and/or Forms) be causes (explain things adequately)?'[97]

[96] An odd and isolated argument at 1084ᵃ27-9 does seem to concern Forms as causes, but is quite irrelevant in context, and may well be a note from *M* 5 that has strayed into an already chaotic section (see note ad loc.)

[97] Cf. Ross's edition, vol.ii: p.462 'In the discussion now entered upon [at *M* 9] two distinct questions arise: (1) whether Ideas and numbers could serve as the elementary principles of things; (2) whether the account given by the Platonists of the principles of Forms and numbers is satisfactory. The two questions are, as Bonitz observes, not kept very clearly apart by Aristotle.'

This does not mean, however, that N as a whole cannot be the 'third inquiry' of M 1 and M 9. For although these two questions are distinct, we can see from the above brief reconstruction of Plato's theories that they hung together very closely. Aristotle could not have dealt properly with the problems involved in giving numbers explanatory status without dealing with the theory of principles in which numbers figured. Moreover, this is an effective way to challenge the Academy—more effective than the comparatively trivial points in sections (k) and (n). None the less, the fact that N does not answer very well to the specifications of M 9 suggests that parts of N may have led an independent life before their incorporation into M-N (and the links between N and Λ confirm this). This does not imply that the whole of N on its own formed a separate course (more on this below), merely that N even more than M has the appearance of various notes assembled on a topic.

M-N is, then, a unity, although a loose one, and one which incorporates what may have originally been independent shorter works. It is noteworthy that all the passages which seem to have been originally independent (sections (e) of M, (i), (j), and (l) of N) are quite specific polemics against the Academy. The over-all picture suggested is that Aristotle in his lecture-course on the philosophy of mathematics used old pieces of polemic by fitting them into a more general framework, the plan set out in M 1. So an attack on Form numbers as sets of combinable units was worked into an attack on platonist theories of number generally, and three attacks on the Academy principles were put together in an attack on the supposed explanatory role of numbers in relation to the world. The fact that the working-up is not complete does not mean that the lectures were given late in Aristotle's lifetime, so that he had no time to polish them up; it just means that M-N was one lecture-course which was left as it stood by his editors, no doubt because they already found the material remote and baffling. M-N is no more ragged than some other parts of the *Metaphysics* which have a rather similar history.

Jaeger's theory about the structure of M-N

The current view of M-N is rather different from the above. Jaeger ((1), (2)) in his 'evolutionary' theory of Aristotle's develop-

ment, put forward a thesis about *M-N* which has won general acceptance outlasting that of his general theory. Perhaps because
M-N has aroused less serious interest than other parts of the *Metaphysics*, it has never been properly tested by critical examination.

Jaeger's theory takes off from the striking discontinuity between
(f) and (g)–the sudden break at 1086ª21. The arresting shift of
topic makes it seem natural to take 1086ª21 ff. with *N* rather than
with the preceding part of *M*; and according to Syrianus (*in Met.*
160. 6-9) some manuscripts made *N* begin at this point. Clearly,
however, this part of *M* 9-10 cannot have formed the prologue to
N as it now stands (the opening sentence of *N* seems to ignore
M 9-10 completely, and would actually fit better on to 1086ª21,
where the sentence is grammatically abrupt and may not be in its
original form). Jaeger's first conclusion ((1), pp. 41-7) was that *M*
9-10 was not an organic part of either *M* or *N*, but a later addition
to *M* by an editor, containing material relevant to *N* and intended by
Aristotle for working-up into a preface to *N*.

This accounts, however, for only some features of *M* 9-10; it fails
to explain the inclusion in it of a discussion of Forms which recalls
M 4 (= *A* 9). What is this doing in a prologue to a discussion of
principles?

In his book *Aristotle* (pp. 176-93, 205-8, 223-7), Jaeger changed
his mind, and found the clue to *M* 9-10 in his 'discovery' that *M*
9-10 was a doublet of *M* 1. Both put forward for discussion the
views of people who accept 'non-sensible substances', abstract
objects, and both divide this view into acceptance of Forms and
acceptance of numbers. Both refer back to the *Physics*. Jaeger also
claimed to find indications showing *M* 9-10 to be the earlier of the
two. It is more 'incohate'. It contains three references to the books
A-B, which for Jaeger are early; there are fewer in the whole of
books *Z-Λ*. At 1086ᵇ16-19 Aristotle uses 'we' of a Platonist doctrine,
and this dates the book in his early, Platonist period. Furthermore,
there is a contrast between *M* 1 and *M* 9-10 which shows the latter
to be the earlier: both refer to the *Physics*, but *M* 1 says explicitly
that the reality of the matter of sensible objects has been dealt with
in the *Physics*, and that of their form later; the most plausible reference for 'later' is the late set of books *ZHΘ*. For Jaeger, *N* is also

early, as is shown by 1091^a32, where Aristotle again uses the first person plural of a Platonist theory.

Jaeger concludes that M 9-10 and N are early: they belong to Aristotle's period at Assos, when he was working in collaboration with Xenocrates (who is treated politely in N) and saw his main target in Speusippus, then head of the Academy. M 1-9, on the other hand, is later, belonging to a time when Xenocrates was head of the Academy and Aristotle, also back in Athens, was head of a rival school; accordingly Xenocrates is treated less politely.

So M 9-10 and M 1-9 do not make up a single course, but are parallel versions of the same course. 'Just as M 9-10 contains the old preface that was replaced by M 1, so in Book N a lucky chance has thrown into the hands of the editors of Aristotle's remains the very portion of the original *Metaphysics* which he meant to replace, in his last version, with the much improved and perfected discussion of M 1-9' ((2), p. 189).

Jaeger's theory has been very influential, and since it is, if any is, the 'received' view of M-N it is necessary for me to clear the way for the account I have offered by showing that several serious objections can be raised to Jaeger's view.

(1). According to Jaeger, use of 'we' at 1086^b19 and 1091^a32 shows that Aristotle there identifies himself as a Platonist; thus M 9-10 is linked with N and both are placed in Aristotle's early, Platonist period. This argument has no force unless Jaeger's main thesis about Aristotle's development is accepted, and even apart from this there are difficulties.

In A 9 Aristotle often uses the first person plural in talking of arguments for Forms, but in M 4-5 where the same material re-appears this is replaced by third person plurals. (There are other minor changes, a list of which I have given.) It seems reasonable to conclude that in A 9 Aristotle is talking as a member of the Academy, whereas in M 4-5 he is not. But it has been shown by Cherniss ((1), App. II) that Jaeger's conclusions on this basis are insecure; even the clear contrast of A 9 and M 4-5 is not reliable, since there is one argument which appears in M but not in A, and it contains a first person plural (1079^b3-11, cf. Cherniss, (1), n. 214). In any case, the difference between using 'we' and using 'they' need not coincide with the difference between being committed to Plato's arguments and rejecting them. Faithful members of the Academy like Speusippus, its next head, rejected some of Plato's ideas, even the theory of Forms. At 992^{a}24–992^{b}1 Aristotle uses 'we' of ideas which he rejects and passes to using 'we' of typically Aristotelian ideas and 'they' of people who reject them. Clearly Aristotle could use 'we' of the Academy as a whole and subdivide this into 'we' and 'they' for allegiance to different ideas. So we cannot read off Aristotle's attitude to Plato from his use of 'we' and 'they'.

Jaeger's case here reduces to his argument that in the two cases in *M-N* where Aristotle uses 'we' he is in fact committed to a Platonist position by the logic of the argument he accepts. I have argued in the notes to these passages that this is not in fact the case.

(2). Jaeger's claim that *M* 9-10 must be early and separate because of its three references to *AB* is unsuccessful, because the reference to *A* could equally well refer to the same material *in M 4*,[98] and the references to *B* do not prove anything conclusive about date. *B* is a collection of philosophical problems which do not seem to be of the same date, and which Aristotle could have used, added to, and consulted at any time. All that a reference to it shows is that *M* is later than some things in *B*; but this is a very weak conclusion.

(3). The apparent reference to *ZHΘ* in *M* 1, though not *M* 9, can be adequately explained in terms of the content of these chapters alone (this is argued in the notes in *M* 9).

(4). Jaeger's theory that *M* 9-10 + *N* and *M* 1-9 are two parallel courses does not solve the problem pointed out by his first theory: why does *N* not fit more closely on to *M* 9-10? According to Jaeger Aristotle was still only intending, at the time of his death, to replace the earlier, much-used lecture-course *M* 9-10 + *N* by the new, superior one *M* 1-9. But the supposedly familiar and much-used course *M* 9-10 + *N* is ragged and badly-organized, and in particular has the notorious gap at the junction of *M* and *N*.

---

[98] Jaeger excludes this possibility (in his Oxford Classical Text apparatus criticus) by assuming the correctness of his own theory, viz. that *M* 9-10 is earlier than *M* 1-9. But this is to beg the question unless it is already settled on independent grounds that *A* 6 is earlier than *M* 9 and *M* 9 earlier than *M* 4; and few would claim that this difficult problem can be settled independently of decisions about just such cross-references as these.

Jaeger ((2), p. 191) has two lines of answer to this problem which do not quite cohere.

(i). M 9-10 + N *do* form a complete whole: the twofold discussion of numbers and Forms promised in M 9 is carried out, Forms being treated in M 9-10 and numbers in N. But neither is in fact the case: N does not in fact limit itself to numbers, but deals with all the Academy theories.[99] And there is nó real criticism of Forms in M 9-10.[100]

(ii). M 10 fits only roughly on to N because a treatment of Plato's Form numbers has dropped out between the treatment of Forms in M 9-10 and the treatment of numbers of N. This is open to the same objection that N does not limit itself to numbers. It is also not clear how the proposed insertion would make the transition any smoother. Jaeger takes the section to have been moved into M 1-9, but there is no part of M 1-9 which appears to do the required job.

The inconsistency of (i) and (ii) indicates that Jaeger has no satisfactory answer to this problem.

(5). Jaeger attempts to order M 9-10 + N and M 1-9 by the attitudes taken up in them to Speusippus and to Xenocrates: in N Aristotle shows 'very natural deference to the view of his fellow-worker in Assos', but in M 1-9 he treats Xenocrates 'with the minimum of flattery' when he was head of the Academy and his opinions 'were beginning to exert a wider influence'.

Aristotle's criticisms throughout M-N, however, are directed not at people but at theories. He attacks Xenocrates' theory as being the worst of the three (quite understandably, because it is), but he never says that Xenocrates is a crude and inferior thinker, as he does with

[99] Cf. 1090a16 ff., 1090b20 ff., where Forms are referred to; b32 ff., where Plato's intermediates figure between Forms and things; and 1093b21-4, where Forms are mentioned. There is also a reference to the Platonic (and non-Speusippean) indefinite two at 1091a4-5.

[100] M 10 deals with those who do not accept Forms as well as with those who do; so treatment of Forms proper is limited to a paragraph in M 9, which analyses the origin of the theory in such a way as to show that it is an impossible search for universals that are also individuals. But even this is not an independent discussion; it refers back to M 4 (or A 6) and is not comprehensible to someone who had not read the earlier account. 'This was stirred up by Socrates through his definitions, as was said before' (1086b2-3) cannot be the first introduction of the topic.

Melissus (986^{b}26-7, *Physics* 185^{a}8-12, 186^{a}6-13). It is surely wrong ·
to accuse Aristotle of changing his mind about theories because of
academic politics, and to date his remarks this way. It is clear from
the content of *M-N* why Aristotle is ruder about Xenocrates in *M*
than in *N*: it is in his theory about numbers and geometrical objects
and their nature that Xenocrates creates real disasters, according to
Aristotle, whereas there is nothing specially disastrous about his
theory of the principles themselves, which is the subject of *N*.

(6). Jaeger ((2), pp. 206-7, 184 n. 2) tries to show that *M* 1 (1076^{a}8
ff.) and *M* 9 (1086^{a}21 ff.) are doublets, but comparison reveals more
differences than parallels. (This is argued in the notes to *M* 9.) Jaeger
does point to the fact that the programme of *M* 1 is recalled in *M* 9,
but this can be accounted for without the doublet theory.

(7). If Jaeger is right and *M* 1-9 was meant to replace *M* 9-10 + *N*,
then *M* 1 is extremely misleading, for *M* 1-9 contains no third inquiry
into principles and elements such as is promised at 1076^{a}29-32.
Aristotle there says that it will be a fuller account, after the treatment of mathematical objects (chs. 2-3) and Forms (chs. 4-5). This
third topic is hardly provided by chs. 6-9, which discuss various
problems with the Academy conception of numbers, units, and
other mathematical objects. It could be objected to this that the
Academy principles *do* in fact figure in the arguments.[101] They
come in, however, only as part of arguments about the nature of
mathematical objects, not as the objects of a critique in their own
right. There is nothing in *M* corresponding to the objections to
numbers as causes in *N* sections (k) and (n).

(8). Finally, it is hard to see how, given the way Jaeger analyses the
contents of *M* 1-9, he takes it to answer to the programme of *M* 1 at
all. He analyses *M* 1-9 into three parts and a conclusion ((2), 178-80).
After the Introduction in ch. 1, Jaeger lists Part One, 'Objects of
Mathematics' (chs. 2-3), Part Two, 'Ideas' (chs. 4-5), and Part Three,
'Numbers as separable substances' (1080^{a}12−1085^{b}34). Part Three
is subdivided into: 1. Derivation of all possible forms of the theory

---

[101] Ross (p. 470) for example says that 'the distinction between *M* and *N*
as dealing, the one with *akinetos ousia* [unchanging reality], the other with its
first principles, is not well maintained; we hear a good deal in *M* of the One
and the indefinite dyad.'

(1080^{a}12–^{b}36); 2. Refutation of these forms: (a) of Plato, 1080^{b}37–1083^{a}17, and (b) of other number-metaphysicians, 1083^{a}20–1085^{b}34. The Conclusion goes from 1085^{b}35 to 1086^{a}20.

This analysis raises several problems. Jaeger takes the full treatment of numbers as separable substances to come *after* that of Forms, i.e. he identifies it with chs. 6-9. But then what of the status of chs. 2-3? This becomes rather mysterious. The plan of *M* 1 has been contradicted, not only in reversing the order of the topics but in taking the promised investigation of mathematical objects to be in fact limited to numbers.

In any case Jaeger's analysis of his Part Three does not do justice to its structure. (The basis for my criticisms is to be found in my actual analysis of the arguments, and the notes on these passages.) Jaeger ignores the fact that his 'Part Three' consists of two very unlike parts, one from 1080^{a}12 to 1083^{b}23 which is a careful and organized refutation of a specific theory, and another from 1083^{b}23 to 1086^{a}21 which is an untidy string of arguments against various targets, not just theories of number. (The section on Speusippus, for example (1085^{b}4-34), is mostly about *geometrical* objects, fitting badly under Jaeger's heading of 'number-metaphysicians'.) Jaeger's 'Part Three' is a unity neither of topic nor of treatment; the first part is self-contained and the untidy second part does not form a refutation of theories classified in the first part.

I conclude that Jaeger's arguments do not in fact support adequately the theory built on them. While Jaeger's theory explains some difficulties it runs into so many others that we should prefer a simpler hypothesis if possible, such as the one I put forward, that *M-N* as it stands is an untidy unity.

It is worth bringing out a general difficulty in Jaeger's theory. He wants to show that *M* 1-9 and *M* 9-10 + *N* are different in subject and aim, in order to show that they are different courses (and in particular that *M* 9-10 belongs with *N* and not with *M*). But reasons for taking them to have different content and purpose are surely reasons *against* taking *M* 1-9 to be *parallel* to *M* 9-10 + *N*, intended to *replace* it. Changing the subject is hardly the same as replacing an old treatment of the same subject by a new one. Jaeger's thesis requires M 1-9 and M 9-10 + N to be different versions of the same course, and also, incompatibly, to be quite different courses.

The arguments brought against the basic Jaeger position hold also against adaptation of it by Von Ivánka[102] and by Düring.[103]

If the above objections have force, the hypothesis that in M-N we have not one but two lecture-courses is misguided, and should be replaced by the simpler alternative, that we have one. Taking M-N as a unity is of philosophical benefit, for the course of Aristotle's argumentation comes out as fairly clear throughout, though the detail of the argument may obscure this at times. The complications introduced by Jaeger's theory do not have any corresponding philosophical advantages in shedding light on difficult arguments or clarifying the course of the thought. So, although we must be prepared for untidiness and digressions, M-N is a single journey we can take with Aristotle from beginning to end.

---

[102] von Ivánka believes that M 9-10 is independent of both M and N, and that there are *three* stages of polemic against the Academy. M 1-9 attacks Forms and numbers as transcendent entities, and is a ground-clearing operation. M 9-10 is also intended to precede a positive Aristotelian exposition, but attacks Forms and numbers as they figured in the kind of theory of principles attacked by Aristotle; N was intended to *follow* Aristotle's positive contribution in a course like Λ. But he cannot account for the polemic against Forms and numbers *in* N (my sections (k) and (n)).

[103] Düring (*Aristoteles*, p. 254) accepts the Jaeger theory and adds some arguments of his own. He takes over from Bonitz the claim that in M 1-9 it is the basic problems that are set, whereas N starts out from specific onslaughts on the Academy theory. But sections (i), (j), and (l) are all systematic attacks on the basic presuppositions of *all* the Academy theories. Düring also finds considerable stylistic contrast between the two books. But style is difficult and elusive as a basis for chronological judgements, especially when dealing with lecture-notes, which would be in constant process of revision. While Düring claims that there is an escalation of polemic in N, Jaeger claims that Aristotle is ruder to Xenocrates in M. In any case, the style of M-N is uneven throughout. While M chs. 2-3 are relatively finished, the style is different from that of the more detailed M 6-8, and both differ from the rougher passage M 8-9. Within N the sections (k) and (n) are rough strings of arguments, while (i), (j), and (l) are more finished, but apparently independent. It is implausible to find a great stylistic gap between M 9-10 on the one hand, and M 1-9 on the other.

NOTES ON THE TRANSLATION

In the translation I have tried to be faithful to Aristotle's style, which suggests that *M-N* is a course of lectures, frequently worked over but never fashioned into a literary whole, and with some sections more stylistically raw than others.

Aristotle's philosophical vocabulary is extremely hard to translate in a way which will both produce reasonable English and translate Greek contexts uniformly. The important verb *einai* covers both 'to be' and 'to exist' (see Kahn). I have translated it as 'exist' in *M-N*, since I take Aristotle's concern there to be what we would call existential questions, even though Greek lacks a distinct verb 'to exist'. (In *N* ch. 2, however, Aristotle is discussing the use of *einai* in different categories, and 'exists' is impossible as a translation, since clearly the verb is thought of as followed by a complement; in this passage I accordingly translate *einai* as 'being'.) Aristotle's difficult technical term *ousia* is cognate with *einai*, and raises corresponding problems. It is traditionally translated 'substance', but while this is helpful in some contexts it darkens rather than illuminates *M-N*. I have translated it as 'reality' or 'real (or "actual") object'. This would be unsuitable in many of Aristotle's discussions of *ousia*, but is appropriate to the ontological concerns of *M-N*.

Another common word in *M-N* is *archē*, which I translate 'principle'. The nearest English paraphrase is probably 'basic term in an explanation', preserving an ambiguity in the Greek as to whether *archai* are linguistic or non-linguistic items. In *M-N* Aristotle chiefly has the Academy's principles in mind; these are certainly non-linguistic, and in *N* he actually discusses whether they are elements (*stoicheia*). The same ambiguity runs through discussions of whether the principles of Forms or numbers can be 'causes' (*aitiai*); only non-linguistic items can be causes, but often the issue seems to be one of types of (linguistic) explanation. *Aitia* is always translated 'cause', even where this makes for rather odd English. One of Aristotle's complaints in *M-N* is that Plato fails to distinguish between different

89

uses of *aitia*; his own well-known discussion can be found at *Physics* Book 2 chapter 3.

Genos is translated 'kind', though occasionally Aristotle makes it bear his more technical sense and it is translated 'genus'. *Eidos* is translated as 'form' rather than 'species' to bring out the fact that it is the same word which Aristotle applies to his own forms and to Plato's Forms (I have marked the difference by capitalizing the 'F' where Plato is in question). However, in the passage *M* 6-8 I have translated 'same (different) in *eidos*' as 'same (different) in kind', since 'form' has the wrong suggestions when applied to numbers; Aristotle means that they are of different sorts.

Phusis (literally 'nature') is translated as 'entity', though occasionally as 'characteristic'. This may sound odd, but a glance at the related system of meanings Aristotle distinguishes for *phusis* at chapter 6 of *Metaphysics* Δ (his philosophical lexicon) may help to explain this.

Pointed brackets in the text contain words inserted to complete the sense of the literal Greek. Square brackets contain words which explain a reference in the text. An asterisk indicates that the passage is discussed in the Notes to the Text. Sub-headings in italics (e.g. *First option*) and numberings of arguments in various styles (e.g. (1), (2), (a), (b) etc.) have been inserted by me to make the course of the argument clearer. The chapter headings are due to a later editor and often cut across the divisions of Aristotle's argument; where they do so I have put them in brackets.

METAPHYSICS BOOK M

CHAPTER 1

We have already said what the reality of perceptible objects is, deal- **1076ª**
ing with matter in the treatise on *Physics*, and later with actual reality.
The present subject of inquiry is whether or not there is any kind of 10
unchanging and eternal real object over and above the perceptible
ones, and, if there is, what it is. So we must first discuss the views of
others, so as to avoid any mistakes they make, and also so as not to
be secretly annoyed with ourselves if there is some opinion common
to us and them; one should be content to put some things better and 15
others no worse.

There are two opinions on this subject. Some people say that
mathematical objects are real objects—I mean numbers, lines, and
things of that kind—while others say that Forms are. Some people
posit these two kinds— Forms and mathematical numbers—as dis- 20
tinct, others posit both as a single type of thing, and others again
say that only mathematical objects are real objects. So we must first
consider mathematical objects, without attaching any other nature
to them (e.g. whether they are in fact Forms or not, and whether or
not they are principles and realities of existing things), but just con- 25
sidering whether, merely as mathematical objects, they exist or not,
and, if they exist, in what way they exist. Then after this we must
separately consider Forms themselves, but only generally and for
completeness' sake, since most of the points are familiar from
published works. Besides, this inquiry is bound to be touched on
again by the fuller argument when we discuss whether the realities 30
and principles of existing things are numbers and Forms; for this is
left as a third inquiry, after Forms.

If mathematical objects exist, they must either exist in perceptible objects as some say, or separate from perceptible objects (some 35
say this too), or, if neither, then either they do not exist or they exist
in some other way. So our debate will be not whether they exist, but
in what way they exist.

CHAPTER 2

As for the impossibility of mathematical objects existing in perceptible objects, this being a fanciful account, it has been pointed
1076^b out in the *Discussion of Problems* that it is impossible for two solids to be in the same place at the same time, and further that by the same argument other powers and characteristics would also be in perceptible objects and none of them separate.

That has already been said; but in addition it is clear that <on
5 this theory> it is impossible for any body to be divided; for it will be divided along a plane, and the plane along a line, and the line at a point, so that if the point cannot be divided, neither can the line, and if the line cannot, the rest cannot either. So what difference does it make whether perceptible bodies are objects of this kind, or whether, while they are not, objects of this kind exist in them?
10 There will be the same result: either they will be divided when perceptible objects are divided, or perceptible objects will not be divided either.

But it is not possible for objects of this kind to exist in separation either. If there are to be solids over and above perceptible solids, separate from them, distinct from and prior to perceptible
15 solids, clearly there must be distinct and separate planes over and above planes, and points and lines—the same argument applies. But if so, there will again be distinct and separate planes and lines and points over and above those of the mathematical solid. (The uncompounded is prior to the compounded, and if there are non-
20 perceptible ones, by the same argument there are planes existing by themselves prior to those in the unchanging solids. So these planes and lines and solids are distinct from those that belong together with the separate solids; the latter belong together with the mathematical solids, while the former are prior to the mathematical solids.) Then
25 again there will be lines belonging to these planes, and there will have to be distinct lines and points prior to them, according to the same argument; and prior to the points in the prior lines there will be distinct prior points, though there are no more prior to them. The piling-up becomes absurd: we get one set of solids over and above perceptible ones, but three sets of planes over and above perceptible
30 perceptible ones, but three sets of planes over and above perceptible

planes (those over and above perceptible planes, those in the mathematical solids, and those over and above the latter), four sets of lines,
and five sets of points. Which of them will be the object of the mathematical branches of knowledge? Not the planes and lines and points in 35
the unchanging solids, for knowledge always deals with what is prior.

The same argument applies also to numbers: over and above each
set of points there will be distinct units, and also over and above
each set of objects, objects of sense and again objects of thought, so
that there will be <infinitely many>* kinds of mathematical
numbers.

Moreover, how can we solve the difficulties reviewed in the 1077^a
Discussion of Problems? There will be objects of astronomy over and
above perceptible objects, just like objects of geometry—but how
can there be a <separate> heaven and its parts, or anything else
with movement? Similarly with the objects of optics and harmonics; 5
there will be utterance and seeing over and above perceptible individual utterances and seeings. Clearly this is true of the other sensings
and objects of sense too—why one rather than another? But if so,
there will be <separate> animals too, if there are <separate> sensings.

Besides, there are some general propositions stated by mathematicians, whose application extends beyond these objects. So there 10
will be another type of object here, between and separate from both
Forms and intermediates, neither number nor point nor magnitude
not time. If this is impossible, clearly it is also impossible for the
former to exist in separation from perceptible objects.

In general, conclusions result which contradict truth and ordinary 15
beliefs, if one takes mathematical objects to exist in this way, as
separate entities. Because they exist in this way they have to be prior
to perceptible magnitudes, but in fact they are subsequent, since incomplete magnitude, while prior in generation, is subsequent in
reality, as is the case with lifeless and living.   20

Besides, what on earth is it in virtue of which mathematical
magnitudes are one?* It is reasonable for things around us to be
one in virtue of soul or a part of soul or something else—otherwise
there is <not one but> many, and the thing is divided up. But these
objects are divisible and quantitative; what can be responsible for

their being one and holding together?

Besides, the point is clear from the way they are generated. First
25 length is generated, then breadth, finally depth, and then it is complete. So if what is subsequent in generation is prior in reality, body
should be prior to plane and to length. It is more complete and
whole in the following way also—it becomes animate. How could
30 there be an animate line or plane? The supposition would be beyond
our senses.

Besides, a body is a kind of real object (for it already has completeness, in a way), but how can lines be real objects? Not by being
form and a kind of shape, as perhaps the soul is, nor by being matter,
like the body, because nothing is seen to be capable of being put
together out of planes or points, though they would have been seen
35 to be capable of undergoing this, if they were some kind of material
reality.

1077ᵇ   Even if they are prior in definition—still, not everything prior in
. definition is prior in reality. Things are prior in reality <to other
things> if more able to go on existing when separated from the
latter, and prior in definition to things whose definitions are compounded from definitions of them. These do not <always>* apply
together. For if there are no attributes over and above real objects
5 (e.g. a moving or a white) then white is prior in definition to white
man, but not in reality, since it cannot exist separately but only
together with the compound (by compound I mean the white man).
So clearly the result of abstraction is not prior, nor the result of
10 addition subsequent, because it is by adding to white that the white
man is spoken of.

It has been adequately shown that <mathematical objects> are
not real objects more than bodies are, that they are not prior to
perceptible objects in reality, but only in definition, and that they
cannot have separate existence. Since they could not exist in per-
15 ceptible objects either, clearly either they do not exist at all, or they
do so in a certain way and so do not exist without qualification—for
we use 'exist' in several senses.

CHAPTER 3

Just as general propositions in mathematics are not about separate objects over and above magnitudes and numbers, but are about these, only not *as* having magnitude or being divisible, clearly it is also 20 possible for there to be statements and proofs about perceptible magnitudes, but not *as* perceptible but as being of a certain kind. For just as there are many statements about things merely as moving, apart from the nature of each such thing and their incidental properties (and this does not mean that there has to be either some moving 25 object separate from the perceptible objects, or some such entity marked off in them), so in the case of moving things there will be statements and branches of knowledge about them, not as moving but merely as bodies, and again merely as planes and merely as lengths, as divisible, and indivisible but with position, and merely 30 as indivisible. So since it is true to say without qualification not only that separable things exist but also that non-separable things exist (e.g. that moving things exist), it is also true to say without qualification that mathematical objects exist, and are as they are said to be. It is true to say of other branches of knowledge, without qualification, that they are about this or that—not what is incidental (e.g. 35 not the white, even if the branch of knowledge deals with the healthy, and the healthy is white) but what each branch of knowledge is about, the healthy if <it studies its subject> as healthy, man if <it 1078^a studies it> as man. And likewise with geometry: the mathematical branches of knowledge will not be about perceptible objects just because their objects happen to be perceptible, though not <studied> as perceptible; but nor will they be about other separate objects over and above these. Many properties hold true of things in their own 5 right as being, each of them, of a certain type—for instance there are attributes peculiar to animals as being male or as being female (yet there is no female or male separate from animals). So there are properties holding true of things merely as lengths or as planes.

The more that what is known is prior in definition, and the simpler, the greater the accuracy (i.e. simplicity) obtained. So there is 10 more accuracy where there is no magnitude than where there is, and most of all where there is no movement; though if there is movement accuracy is greatest if it is primary movement, this being the simplest, and uniform movement the simplest form of that.

The same account applies to harmonics and optics; neither

15 studies its objects as seeing or as utterance, but as lines and numbers
(these being proper attributes of the former); and mechanics likewise.

So if one posits objects separated from what is incidental to them,
and studies them as such, one will not for this reason assert a falsehood, any more than if one draws a foot on the ground and calls it
20 a foot long when it is not a foot long; the falsehood is not part of
the premises.

The best way of studying each object would be this: to separate
and posit what is not separate, as the arithmetician does, and the
geometer. A man is one and indivisible as a man, and the arithmetician posits him as one indivisible, then studies what is incidental
25 to a man as indivisible; the geometer, on the other hand, studies him
neither as man nor as indivisible, but as a solid object. For clearly
properties he would have had even if he had not been indivisible can
belong to him without them. That is why geometers speak correctly:
30·they talk about existing things and they really do exist—for what
exists does so in one of two senses, in actuality or as matter.

Since the good is different from the beautiful (because the good
is always found in some action, while the beautiful is found also in
unchanging things), those who say that mathematical branches of
knowledge do not speak about the beautiful or the good are wrong.
They do speak about and demonstrate a good deal about them; just
35 because they do not name them in demonstrating their effects and
relations, it does not follow that they are not speaking about them.
1078ᵇ The main forms of the beautiful are order, symmetry, and definiteness, which are what the mathematical branches of knowledge
demonstrate to the highest degree. Since these (I mean order and
definiteness, for instance) evidently are causes of a lot of things,
clearly they are in a sense speaking about this sort of cause too—
5 namely the beautiful as cause. But we will speak about this more
intelligibly elsewhere.

CHAPTER 4

As for mathematical objects, then, so much must suffice—that they
really exist and the way in which they really exist, and the way in
which they are prior and that in which they are not prior. Now as

regards Forms, we must first examine just the theory of the Form,
not connecting it at all with the nature of numbers, but just as the 10
people who first said that there were Forms understood it at the
outset.

The theory of Forms occurred to the people who stated it because
as regards truth they were convinced by the Heracleitean arguments
that all perceptible things are always in flux, so that if there is to be
knowledge of anything, or understanding, there must be some other, 15
permanent kinds of thing over and above perceptible things, because
there is no knowledge of things in flux.

Now Socrates gave his attention to virtues of character, and tried
in connection with them to give general definitions. He was the first
to do so, for among the natural scientists Democritus touched on
this only slightly and defined the hot and the cold, after a fashion, 20
while the Pythagoreans had already done so in the case of a few
things whose definitions they reduced to numbers, e.g. what opportunity is, or the just, or marriage. But it was natural for Socrates to
try to find what a thing is, because he was trying to reason formally,
and the starting-point of formal reasoning is what a thing is. For at
that time there was not yet the dialectical power to enable people to 25
consider opposites apart from what a thing is, and whether the same
branch of knowledge deals with contraries; for there are just two
things one might fairly ascribe to Socrates, arguments from particular to general and general definitions, both being concerned with the
starting-point of knowledge. —Well, Socrates did not take the uni- 30
versals to be separate, nor the definitions, but *they* [the Platonists]
made them separate, and called such entities Forms.

So it followed for them almost by the same argument that there
are Forms of everything to which we apply general terms, rather as
if someone who wanted to count things thought that he would not
be able to do so while there were only a few, but made more before 35
counting them. For the Forms are, one may say, more numerous
than perceptible particulars (though it was in seeking causes for the 1079^a
latter that they went on from them to Forms), because in each case
there is, over and above the real objects, something else with the
same name, both for things around us and for eternal things.*

Besides, none of the ways of proving that there are Forms is 5

97

decisive. Some do not logically imply their conclusion; others produce Forms of things of which they do not think there are Forms. According to the arguments from the branches of knowledge there will be Forms of everything of which there is a branch of knowledge; according to the One over Many there will be Forms even of nega-
10 tions; according to the Thought of what Perished there will be Forms of perishable things, since we have a kind of image of them. Besides, among the most precise arguments some produce Forms of relatives, of which they deny that there is an independent class, and others involve the Third Man. Altogether, the arguments for Forms
15 do away with things whose existence the believers in Forms put before the existence of Forms; for the result is that it is not the two that is primary but number, and the relative prior to that, the relative being prior to the independent—not to mention all the ways in which people who have followed up the theory of Forms contradict the principles.
20   Besides, given their argument for the existence of Forms, there will be Forms not only of actual objects but of many other things too, because there is a single concept not only for a real object but also in the case of things that are not objects, and there are branches of knowledge for things other than objects. And thousands of other such problems result. By necessity and according to the theory, if
25 Forms can be participated in then there must be Forms only of real objects, since they are not participated in accidentally; a Form must be participated in in so far as it is not said of a subject. I mean, for example, if something participates in the original Double, the same thing participates in eternal, but only accidentally, since the Double
30 is, accidentally, eternal. So Forms will be real objects. But the same terms signify being an object yonder as do so here. Otherwise what will be the point of saying that there is something over and above these objects (the One over Many)? If Forms and particulars have the same form, there will be something common (for why is two one
35 and the same in the case of perishable twos and of the many but eternal twos, any more than in the case of the original Two and a particular two?). But if the form is not the same, they will be merely
1079ᵇ homonymous, as if one were to call Callias and a block of wood 'man', having observed nothing in common between them.

If we are to suppose that in other respects the common definitions fit the Forms, for instance, plane figure and the other parts of
the definition in the case of the original Circle, but that *what it is* 5
must be added, then we should consider whether this is not completely vacuous. To what will it be added, to centre or to plane, or
to all of them? All the <elements> in its reality are Forms, e.g.
animal and two-footed. Besides, clearly there will have to be such a
thing as Original, just like plane, some sort of entity which will be 10
present in all the Forms as their genus.

CHAPTER 5

Most of all one might puzzle over what on earth Forms contribute
either to eternal perceptible objects or to those that come into being
and pass away. They are not causes of movement, nor of any change
in them. 15

But neither are they any help toward knowledge of the other
things (they are not their reality, or they would have been in them)
nor towards their being <what they are>, not being present in their
participants. If they were, they might perhaps seem to be causes, as
white is of a thing's being white, by being mixed in. But this account,
given first by Anaxagoras and later by Eudoxus in his discussions, 20
and by some others, is very simple to upset; it is easy to collect
many absurdities against such a theory.

But nor can other things come 'from' the Forms in any ordinary
way of speaking.

Saying that they are paradigms and that other things participate 25
in them is vacuous, use of poetic metaphor. What is it that works
looking towards the Forms?

And anything can both exist and come into existence without
having been copied <from something else>, so that someone like
Socrates could come into being whether Socrates exists or not; and
clearly it is the same even if Socrates were eternal. 30

And there will be several paradigms (and so Forms) of the same
thing, e.g. Animal and Two-footed will be paradigms of man, at the
same time as the original Man.

Besides, Forms are paradigms not only of perceptible things but
also of themselves, e.g. the genus is the paradigm of the forms of

35   of the genus. So the same thing will be both paradigm and likeness.

Besides, it would seem impossible for a thing's reality to exist separately from the thing whose reality it is; so how could Forms

1080ᵃ   exist separately, if they are the reality of things?

In the *Phaedo* it is put this way: Forms are causes both of being and of coming into being. Yet even if Forms exist there is still no coming into being unless there is something to start things moving;

5   and many other things come into being, like a house or a ring, of which they say there are no Forms. So clearly those things of which they do say there are Forms can also be and come into being because of causes like those of things just mentioned, and not because of Forms.

So as regards Forms one can collect many objections like those

10   considered, both in this way and by more formal and precise arguments.

CHAPTER 6

Now that these matters have been settled, it is a good idea to consider again what consequences there are as regards numbers for the people who hold that they are separate real objects and the primary causes of existing things.

15   If number is a kind of entity and its reality is nothing else but number, as some say, then it follows that *either*

(I) there must be a first number and a next in succession, each being different in kind, and this applying directly to the units, any unit being non-combinable with any other.* *Or*

20   (II) units are all directly successive and any one combinable with any other one, as they say is the case with mathematical number (in mathematical number no unit is in any way different from another). *Or*

(III) some units are combinable and some not, e.g. if after one there is first two and then three and so on for the rest of the numbers, and

25   the units in each number are combinable (those in the first two, for example, being combinable between themselves and those in the first three among themselves, and so on with the other numbers), but those in the original Two are non-combinable with those in the original Three, and similarly with the other numbers in succession.

30   (This is why *mathematical* number is counted as follows: after one,

two—another one added to the one before—and then three—another
one added to those two—and the remaining numbers likewise; but
this sort of number is counted as follows: after one a distinct two
not including the first one, and three not including two, and the
other numbers similarly.) *Or*
(IV) one kind of number is like the first mentioned, another like the   35
sort spoken of by mathematicians, and a third is that named last.

     Besides, these numbers must either be separate from things, or
not separate but in perceptible objects (but not in the way we dis-   **1080ᵇ**
cussed at first, rather in the sense that perceptible objects are made
up of numbers present in them), or some are and some are not, or
all are.

     These are necessarily the only ways in which numbers can exist.   5
Among people who maintain that one is the principle and reality
and element of everything, and that number comes from it and
something else, nearly every one has maintained one of these ways
(except the one that all units are non-combinable). Nor is it surprising that this has happened, since there cannot be another way over   10
and above those mentioned. Some say that both sorts of number
exist, the sort with a before and after being Forms, and mathematical number being distinct from both Forms and perceptible
things, but both being separate from perceptible things. Others say
that only mathematical number exists, number, that is, that is
primary among existing things, separate from perceptible things. The   15
Pythagoreans say there is only one kind, mathematical number, only
they say it is *not* separate but that real perceptible objects are composed of it; they construct the whole universe out of numbers, only
not numbers made up of abstract units, since they suppose the units to
have magnitude. But they seem at a loss to say how the first one   20
came together possessing magnitude. Someone else says that the first
kind of number, Form number, is the only kind, and some say that
mathematical number is the same as this.*

     Similarly with lengths, planes, and solids. Some think that mathe-
matical objects and the objects after the Forms are different; and   25
among people who give other accounts some discuss mathematical
objects in a way appropriate to mathematics (namely those who do
not make Forms numbers, and even deny that there are Forms),

while others discuss mathematical objects in a way inappropriate to mathematics (they say that not every magnitude is divided into magnitudes, and that not any units make up two).

30 All those who say that one is an element and principle of existing things take their numbers to be composed of abstract units, except the Pythagoreans: *they* say that <units> have magnitude, as has already been stated.

35 It is apparent from this how many theories there can be about number, and also apparent that all the ways have been mentioned. They are all impossible, but perhaps some more so than others.

(CHAPTER 7)

First, then, we must see whether units are combinable or non-combin-
1081ᵃ able, and, if non-combinable, in which of the ways we distinguished. It is possible for any unit to be non-combinable with any other unit, and also possible for those in the original Two to be non-combinable with those in the original Three, and those in each first number non-combinable with one another in this way.

Second option (1080ᵃ20-3)

5   If all the units are combinable and without difference, mathematical number results and only this one kind, and Forms cannot be numbers. (What sort of number will the original Man be, or Animal or any other Form? There is one Form of each thing, e.g. one of the
10 original Man and another of the original Animal; but these similar and undifferentiated numbers are limitless, so this particular three cannot be the original Man any more than any other.) But if Forms are not numbers, they cannot exist at all. (From what principles will Forms come? Number comes from one and the indefinite two, and
15 the principles and elements <of things> are said to be <the principles and elements> of number;* but Forms cannot be ranked either before numbers or after them.

First option (1080ᵃ17-20)

But if units are non-combinable, in the sense that none is combinable with any other, then this number cannot be mathematical number, since mathematical number is made up of undifferentiated
20 units, and results proved of it fit it as such. But it cannot be Form number either. For:

(a) Two will not be the first product of one and the indefinite two, followed by the numbers in succession, as one says, 'two, three, four . . .' This is because the units in the first two come into being simultaneously (either in the way the founder of the theory held, from the equalization of unequals, or in some other way).   25

(b) Besides,* even if one unit does come before the other, it will also come before the two made up of both. For whenever one thing is prior and another subsequent, a thing made up of both of them will be prior to the latter and subsequent to the former.

(c) Besides, since the original one is first, and then there is a one first among the others but second after it, and again a third, second   30
after the second one and third after the first one—so that the units will come before the numbers after which they are named. For example, there will be a third unit in two before three exists, and a fourth in three, and a fifth, before these numbers exist.

(d) Nobody has said that units are non-combinable in this way,   35
but even this is reasonable according to their principles, though in fact impossible. It is reasonable for units to be prior and subsequent,   1081^b
if there is both a first unit and a first one, and similarly with twos, if there is a first two. After the first it is reasonable, indeed necessary, for there to be a second, and, if a second, a third, and similarly with   5
the others in succession. (It is impossible to say both that a unit comes first after one, and another unit comes second, and also that two comes first.) But they make a first unit, and a first one, but not a second and third, and a first two, but not a second and third.

(e) Clearly is it not possible for there to be an original Two and   10
Three, and so on with the other numbers, if all the units are non-combinable. Whether units are undifferentiated or each different from each other, number must be counted by addition, two for example by adding another one to one, three by adding another one   15
to two, and four likewise. But if this is so, number cannot be generated as they generate it, from the two and one. Two becomes *part* of three and three of four, and this happens in the same way to the   20
following numbers, but <for them> what came from the first two and the indefinite two is four—two twos other than the original Two. (Otherwise the original Two will be part of it, with the addition of one other two.) And two, also, will result from the original One

103

25 and another one—but if so the other element cannot be the indefinite two, because it generates one unit rather than a definite two.
Again, how can there be other threes and twos besides the original
Three and the original Two? In what way do they consist of prior
30 and subsequent units? This is all absurd and strained, and it is impossible for there to be a first two and then an original Three. But
there must be, if one and the indefinite two are to be the elements.
But if the consequences are impossible, it is also impossible for these
to be the principles.

So if any unit is different from any other, these and the like are
the necessary consequences.

Third option (1080ª23–35).

35   If units in a different number are different, and only those in the
same number undifferentiated from one another, there are just as
many awkward consequences.

1082ª   (i) For example, in the original Ten there are ten units, and ten is
composed both of these and of two fives. Since the original Ten is
not just any number and is not composed of just any fives. (or just
5   any units) the units in this ten must differ. If they do not differ, the
fives of which the ten consists will not differ either, but since they
do differ, the units will differ too. But if they do differ, will there be
no other fives in <the ten> but only these two, or will there be? It
is absurd if there are not; but if there are, what kind of ten will be
10 composed of them? There is no other ten in the ten over and above
itself. But it is indeed necessary that <on their view> four should
not consist of just any twos: the indefinite two, so they say, took
the definite two and made two twos, since it was a duplicator of
what it took.

15   (ii) Besides, how can it be that two is an entity over and above
the two units, and three over and above the three units? Either one
thing will partake in the other, as there is white man besides white
and man, since it partakes in them—or one is some differentia of the
20 other, as there is man besides animal and two-footed. Besides, some
things are one by contact, some by mixture, some by position, but
none of these can apply to the units of which two and three are
made up. Two men are not some one thing over and above both of
them, and this must be so with units too. Their being indivisible will

make no difference; points are indivisible too, but still two of them 25
do not make up anything over and above the two.

(iii) We should not fail to notice the following too: it follows
that there are prior and subsequent twos, and similarly with the
other numbers. Suppose the twos in four come into being simultaneously; they are still prior to those in eight, and just as two
generated them they generated the four in the original Eight. So if 30
the first two is a Form* these will themselves be a kind of Form.
The same argument applies to the units, since the units in the first
two generate the four units in four. So all units become Forms and
a Form will consist of Forms. Clearly then the things of which these 35
are in fact the Forms will also be composite—as if, for example, one
were to say that animals are composed of animals, if there are
Forms of them.

(iv) In general, making units different in *any* way is absurd and 1082ᵇ
strained (by strained I mean forced in order to fit one's assumptions).
We can see no difference between unit and unit in quantity or in
quality. And number must be either equal or unequal (all kinds but 5
especially number made up of abstract units), so that if a number is
neither larger nor smaller <than another> it is equal to it—and with
numbers we suppose that what are equal and completely undifferentiated are the same. Otherwise not even the twos in the original
Ten will be undifferentiated, though they are equal—what reason 10
will anyone be able to give who asserts that they are undifferentiated?

(v) Besides, if every unit and another unit make two, there will
be a two made up of a unit from the original Two and another from
the original Three, which will thus be made up of differentiated
units. Also, will it be before three or after it? It seems rather as if it
must be before, since one of the units comes about together with 15
three, and the other together with two. *We* suppose that in general
one and one make two, whether they are equal or unequal—good
and bad, for instance, or man and horse; but people with these
views suppose that not even any two *units* make two.

(vi) It is surprising if the original Three is not a larger number 20
than two, but if it is larger, clearly there is a number in it equal to
two, and so undifferentiated from the original Two. But this is im-

105

possible, if there is a first and then second number of some kind.

(vii) Nor will the Forms be numbers. The people who claim that
25 if there are to be Forms the units must differ are right on this point,
as was said earlier, for a Form is unique, but if the units are undifferentiated the twos and three will be undifferentiated also. That
is why they have to say that counting 'one, two . . .' does not proceed by adding to what we have already; because if so number will
30 not be generated from the indefinite two, and cannot be a Form,
since then one Form will be present in another and all the Forms
will be parts of a single Form. Thus in the light of their assumptions
what they say is correct, but it is wrong in general, since their theories
cause havoc. They will actually say, for example, that *this* is a
35 problem: when we count and say 'one, two, three . . .', do we count
by adding on or by separate parts? But we do it in both ways, which
is why it is absurd to trace it back to such a vast difference of real
object.

(CHAPTER 8)

1083^{a} (viii) First of all it is a good idea to determine what the differentia of
a number is, and of a unit if it has one. Units must differ either in
quantity or in quality, but neither of these seems to apply. Number
as number differs in quantity. If units *did* differ in quantity too,
5 then a number could differ from another number even when equal in
quantity of units. Besides, are the first units bigger or smaller, and
do the later ones increase or the reverse? All this is absurd. But they
cannot differ in quality either, since no attribute can apply to them
10 (to numbers, indeed, they say that quality applies, but only after
quantity). Besides, <quality> could not come to <units> from one
nor from the two, since the former has no quality and the latter is
quantity-producing, this entity being the cause of plurality. If in fact
15 matters are different in any way, they should state this right at the
outset and determine the differentia of a unit, and especially why
there must be one. Otherwise, what do they mean by it?
Conclusions

Clearly, then, if Forms are numbers, the units can neither be all
20 combinable, nor non-combinable with one another in either way.

The way some other people speak about numbers is not correct either. These are people who believe that Forms do not exist, either straightforwardly or as being a kind of number, but that mathematical objects exist and that numbers are primary among existing things, their principle being the original One. Now it is absurd for there to be a one beginning a series of ones, as they say, but not a two begin- 25 ning a series of twos, or a three of threes, since the same argument applies to them all. If this is how things stand with number, and only mathematical number is supposed to exist, one is not the principle: such a one would have to be different from the other units, and if so there would have to be some two first among the other twos, and 30 similarly with the other successive numbers. If on the other hand one *is* the principle, facts about number must rather be as Plato used to say: that is, there is a first two and three, the numbers being non-combinable with one another. But then again, if one supposes this, 35 we have said that many impossibilities result. However, it is surely necessary for one or the other to be the case, so, if neither is, number cannot be separate.

It is apparent also from this that the worst account is the third 1083ᵇ say—that Form number and mathematical number are the same sort of number. This one theory must be the product of two mistakes. Mathematical number cannot exist in this fashion; he has to set up 5 his own assumptions and spin things out. And he has to admit also all the consequences of the theory that numbers are Forms.

The Pythagoreans' version has fewer difficulties than the above-mentioned in one way, but in another way has others of its own. Many impossibilities are done away with by not making number 10 separate; but for bodies to be composed of numbers, and for this to be mathematical number, is impossible. It is not true to say that there are atomic magnitudes, and even granting fully that there were, units at least have no magnitude. And how is it possible for a magni- 15 tude to be composed of indivisibles? Arithmetical number, at any rate, is composed of abstract units. But the Pythagoreans say that things are number—at any rate they apply their theorems to bodies as though the latter were made up of those numbers.

So, if it is necessary for number to exist in one of the above- 20 mentioned ways, if it exists independently, but none of these is possible, clearly number has no such character as is set up by those who make it separate.

*   *   *

Besides, does each unit come from the great and small when they are equalized, or one from the small and the other from the great? If the
25 latter, each will not come from all the elements, and the units will not be undifferentiated—in one the great will occur and in the other the small, whose nature is the opposite.

Besides, what about the units in the original Three? One is odd. Perhaps this is why they put the original One midway in the odd.

And how can two, which is a single entity, come from the great
30 and small, if each of its units comes from the equalization of both the principles? How will it differ from the unit? Besides, the unit is prior to two (when it is taken away two is taken away). So it must be the Form of a Form, because prior to a Form, and must come
35 into being before it. From what, then? The indefinite two produces *twos*.

Besides, number must be either infinite or finite, since they make
1084ᵃ number separate, so one of the two must be the case. Clearly it cannot be infinite. Infinite number is neither odd nor even, but generation of numbers is always of an odd number or an even one. An odd number is generated when one applies to an even number;
5 the numbers doubled from one when the two applies [i.e. the powers of two] ; and the other even numbers when the odd numbers <apply>. Besides, if every Form is a Form of something, and the numbers are Forms, infinite number also will be a Form of something, either a perceptible thing or something else. But this is not possible consistently either with their assumption or with the argument (though
10 they do arrange Forms in this way*).

But if the number is finite, how far does it go? Not only the answer but the reasoning should be stated. If number goes up to ten, as some say, firstly Forms will soon run out—if three is the original Man, for example, what number will the original Horse be? The
15 numbers which are each originals go up to ten, so it must be one of the numbers in these (these being real objects and Forms), but they will still run out, since the forms of animal will exceed them.

At the same time it is clear that if it is in this way that three is the original Man, then so are the other threes (since those in the same numbers are similar), so that there will be infinitely many men—if each three is a Form, they will all be the original Man, and if not they will at least be men.

Also, if a smaller number is part of a larger (number, that is, of units combinable in the same number), then if the original Four is a Form of something, e.g. horse or white, then if man is two, man will be part of horse.

It is absurd for there to be a Form of ten but not of eleven and the succeeding numbers.

Besides, some things exist and come into existence of which there are no Forms, so why are there not Forms for these too? So Forms cannot be causes.

Besides, it is absurd for number up to ten to be more of a reality and Form than the original Ten, while there is no generation of the former as a single thing, as there is of the latter. But they proceed as though number up to ten were complete. At any rate they generate the things that follow—e.g. the void, proportion, the odd, and others of this sort—within the numbers up to ten. Some things they assign to the principles, e.g. change and rest, good and bad, but others to the numbers. That is why the odd is one: if it were in three, how could five be odd? Again, magnitudes and things of that kind go up to a definite number e.g. the first, indivisible line, then two, then more of these up to ten.

Besides, if number is separate, one might raise the problem whether one comes first, or three or two. In so far as number is composite, it is one that comes first, but in so far as the universal and form are prior, it is number that comes first; each of the units is part of a number as matter, but the number is their form. In a sense, too, the right angle is prior to the acute angle, because it is determinate and because of its definition; but in a sense the acute angle is prior, because it is a part such as the right angle is divided into. As matter, then, the acute angle, the element, and the unit are prior, but regarded as form and the real thing according to the definition it is the right angle which is prior, and the whole made up of matter and form. (What is both <form and matter> is nearer to the form

and the object of definition, though later in generation.) In what way, then, is one a principle? Because it is not divisible, they say— but both the universal and the particular and element are indivisible.
15 But <they are principles> in different ways, the one in definition, the other in time. In which way, then, is one a principle? As we have said, the right angle seems to be prior to the acute angle, *and* the acute angle to the right angle, and each is *one*. So *they* make one a principle in both ways. But this is impossible; in one way <a principle
20 is> as form and reality, in another as part and matter. In a way, each of them is one. But in fact it is only potentially, and not in actuality, that each of the two units exists (at least if the number is a unity and not like a heap, and if different numbers are made up of different units, as they say).

The cause of the mistake they made was the fact that they were making their search at one and the same time from the side of
25 mathematics and from that of definitions of universals. From the former side they regarded one, their principle, as a point. (A unit is a point without position. So they put things together from minimum parts, as others have done, and the unit becomes the matter of numbers, and at the same time prior to two—though also subsequent,
30 in fact, because two is a whole and a unity and form.) But because they were looking for the universal they treated the one that is predicated as also being a part even so. But it is impossible for both of these to apply simultaneously to the same thing.

If the original One must be merely without position* (there being no difference <between it and the other ones> except that it is a principle) and two is divisible but a unit not, then a unit is more like
35 the original one. But if a unit <is more like it> then it must be more like a unit than like two; so each of the units in two must be prior to two. But they deny this; at least they generate two first.

1085^a Besides, if the original Two is a one, and so is the original Three, both together are two. What, then, does this two come from?

(CHAPTER 9)

One might well raise this problem: since there is no contact in numbers, only succession, applying to units between which there is
5 nothing—those in two, for example, or three—do these succeed the

original One, or not? And is two first in the succession, or one of the units in two?

There are similar awkward consequences with the classes after number—line, plane, and body.

Some produce these out of forms of the great and small—lengths for example from long and short, planes from broad and narrow,   10
masses from deep and shallow (these being forms of great and small). The principle answering to one is posited by different people in different forms. Here we can find hosts of impossible notions, strained and contrary to all reason. <The classes> turn out to be   15
cut off from one another, unless indeed the principles imply one another, so that the broad and narrow is also long and short—but if so, a plane will be a line and a solid will be a plane. Besides, what account can be given of angles and figures and the like?

There is also the same consequence as with number: these are   20
attributes of magnitude, not what magnitude consists of, just as length does not *consist of* straight and curved, and solids do not *consist of* smooth and rough.

Common to all these is a problem arising with forms of a genus, if one posits* universals: is it the original Animal that is in an animal   25
or something other than the original Animal?* This creates no difficulty if the universal is not separate; but if one and numbers are separate, as the people who hold this theory say, then it is not easy to solve—if one can call something impossible 'not easy'. When one apprehends one(ness) in two and in number generally, does one   30
apprehend an original or something else?

Some people, then, generate magnitudes from this kind of matter, others from the point (they think the point is not one but is like one) and another matter, like plurality only not plurality. The same problems arise for this account none the less. For if the matter is one, line, plane, and solid will be the same (what comes from the   35
same <principles> is one and the same). But if there is more than   **1085ᵇ**
one matter—one for the line, another for the plane, another for the solid—then either they imply one another or not, so we get the same results this way too: either a plane will not contain a line, or it will be a line.

Besides, no attempt is made on the problem of how number can

5 come from one and plurality. Whatever they say the same difficulties arise as for those who <produce> number from one and the indefinite two. While some generate number from plurality predicated in general, not a particular plurality, others generate it from a particular plurality, namely the first (two being the first particular
10 plurality). So there is no difference to speak of: the same difficulties will follow—<is it> mixture or position or blending or generation?— and so on.

One could inquire in particular what each unit comes from, if it is one: each of them cannot be the original One. It must come from
15 the original One and plurality or part of plurality. It is impossible to say that a unit is a plurality, because it is indivisible. But if it comes from a part <of plurality> there are many other problems. Each of the parts must be indivisible (or it will be a plurality and the
20 unit will be divisible). So, since each unit does not come from plurality and one, the element cannot be one and *plurality*. Besides, the person holding this view does nothing but produce another number: this plurality of indivisible parts is <just> number.

Besides, we should inquire in the case of this theory too whether number is infinite or finite. There was, so it appears, a finite plurality,
25 from which, together with one, come the finite number of units. But there is also another original plurality, infinite plurality. So which kind of plurality is an element, together with one?

One could ask similar questions about the point and the element from which they produce magnitudes. This is not the one and only point—so what does each of the *other* points come from? Hardly
30 from some distance and the original Point. Anyway, there cannot be indivisible parts of a distance, as there can be of the plurality that units come from; for while number is composed of indivisible parts, magnitudes are not.

All these and other arguments make it clear that number and
35 magnitudes cannot exist separately. Besides, the discord between the theories about number is an indication that it is really incorrectness
1086ᵃ in their facts which produces their confusion. The people who posit only mathematical objects over and above perceptible objects saw the difficulties and fictions surrounding Forms, and so rejected
5 Form number and set up mathematical number. The people who

want to posit Forms and numbers at the same time could not see how mathematical number could exist over and above Form number if one posits only these principles, and so set up Form number and mathematical number as identical—in name, since in fact mathematical number is done away with (the assumptions they make are peculiar to them, and unmathematical). But the first person to hold that Forms exist, that Forms are numbers, and that mathematical objects exist naturally separated them. So the result is that all of them are correct in some way, but wrong over all. They themselves confirm this, in not agreeing but contradicting one another. The reason is that their assumptions and principles are false. It is hard to say what is right starting from what is wrong; as Epicharmus says, no sooner is it said than it is seen to be wrong.

About numbers we have gone through enough problems and distinctions. Someone already convinced might be convinced still further as the result of more, but someone not convinced would come no nearer to conviction.

* * *

As regards primary principles and primary causes and elements, some of what is said by people who treat only of perceptible reality has been discussed in the *Physics*, and some is irrelevant to the present inquiry, but a treatment of the views of people who assert that there are other real objects over and above perceptible objects does form a sequel to our previous discussion. So since some people say that Forms and numbers are such objects, and that their elements are the elements and principles of existing things, we must examine what they say on the subject and what they mean by it.

The people who posit only numbers (mathematical numbers, that is) are to be examined later. One might well, however, take a look at the version of those who say that there are Forms, and at the same time note the problem they meet. For they posit Forms at one and the same time as universal and also as separate and individuals; but it has already been argued that this is not possible. The reason they made this conflation and made real objects universal was that they took real objects to be non-identical with perceptible things. They

judged that with perceptible things the individuals were in flux, none
1086^b of them being permanent, while the universal both existed over and
above them, and was different from them. This, as has already been
said, was set going by Socrates through his definitions, but he at
least made no separation from the individuals, and was right not to
5 make a separation. This is clear from the results: for without universals knowledge cannot be achieved, but separating them is responsible for the resulting difficulties with Forms. But since they
took it to be necessary for any real objects other than perceptible
ones and those in flux to be separate, and they had no others, they
10 set up these universal predicates, with the consequence that universals
and particulars were almost the same sort of thing. This in itself
would be one problem for the view outlined.

CHAPTER 10

Let us now discuss an issue which contains a problem both for those
who believe in Forms and for those who do not, and has already been
15 mentioned at the start in the *Discussion of Problems*. If one does not
take real objects to be separate, in the way in which individual existing things are said to be separate, one will do away with reality as
we want to describe it. But if one does take real objects to be separate, how is one to take their elements and principles?
20   (a) If they are individual and not universal, then (i) there will be
as many existing things as elements, and (ii) the elements will not be
knowable.

(i) Suppose syllables in speech are real objects and their elements
<=letters> are elements of real objects. Then there must be only
one **BA** and one of each other syllable, since they are not universal
25 and the same in form; each is one in number and a particular and
not the same in name <as any other>. (Besides, they do take it that
the original is in each case one*.) But if this is true of the syllables,
it is true of their letters <=elements>; so there will not be more
than one **A**, nor more than one of any letter <=element>, by the
30 same argument which shows that there cannot be more than one of
the same syllable.* But if this is the case, there will be nothing else
existing over and above the elements, only the elements.

(ii) Again, the elements will not be knowable, because they are not universal, while knowledge is of universals. This is clear from proofs and definitions; we cannot validly reason that this triangle has its angles equal to two right angles, unless every triangle has its angles equal to two right angles; nor that this man is an animal, unless 35 every man is an animal.

(b) But if the principles *are* universal, either the real objects that come from them are universal, <or>* objects that are not real will 1087^a be prior to those that are. For a universal is not a real object, but an element or principle is universal, and an element or principle is prior to the things whose element or principle it is.

All this, then, is a natural result when they make Forms out of elements and also claim that there is a single separate entity over and 5 above the real objects that have the same form. But there is nothing to stop there being many As and Bs (as with elements of speech) without there being an original A and an original B over and above the many; and if so then as far as this is concerned there will be infinitely many similar syllables.

The fact that all knowledge is universal, so that the principles of 10 existing things must be universal and not separate real objects, contains the greatest problem among those mentioned, but none the less the statement is true in one way but not in another. Knowledge, like knowing, is of two kinds, one potential, one actual. Potentiality, 15 being (as matter) universal and indefinite, is of what is universal and indefinite, but actuality, being definite, is of something definite, and being individual, is of an individual. It is <only> incidentally that sight sees universal colour, because this <individual> colour which 20 it sees is *a* colour; and the grammarian's object of study, this individual A, is *an* A. If principles must be universal, so must what comes from them be universal, just as in proofs; but if this is so nothing will be separate or a real object. Anyway clearly knowledge is in one way universal and in another not. 25

CHAPTER 1

This concludes our discussion of this sort of reality.

30   Now everyone makes their principles contraries, for unchanging objects too, just as they do in natural science. There cannot, however, be anything prior to a principle of everything, so it must be impossible for it to be a principle as being something else. (This would be as if one were to say that white is a principle, just as white, not as being something else, but yet also that it belongs to an under-

35 lying subject, and is white as being something else.) For that thing will be prior to it. However, everything comes into existence from contraries as belonging to a subject underlying them; this must therefore apply above all to contraries. So all contraries always belong to

1087^b an underlying subject, and none are separate. (A real object, however, has no contrary. This seems obvious and is confirmed by argument.) Something else, then, and not a contrary, is the principle of everything in the proper sense.

They [the Platonists], however, put forward one contrary as

5 matter. Some of them make the unequal (taking this to be the nature of plurality) the matter for one. (i.e. the equal).* Another makes plurality the matter for one. (Numbers are generated for the former from the two <consisting> of the unequal, and for the latter from plurality, but for both they are generated by one as their reality.) The person who takes the unequal and one as elements, the unequal

10 being a two made up of great and small, <really> takes the unequal and the great and small to be one thing, not drawing the distinction that they are one in definition but not in number.

They do not even give a good account of the principles they call elements. Some talk of the great and the small, along with one,

15 taking these three to be elements of number, the two as matter and one as form. Others talk of 'the many and few', because 'the great and the small' are more appropriate in character to magnitude; while others talk instead of the universal character covering these, 'the exceeding and the exceeded'. None of these differ to speak of as far

as concerns any of the consequences, except the formal difficulties,
which they try to avoid because the proofs they themselves put   20
forward are formal.—Except that the argument that makes the
exceeding and exceeded principles, not the great and the small,
implies that number comes before two from the elements, since in
both cases you have the more universal. As it is, however, they admit 25
one but not the other. Others, again,' oppose the different and the
other to one, yet others oppose plurality and one. Suppose, however,
that existing things do come from contraries, as they like to think,
and suppose one has no contrary, or, if it has, it is plurality (unequal being contrary to equal, different contrary to same, and other
contrary to identical) then the people who oppose one to plurality   30
are the ones who have the most plausible view—though still an inadequate one, since one will then be few (plurality being opposed to
fewness, and many to few).

It is obvious that one means a measure. In every case there is
something else which is the subject, a quarter-tone in a musical scale,
a finger or foot or the like in magnitude, in rhythms a beat or syl-   35
lable, and similarly in weight a defined standard weight. So it is in
all cases, a quality for qualities, a quantity for quantities. (The   1088^a
measure is indivisible in kind for qualities, and indivisible to percep-
tual test for quantities.) For one is not a real object in its own right.
And this is only reasonable: one means a measure of some plurality,
and number means a measured plurality and a plurality of measures.   5
(Thus there is good reason for one not to be a number: a measure is
not itself measures. The measure and one are both principles.) The
measure must always be some one and the same thing applying to all
cases; for example, if there are horses the measure is horse, if men it
is man.* If there are a man, a horse, and a god, the measure will per- 10
haps be living thing, and their number will be a number of living
things. If there are a man, white, and walking, they will hardly have
a number, because they all belong to the same thing which is numerically one. Still, they will have a number of categories or some such
term.

The people who posit the unequal as one thing, and posit the   15
indefinite two of great and small,* have a highly implausible and
impossible view. For these are characteristics and features, not what

underlie numbers and magnitudes—many and few being characteristics of number and great and small characteristics of magnitudes—
20 just like even and odd, smooth and rough, straight and curved.

Besides, apart from this mistake, the great and the small, and the
like, must be relative. But relatives least of all are entities or real
objects, coming as they do after both quality and quantity. A
25 relative is a characteristic of quantity, as has been said, not matter,
since there is something else <serving as matter>* for both relative
in general and its parts and forms. There is nothing either great or
small, many or few, or relative in general, which is not many or few
or small or relative as being something else. An indication that a
30 relative is least of all a kind of real object and existing thing is the
fact that relatives alone do not come into being or pass away or
change in the way that increase and diminution occur in quantity,
alteration in quality, locomotion in place, sheer coming into being
and passing away in the case of a real object. There is none of this
with relatives. A thing will be greater or less or equal without itself
35 changing if *another* thing changes in quantity. Also, the matter of
1088ᵇ each thing (and thus of a real object) must be that kind of thing
potentially; but a relative is neither potentially nor actually a real
object. It is absurd, or rather impossible, to make what is not a real
object an element of and prior to a real object, for all the categories
come later.

5   Besides, elements are not predicated of the things they are elements
of, but many and few are predicated of number both separately and
together, while long and short are predicated of a line, and planes are
both broad and narrow. If there really is a plurality of which 'few' is
always true,* two for example (if it were many, then one would be
10 few), then there must also be an absolute many, e.g. ten would be
many, if there is no number greater than ten, or ten thousand. How
then can number be composed in this way of few and many? Either
both would have to be predicated, or neither; but as it is only one of
them is.

CHAPTER 2

We must examine this question generally: is it possible for eternal
15 things to be composed of elements? In that case they will contain

matter, since everything composed of elements is composite. Now a thing must come into being from what it consists of, whether it exists for ever or would have come into being; and everything comes into being out of something which is potentially what it comes to be (it could not have come into being from, or consist of, what lacked that potentiality). And what is potential can be actualized or not. So however true it is that number '(or anything else containing 20 matter) exists for ever, it *could* fail to exist, just like a thing after one day, or after any number of years: if these could fail to exist, so could something even after so long a time as to be without limit. Therefore they cannot be eternal, since what can fail to exist is not eternal, as we have had occasion to discuss in another work. If the present statement—that no real object is eternal except actuality—is 25 universally true, and elements are the matter of a real object, then no eternal real object can have elements present in it from which it is composed.

There are some people who make the element along with one an indefinite two, and object to the unequal, reasonably in view of the impossible consequences. But they only get rid of those difficulties 30 which that theory encounters because it makes the unequal and relative an element; all the difficulties apart from this idea must apply to them too, whether it is Form number they produce from the elements or mathematical number.

There are many reasons for their being led astray towards these 35 causes, but the main one is their old-fashioned way of putting the 1089^a problem. They thought that all existing things would be one, the original Being, unless one could refute and come to grips with Parmenides' words, 'Never shall this be forced through, that things that are not, are.' They thought it necessary to prove that what is not, is; for only in this way—from being and from something else— 5 would it be possible for there to be many existing things.

However, in the first place, 'being' has many senses: sometimes it means real objects, sometimes quality, sometimes quantity and the other categories. So if there is no not-being, what kind of one will all existing things be? Will it be real objects, or qualities, and the rest 10 similarly? Or will they all—'this' and 'such' and 'so much' and everything else signifying one kind of thing—be one? It is absurd, or rather impossible, for a single kind of thing to become responsible for one thing's being this, another's being such, another's being so much, another's being somewhere.

15   Further, what kind of not-being and being do existing things come from? 'Not-being' too has many senses, since 'being' has: not being a man means not being a 'this'; not being straight means not being 'such', not being three cubits long means not being 'so much'. So from what kind of being and not-being do existing things come to be many?

20   *He* [Plato] means falsity and that kind of thing by not-being, from which, together with being, there come to be many things. That is why it used to be said that you have to assume something false, like geometers when they assume a line to be a foot long when it is not a foot long. But this cannot be right. Geometers do not make any false assumptions (it is not a premise in their reasoning). 25 And it is not this kind of not-being that existing things come into being from or pass away into. Not-being in its different cases has as many senses as there are categories, and in addition to these is used to mean what is false and what is potential; and it is from this last that coming into being takes place. A man comes into being from what is not man but is potentially man, and white comes into being 30 from what is not white but is potentially white, and similarly whether it is one thing that comes into being or many.

Obviously their inquiry is how there can be many beings in the sense of real objects: it is numbers and lengths and bodies that are generated. Now it is absurd to ask how there can be many beings in the 'what it is' sense, and not how there can be many in the case of 35 quality or quantity. For the indefinite two or the great and small is hardly responsible for there being two whites or many colours or **1089ᵇ** flavours or shapes, or these would have been numbers and units. However if they had approached these questions, they would have seen what was responsible in the former case too, since what is responsible is the same thing, or something analogous.

The same aberration explains also why those who search for the 5 contrary of being and one (from which together with them existing things come) set up the relative and unequal—but this is not the contrary or negation of these, but just one sort of being, like the *what* category or quality.

They should also have looked for the way relatives can be many and not one. But as it is they ask how there can be many units besides the first one, but not how there can be many sorts of un- 10 equal besides the unequal. They make use of them, however, talking about great and small, many and few (from which come numbers), long and short (from which comes length), broad and narrow (from which comes the plane), deep and shallow (from which comes masses). And they mention even more types of relative. What is responsible for these things being many?

It is indeed necessary, as we ourselves say, to assume for each 15 thing something which potentially is that thing. But the holder of this theory went on to declare what it is that is potentially a *this*, a real object, but has no independent being. He said that it is the relative—rather as though he had said quality. But this is not potenti- ally one or potentially being, and not the negation of one or being either. It is just one kind of being. And since he was asking how there can be many existing things, it was even more necessary, as we 20 said, not only to ask about things in the same category—how there can be many objects or many qualities—but to ask how existing things in general can be many, some of them being objects, some characteristics, some relatives.

In the case of the *other* categories, another thing to give us pause is the question how there can be many items. Because they are not 25 separable, it is through their underlying subject's coming to be and being many that qualities and quantities are many. But there ought to be a type of matter for each category, except that it cannot be separated from the actual objects.

In the case of items that are a *this*, however, it is intelligible how there can be many of them, unless there is to be something which is both a this and an entity of a certain kind. The real problem here is 30 rather how there can be many objects rather than one in actuality.

Further, if *this* and quantity are not identical, we have not been told how and why there are many things, but how there are many quantities. All number means a kind of quantity, and so does unit, if it does not mean a kind of measure or what is quantitatively in- 35 divisible.* If then quantity and the *what* category are *different*, we

have not been told from what <principle> or how the *what* items
are many. If they are identical, many inconsistencies face the holder
of the theory.

*   *   *

One might also fix on this question about numbers: where are we
to find reasons for believing that they exist? For someone who accepts
Forms they provide some kind of explanation for things, since each
5   number is a Form and a Form is an explanation of the being of other
things somehow or other (we shall grant them this assumption). But
what about the person who does not hold this sort of view through
seeing the difficulties over Forms latent in it, so that this is not his
reason for taking there to be numbers, but who still takes there to be
1C   mathematical number? Why should we credit him when he says that
this sort of number exists, and what use is it to anything else? There
is nothing which the man who believes in it *says* it causes; he just
says it is a kind of independent entity. Nor is it *obviously* a cause,
for arithmeticians' theorems will all apply just as well to perceptible
15   things, as we have said.

(CHAPTER 3)

The people who take Forms to exist, and to be numbers, take each
to be one thing in virtue of their. method of setting each one out
over and above the many <individuals>; so they at least attempt to
say in a way why <number> exists. However, since these considerations are neither necessary nor possible, one should not assert that
20   number exists because of them, at any rate.

As for the Pythagoreans, it was because they saw that many attributes of numbers apply to* perceptible bodies that they made
actual things to be numbers—not separate, however, but they made
actual things consist of numbers. Why? Because the attributes of
numbers apply in a musical scale, in the heavens, and in many other
25   cases. People who assert that only mathematical number exists cannot say anything like this, on their own assumptions; so it used to
be said that branches of knowledge cannot have <perceptible>
things as their objects. But we say that they can, as we said before.

And clearly mathematical objects are not separate; if they were
separate their attributes would not apply to bodies. The Pythagoreans 30
are not open to any objection on this score; but in producing physical
bodies out of numbers, things with lightness and weight out of
things with neither lightness nor weight, they seem to be talking
about a different heaven and different bodies, and not the perceptible
ones. As for the people who make <number> separate,* however, 35
they suppose it to exist and to be separate on the grounds that
axioms will not be true of perceptible things, while <mathematical>
statements *are* true and appeal to the soul; and similarly with mathematical magnitudes. Clearly the opposing theory will say the opposite, **1090^b**
and the problem just raised has to be solved by those who hold these
views: why, if numbers are in no way present in perceptible things,
their attributes apply to perceptible things.

   There are some people who think that there must be entities of 5
this sort, because the point is the limit and extreme of the line, the
line of the plane, and the plane of the solid. We must therefore have
a look at this argument too, and see whether it is not extremely
feeble. Extremes are not real objects; they are all rather limits. (Even
walking, and movement in general, has a sort of limit; so this would 10
be an individual and a real object, which is absurd.) But even if they
are, they will all belong to the particular perceptible things (it was to
these that the argument applied); so why should they be separate?

   Besides, if one is not too complacent, one might go on asking
questions about all <kinds of> number and mathematical objects, 15
and the way they make no contribution to one another, the ones
coming before to the ones coming after. If number did not exist,
magnitudes would exist none the less, on the theory that only mathematical objects exist; and even if these did not exist soul would,
and perceptible bodies. However, judging by what we can observe,
nature is not a mere series of episodes, like a bad tragedy. 20

   This objection does not touch the people who posit Forms,
because they produce magnitudes out of matter and number: lengths
from two, planes from three, presumably, and solids from four, or
from other numbers too—it makes no difference. But will these
<objects> be Forms, or what kind of existence will they have? 25

And what do they contribute to things? Nothing; like mathematical objects they too contribute nothing. Nor even does any mathematical theorem apply to them, unless one wants to interfere with mathematics and make up one's own theories; it is not hard to assume any
30 hypothesis whatever and spin out conclusions at vast length. So these people are wrong here, in trying to pull mathematical objects and Forms together. The first people, however, who set up two sorts of number, Form number and mathematical number, said nothing at all, and cannot say, as to how and whence mathematical number is
35 to exist. They put it between Form number and perceptible number. But if it comes from the great and small, it will be the same as Form number (and from what *other* small and great can he produce magni-
1091^a tudes?). And if he names some other element, there will be rather a lot of elements to name. Also, if a one is the principle of both kinds, one will be common to them, and we should ask how one can be these many things, while according to him number cannot be pro-
5 duced otherwise than from one and an indefinite two.

All this is absurd, and conflicts both with itself and with what is reasonable. They seem to be a case of Simonides' long story; we get a long story like that of slaves when what they say is dubious. The
10 very elements, too, the great and the small, seem to cry out as though they were being manhandled; they cannot generate number at all except the numbers doubled from one [i.e. the powers of two].

It is absurd—or rather one of the impossibilities—to have a generation of things that are eternal. There is no need to doubt whether the Pythagoreans do or do not have a generation; they say clearly
15 that when one had been composed (out of planes or surface or seed or something that they are at a loss to express), then forthwith the nearest part of the unlimited was drawn in and limited by the limit. But since they are giving a cosmogony and mean to speak as natural scientists, we owe it to them to examine their account of nature, but
20 to release them from the present inquiry; we are examining principles among *unchanging* things, so it is this sort of numbers whose generation we should study.

(CHAPTER 4)

They say that there is no generation of the odd, clearly implying

124

that there *is* generation of the even. As for the even, some produce it
as the first thing to come from unequals, the great and small, when 25
equalized. So it follows that inequality must have applied to them
before the equalization. If they had always been equalized, they
would not have been unequal before (there is nothing before *always*).
So clearly it is not <just> as a theoretical analysis that they set up
the generation of numbers.

*   *   *

It is a puzzle (which it is discreditable to be complacent about) how 30
the elements and principles are related to the good and the beautiful.
The problem is whether any of the elements is the sort of thing we
mean in speaking of the original Good and the best, or whether this
is not so, these being produced later.

People who tell stories about the gods seem to agree with some
present-day thinkers, who say it is not so: it is only as the nature of
things progresses that the good and the beautiful make their appear- 35
ance. (They do this to avoid a real difficulty which faces people
who make one a principle, as some do; the difficulty, however, **1091ᵇ**
comes not because they ascribe the good to their principle, but
because they make one a principle—and a principle in the sense of
an element—and because they make number come from one.) The
early poets agree, in so far as they describe as sovereign and ruler not
the first comers, night for example or heaven or Chaos or Ocean, but 5
rather Zeus. But still, they are led to say such things because their
rulers of the world change. Those of them whose works are a mixture,
in that not everything is said in myth, like Pherecydes, and some
others, *do* make the first productive principle the best. So do the 10
Magi and some later philosophers, like Empedocles, who made Love
an element, and Anaxagoras, who made Mind a principle. Among the
people who assert the existence of unchanging real objects some say
that the original One is the original Good, but they thought that its
reality lay primarily in its being one.

This, then, is the problem, which theory one should hold. It would 15
be surprising if what is primary and eternal and most self-sufficient
did not posses this very thing—self-sufficiency and self-maintenance—

primarily as a good. In fact it cannot be indestructible or self-sufficient because of anything other than being good. So saying that a principle has this character may very well be true.

20 But it is impossible for it to be one, or, if not that, anyway an element, and an element of numbers. Huge difficulties follow (to avoid which some people have rejected the theory, agreeing that one is the primary principle and element, but only of *mathematical*

25 number). For all units become sorts of good, so that there is rather a plethora of goods. Besides, if Forms are numbers, all Forms are kinds of good. But suppose there are Forms of anything one pleases. If there are Forms only of goods, Forms will not be real objects; but if there are Forms of real objects too, then all living creatures and plants and everything participating in Forms will be good.

30 These absurdities follow, and it also follows that the opposite element (whether plurality or the unequal and great and small) is the original Evil. (This is why one person used to avoid attaching the good to one, on the ground that since generation is from contraries, evil would necessarily be the nature of plurality. Others say that it is

35 the unequal that is the nature of evil.) It follows that all things partake of evil except one, the original One, and that numbers partake of it in a less diluted form than magnitudes. It also follows that evil

1092ᵃ is the area of the good, and that it partakes of and desires what tends to destroy it (contraries tend to destroy each other). Also, if, as we were saying, matter is what is potentially each thing (e.g. the matter of actual fire is what is potentially fire) then evil will be precisely the

5 potentially good.

All this follows partly because they make every principle an element, partly because they make contraries principles, partly because they make one a principle, and partly because they make numbers the primary real objects, separate and Forms.

(CHAPTER 5)

If, then, it is impossible either not to place the good among the principles or to place it there in this way, clearly their account of the

10 principles and primary real objects has been incorrectly given. Nor is someone correct who compares the principles of the universe to that of living things and plants, on the ground that the more complete

always comes from what is indefinite and incomplete (this being his reason for saying that this applies to the primary principles too, so that the original One is not even an existing thing). For even in this case the principles from which these things come *are* complete; it is a man that produces a man, and it is not true that the sperm is primary.

*   *   *

It is absurd to produce place simultaneously with mathematical solids (place is peculiar to individual things, which is why they are separated by their place, while mathematical objects are not anywhere); <it is also absurd> to say that they are somewhere, but not to say what their place is.

People who say that existing things come from elements, and that numbers are primary among existing things, ought to have distinguished the ways in which one thing comes *from* another, and then told us the way in which number comes from the principles. Is it by mixture? But not everything can be mixed; and what is produced will be different from its elements; and one will not be separate and a distinct entity, which they want it to be. By juxtaposition, like a syllable? But then the elements will have to have position, and when one thinks of one and plurality one will think of them separately; so this is what number will be: a unit *and* plurality, or one *and* unequal.

Also, coming from things means in one way that they are still present, and in another that they are not, so which is the case with number? The case where they are present is only possible for things that have generation. Is it then like coming from sperm? Nothing can come from what is indivisible. Is it then like coming from a contrary that does not persist? But everything of this type comes from something else too, that *does* persist. Then since one is posited by one person as contrary to plurality, and by another (who treats one as equal) to the unequal, number must be, according to this, produced from contraries. So there is something else persisting, from which, together with one other factor, number is or has been produced.

Besides, why ever is it that everything that comes from contraries

15

20

25

30

35

1092ᵇ

127

or has a contrary perishes (even if it came from the entire contrary)
5 while number does not? Nothing is said on this point. But a contrary
always destroys <a contrary> whether as an ingredient or not, just
as Strife destroys the Mixture (it shouldn't, however, because it is
not *its* contrary).

*   *   *

Nothing has been defined about the way in which numbers are causes
of real objects and of being.

Is it as boundaries, the ways points are boundaries of magnitudes,
10 and the way Eurytus used to draw up what a thing's number was
(e.g. this is the number of man, and that of horse), making likenesses
of the forms of living things with his pebbles, like people putting
numbers in the shapes of a triangle or a square?

Or is it because harmony is a ratio of numbers, and so is man and
15. everything else? But how are characteristics numbers—white, sweet,
hot? Clearly it is not numbers that are the thing's reality and the
cause of its form; it is the ratio that is the reality, and number the
matter.* For example, number is the reality of flesh and bone
<only> in this sense, that it is three parts of fire to two of earth.
A number, whatever it is, is always a number *of* something, of fire or
20 earth or units; but the actual being of the things consists in there
being so much to so much in the mixture; and this is no longer a
number but a ratio of mixture in numbers, whether these are bodily
or of some other kind.

Number, then, is not a cause by producing things (whether
number in general or number composed of units), nor as matter, nor
25 as ratio and form of things. Not that it is the final cause either.

(CHAPTER 6)

One might raise the question: what is the good got from numbers in
the fact that a mixture is expressible by a number, whether an easily
calculable one or an odd one? In fact honey-water is no more
wholesome if mixed in 'three times three' proportion; it would be
more use if mixed in no proportion but diluted than it would if
30 mixed by number but not diluted <enough>.

Besides, ratios of mixtures are expressed by adding numbers, not just by numbers, e.g. 'three to two', not 'three times two'. For in multiplication the factors must be of the same kind; the product of $1 \times 2 \times 3$ must be measured by 1, and that of $4 \times 5 \times 7$ by 4. So all products of the same factor must be measurable by that factor. So it cannot be the case that the number of fire is $2 \times 5 \times 3 \times 7$ and that of water 2×3. 35

If everything must share in number, many things must turn out to **1093ᵃ** be the same, and the same number must belong to one thing and also to something different.

Is number a cause, then, and is this why the thing exists? Or is this unclear? The sun's motions have a number, and so again do the moon's, and so does the life and maturity of any animal. What is 5 there to prevent some of these being square numbers, and some cubes, and some equal and others double? There is nothing to prevent it; indeed they would necessarily fall within these types if everything shared in number.

It was also possible <on their view> for different things to fall under the same number; so that if things happened to have the same 10 number, they would be the same as one another, having the same kind of number. The sun and moon, for example, would be the same.

Why, however, are these numbers causes? There are seven vowels, the scale has seven strings, there are seven Pleiads, animals lose their teeth at seven (some anyway; some don't), and there were seven 15 against Thebes. Is it because the number is the sort of number it is that there were seven of them, or that there are seven stars in the Pleiad? Surely there were seven heroes because of the gates or some other reason, and while we count the Pleiad as seven and the Bear as twelve, others count more stars in them.

They even say that <the double consonants> *xi, psi* and *zeta* are 20 concords, and that there are three of them because there are three concords. They ignore the fact that there might be thousands <of such letters>—there might be one symbol for *gamma* and *rho* together. If they say that it is because each of these is equal to two other letters, while no other letters are, and that this has an explanation (there are three regions <of the mouth> and one letter is applied to *sigma* in each)—well, that is why there are only three of

129

25 them, and not because there are three concords. There are more
    <than three> concords, in fact, but there cannot be more <than
    three double consonants>.

    These people are like the Homeric scholars of old, who see small
    resemblances and overlook important ones.

    Some people go on to describe many such cases. For example, the
    middle notes are 9 and 8; the epic hexameter has 17 syllables, which
30 is equal to their sum, and scans with 9 syllables in the right-hand
1093ᵇ part, and 8 in the left-hand part. They say also that the distance in
    letters from *alpha* to *omega* is equal to that from the lowest to the
    highest note on a flute, and this number is equal to the whole sys-
    tematic harmony of the universe. We should suspect, however, that
5   nobody need be at a loss to state or discover such facts in the sphere
    of the eternal, since they occur even among things that perish.

    However, the celebrated characteristics of numbers and the con-
    traries to them, and mathematical facts generally, as described by
    some people who make them causes of nature, seem, viewed in this
10 light, to slip away, for none of them is a cause in any of the ways
    distinguished in reference to the principles.

    The way they proceed does, however, make it clear that the
    good has application, and that we do find odd, straight, equal-by-
    equal, and the powers of some numbers in the column of the beauti-
    ful. The seasons and a certain sort of number go together; and this
15 is the force of all the other examples they collect from mathematical
    theorems. Hence they are like coincidences; they are incidental
    (though all appropriate to one another) but one by analogy. For
    there is an analogous item in each category of being; straight in
20 length is as level in surface, and perhaps as odd in number and white
    in colour.

    Besides, it is not the numbers among the Forms that are causes of
    harmonic relations and such. They differ from one another in form
    even when equal, because their units differ. So we need not posit
    Forms for this reason anyway.

    These, then, are the consequences <of the theories> and even
25 more might be brought together. The many troubles they have with
    the generation of numbers and their inability to systematize in any
    way seem to be an indication that mathematical objects are not
    separate from perceptible objects, as some say, and that these are
    not the principles.   130

THE RELATION OF M 4-5 to A 6 and A 9

1078^b7-34 recasts some of the material in A 6, but with major changes. $1078^b34-1080^a8$ corresponds to A 9, 990^b2-991^b9, except that (i) 1079^b3-11 has been inserted (a new argument) and (ii) 991^b8-993^a10 has disappeared; the arguments it contains are partly omitted and partly developed through M-N.

1078^b36 πλείω γὰρ ἐστι τῶν καθ᾽ ἕκαστα αἰσθητῶν ὡς εἰπεῖν τὰ εἴδη replaces σχεδὸν γὰρ ἴσα–ἢ οὐκ ἐλάττω–ἐστι τὰ εἴδη τούτοις at 990^b4.

1079^a2 καθ᾽ ἕκαστόν τε γὰρ ὁμώνυμον ἔστι replaces καθ᾽ ἕκαστον γὰρ ὁμώνυμόν τι at 990^b6, and 990^b7 contains ὦν which is omitted in 1079^a3. (J. and R. emend differently: see the Textual Notes.)

1079^a5 δείκνυται; δείκνυμεν at 990^b9.

1079^a7 οἴονται; οἰόμεθα at 990^b11.

1079^a11 ἀκριβέστατοι; ἀκριβέστεροι at 990^b15.

1079^a12 φασιν; φαμεν at 990^b16.

1079^a14-15 βούλονται; βουλόμεθα at 990^b18 in some MSS (the reading accepted by J. and R.).

1079^a17 καὶ τούτου τὸ πρός τι, καὶ τοῦτο τοῦ καθ᾽ αὐτό replaces καὶ τὸ πρός τι τοῦ καθ᾽ αὐτό. at 990^b20-1.

1079^a20 φασιν; φαμεν at 990^b23.

1079^a20 ἔσονται εἴδη; ἔσται εἴδη at 990^b24.

1079^a21 ff. ἀλλὰ καὶ ἄλλων πολλῶν (τὸ γὰρ νόημα ἕν οὐ μόνον περὶ τὰς οὐσίας ἀλλὰ καὶ κατὰ μὴ οὐσιῶν ἐστί, καὶ ἐπιστῆμαι οὐ μόνον τῆς οὐσίας εἰσί)· συμβαίνει δὲ καὶ ἄλλα μυρία τοιαῦτα replaces ἀλλὰ πολλῶν καὶ ἐτέρων (καὶ γὰρ τὸ ᾽νόημα ἐν οὐ μόνον περὶ τὰς οὐσίας ἀλλὰ καὶ κατὰ τῶν ἄλλων ἐστί, καὶ ἄλλα δὲ μυρία συμβαίνει τοιαῦτα). at 990^b24 ff.

1079^a28 λέγονται; λέγεται at 990^b31.

1079^a35 At 991^a4 τῶν δυάδων is omitted.

1079^a36 J. adds $<εἶναι>$ 'ex A', where however it does not appear in the text but in the apparatus as the reading of one manuscript and of Alexander.

1079^b12 συμβάλλονται τὰ εἴδη; συμβάλλεται τὰ εἴδη at 991^a9.

1079^b21 Εὔδοξος δὲ ὕστερος ἔλαγε διαπορῶν replaces Εὔδοξος δ᾽ ὕστερον at 991^a17.

1079^b28 Cf. 991^a24; M omits ὅμοιον.

1079^b34 οἶον τὸ γένος τῶν ὡς γένους εἰδῶν replaces οἶον τὸ γένος, ὡς γένος εἰδῶν at 991^a30-1.

1080^a2 τοῦτον λέγεται τὸν τρόπον; οὕτω λέγεται at 991^b3.

1080^a2 λέγεται. At 991^b3 λέγομεν has been proposed by J., as found in Alexander and Asclepius (not in the OCT; see P. Merlan, 'War Aristoteles je Anhänger der Ideenlehre? Jaegers letztes Wort', *Archiv für Geschichte der Philosophie*, 1970).

1080ª4 Cf. 991ᵇ5. *M* omits τὰ μετέχοντα.

1080ª6 κἀκεῖνα, ὧν φασιν ἰδέας εἶναι replaces καὶ τἆλλα at 991ᵇ7.

1080ª6 φασιν; φαμεν at 991ᵇ7.

1080ª8 Cf. 991ᵇ9. *M* adds ἀλλ᾽ οὐ διὰ τὰ εἴδη.

NOTES ON THE TEXT

The text translated is that of W. Jaeger in the Oxford Classical Text (Oxford 1957). The places at which I disagree with Jaeger's text are marked in the translation by an asterisk and discussed in the following notes. The following abbreviations are used:

J. = W. Jaeger, Oxford Classical Text of the *Metaphysics* (Oxford 1957).

R. = Sir D. Ross, Text of the *Metaphysics* with Introduction and Commentary, 2 vols. (Oxford 1924).

Em. = Jaeger, 'Emendationen zur aristotelischen Metaphysik (II)', in *Sitzungsberichte der Preussischen Akademie der Wissenschaften*, Berlin 1923, pp. 263-79 (this is referred to by J. in his OCT apparatus as 'BBA'). I refer to it as reprinted in Jaeger, *Scripta Minora* vol. 1 (Rome 1960), pp. 257-80.

1076^b39 J. inserts $<ἄπειρα>$ (Em. p. 278), taking the argument to be incomplete otherwise. This is not so if the argument is taken in close connection with the one preceding, but J.'s insertion makes better sense of the way the argument develops. See the notes on this passage.

1077^a20 The OCT text of J., and R., both read the MSS. τίνι καὶ πότ' which means, 'in virtue of what, and when . . .? But 'when' seems to make no sense here. J. in his apparatus mentions Bonitz's suggestion that καί and ποτ' (enclitic) are alternatives which have got conjoined in our text. I accept this and translate accordingly, without 'when?'

1077^b4 I take 'always' to be necessary here, and assume with Bywater that ἀεί has fallen out after ὑπάρχει.

1079^a2 The reading here is καθ' ἕκαστόν τε γὰρ ὁμώνυμον ἔστι while at 990 $^b6$ it is καθ' ἕκαστον γὰρ ὁμώνυμόν τι J. here brackets [τε], while R. inserts $<τι>$ from the A passage, which I accept. J. brackets [καὶ παρὰ τὰς οὐσίας] where it stands in the text and inserts it after πολλῶν, and inserts $<ὧν>$ after ἄλλων on the ground that this is the reading of the A text. I follow R. who excises ὧν from the A text–'the balance of evidence is against it, and the construction without it is at any rate not more difficult than that which we get by reading it' (i, p. 191). Accordingly I translate the text here without J.'s transpositions.

1080^a18 I suggest omitting ἤ before ἐπί, in order to remove incoherence in the argument of chs. 6–7. See the notes on the passage.

1080^b22-3 Jaeger proposes to omit two words: ἕνα εἶναι [ἔνιοι] δὲ καὶ τὸν μαθηματικὸν τὸν αὐτὸν τοῦτον [εἶναι] (this suggestion appears in Em. p. 266 and the OCT apparatus, though not the text). This has the effect of collapsing the two views here into one, to match the later passage 1083^b1 ff. But as R. points out, Alexander read our text, and the inconsistency is not a major problem: Aristotle's summaries of opposing views vary considerably throughout M-N.

1081ᵃ15 I reject J.'s insertion of $<αὗται>$ as making the sentence long-winded and the argument obscure.

1081ᵃ25 J. accepts R.'s emendation of ἔπειτα to ἐπεὶ in order to make one argument out of two, but I reject this on the grounds that there are two distinct arguments, and read the MSS. ἔπειτα (see notes on the passage).

1082ᵃ31 J. obelizes the OCT text because of the plural ἰδέαι in 1. 32. In Em. pp. 278-9 he proposes to insert $<ἡ πρώτη τετράς>$ after εἰ to render the text grammatically consistent. But it is much easier to alter ἰδέαι to ἰδέα, as R. does, in spite of weaker MS. support; and I follow him here.

1084ᵃ10 J. has τάττουσι δ' οὕτω τὰς ἰδέας. R. accepts Schwegler's γ', which has the effect of taking τάττουσι as dative participle instead of third person indicative and changing the sense from 'it is against reason *but* they (still) arrange Forms this way' to 'it is against reason for them to do it because they arrange Forms this way'. It is hard to choose, because the force of τάττουσι is hard to understand here.

1084ᵇ33 J. marks the OCT as corrupt at this point (as does R.) I translate it as it stands, but it makes little sense. Suggested alternatives do not seem satisfactory (see notes on this passage).

1085ᵃ25 I follow R. in accepting θῇ , which J. obelizes.

1085ᵃ26 I keep ζῴου with the MSS. (and R.) against J.'s ζῷον.

1086ᵇ27 J. brackets this sentence on grounds of irrelevance, but I accept R.'s defence of it (ii, pp. 463-4).

1086ᵇ30 I follow R. in excising ἄλλων, which J. accepts.

1086ᵇ37–1087ᵃ1. I follow R. in assuming ἢ to have fallen out before ἔσται. This is more economical than J.'s solution (Em. pp. 268-9) of bracketing the whole first clause as a marginal gloss.

1087ᵇ5 J. brackets τῷ ἴσῳ, 'the equal', on the ground (Em. p. 273) that if the one were already taken to be identical with the equal and thus the opposite of the unequal, it would be superfluous to point out that inequality is the nature of plurality. This is weak in the face of 1092ᵃ35-ᵇ1, which shows that some people in the Academy at least did vaguely identify the one with the equal. This together with the Hermodorus fragment (Simp. *in Phys.* 247.30) and Alexander *in Met.* 56.13 ff., suggests that this passage should be left and regarded as part of our evidence on the subject, not altered to fit any theory.

1088ᵃ9 I accept Bonitz's and R.'s εἰ ἵπποι, τὸ μέτρον ἵππος, καὶ εἰ ἄνθρωποι, ἄνθρωπος. J.'s reading, εἰ ἵππος τὸ μέτρον, ἵππους καὶ εἰ ἄνθρωπος, ἀνθρώπους, demands a very harsh ellipse of 'must be the number' or something similar.

1088ᵃ16 I do not accept J.'s insertion of ἐκ, 'out of'.

1088ᵃ25 I agree with R. that there is no difficulty supplying ὕλη ἐστι or the like, and J.'s insertions of ἢ before εἰ and ὑπόκειται (with Christ) after ἕτερον are not necessary.

1088^{b}8-9 J. marks the text as corrupt. I follow R. in taking it to be satisfactory if one inserts τό before ὀλίγον and a comma after ἀεί, and understands 'is true of' or the like.

1089^{b}35 I follow R.'s καὶ ἡ μονάς, εἰ μὴ μέτρον καὶ τὸ κατὰ τὸ ποσὸν ἀδιαίρετον rather than J.'s καὶ ἡ μονάς, εἰ μὴ μέτρον ὅτι τὸ κατά.

1090^{a}22 J.'s ἐν, 'in', is not necessary (though it has parallels in sentences nearby).

1090^{a}36 J. suspects a lacuna, partly because χωριστά in 1.37 should be χωριστόν (as in 1.35) to be grammatical. But Aristotle is here thinking of a 'vague subject such as ταῦτα' (Ross) and there is no serious gap in the train of thought.

1092^{b}18 J. accepts Schwegler's ὕλης for ὕλη because of 1.24 where it is denied that number is matter. R., however, shows convincingly that the two points are not in conflict. In this line I follow R.'s text and punctuation rather than J.'s.

NOTES

BOOK M

CHAPTER 1

This chapter sketches the course of *M-N* in a very rough way. (See the Introduction, pp. 78-81), for discussion of some complications.) Aristotle's introduction shows clearly that *M-N* is a response to platonist theories, especially those developed in the Academy. Instead of beginning in his usual way, by carefully collecting all the relevant opinions on a topic, he here analyses and classifies an already demarcated theory. *M-N* is unusual among Aristotle's works in that normally he is not much interested in problems created entirely by the theories of other philosophers. But platonism (in both the forms mentioned here) strikes him as a particularly pernicious view which it is important to combat in the interests of the truth.

The classification already makes it clear that the theory of Forms is of merely subordinate interest in this context, especially as it has already received so much attention, and there are few new arguments against it. The main theme is now platonism in general, especially in the philosophy of mathematics, where it has never been adequately challenged (apart from a few arguments in *A* 9). The three views distinguished are those of Plato, who accepts the existence of both Forms and numbers, Xenocrates, who accepts both but identifies them, and Speusippus, who accepts only numbers. (Aristotle is slightly careless here; in line 20 we should understand 'mathematical objects' for 'mathematical numbers'.) The Pythagoreans do not fit into this classification, because they are not platonists; they do not believe in the reality of *abstract* objects. In *M-N* the references to them are always clearly marked as incidental to the main theme.

The final paragraph again sharpens the alternatives as Aristotle sees them. If numbers do not exist in either of the two ways open to a platonist (as Aristotle will try to show in ch. 2), then either they do not exist at all or only in a sense. Aristotle is clearly caught in the difficult position of anyone wanting to deny the existence of abstract objects. He is not denying that mathematical objects exist in any sense, which would be absurd. He wants to deny that they exist as the platonists understand this, that is, in virtue of having independent existence, distinct from physical objects. For Aristotle they do exist in a sense which he will try to explain in chapter 3, which does not imply that they are separate from physical objects.

1076ª28-9: 'Published works' is meant to reproduce the ambiguity of the Greek *exōterikoi logoi*; Aristotle is probably referring to his early work *On the Forms*, referred to in chapter 4, but may also mean the work of others. Cf. Düring, *Aristotle in the Ancient Biographical Tradition*, pp. 426-44, Cherniss (1), n. 107.

CHAPTER 2

In this chapter Aristotle demolishes the platonist conception of mathematical objects before offering his own alternative in chapter 3. For most of this chapter he attacks platonism as the theory that, since mathematical statements do not apply to the world in the sense of describing it directly, mathematics is not about the physical world at all, but about a quite different and superior subject-matter—numbers and ideal geometrical objects which, while not in space and time, have nevertheless real, mind-independent existence. This is the theory that mathematical objects are 'separate'.

He first, however, deals with another theory, which resembles platonism in taking the objects of mathematics to have real existence independent of the mind, and in denying that mathematics directly describes the world, but differs from platonism in not taking mathematical objects to be quite separate and distinct from physical objects, supposing them to exist in physical objects. I shall call this 'partial platonism'.

This view sounds absurd: how could anybody believe that mathematics deals with objects that are indivisible (1076ᵇ7) but literally in physical objects? But the position may not be as straightforwardly absurd as is suggested by Aristotle's stress on the locution of 'in physical objects'. The partial platonist can be characterized as someone who accepts the platonist's premise that mathematics does not describe the actual behaviour of physical objects since its truth is independent of such behaviour, but who fights shy of the platonist conclusion that therefore mathematics is not about the actual world at all, but a quite separate one. The partial platonist agrees that mathematical objects are in some way ideal—mathematical points, for example, are not divisible the way dots on paper are—but rejects the idea that their existence is quite independent of drawing dots on paper. For him mathematics is about ideal objects, but still applies directly to physical objects. Aristotle represents this as a confused failure to distinguish ideal from physical objects.

Partial platonism is obviously a muddle, and Aristotle is brusque with it. Why does he give it space at all? The partial platonist may be muddled, but from Aristotle's point of view his confusions derive from the right instinct: both in recognizing that mathematics does not straightforwardly describe the physical world, and in refusing to recognize the existence of an extra world for it to describe, the partial platonist is confusedly groping after something like Aristotle's own position. For the moment, however, Aristotle merely shows that the partial platonist does not provide a real alternative to the platonist's postulation of an extra world of ideal objects, the theory to which the rest of the chapter is devoted.

1076ᵃ37–1076ᵇ11: This section deals with the partial platonist. Aristotle refers to two arguments in *Metaphysics B*, and adds a third.

The reference to *B* (998ᵃ7 ff.) is not as straightforward as it appears, since the passage there argues against people who hold that the *intermediates* exist, but in physical objects. Aristotle is assuming without argument that an objection against one type of mathematical object will hold against all types that might be recognized by a platonist.

The two arguments in *B* corresponding to the ones here are: (i) 998ᵃ13-14: On this theory there would be two solids in the same place. This is not further developed in either passage. It shows that Aristotle's main point is not the absurdity of holding that ideal objects exist *in* physical objects, for then one could retort that they might exist in them as parts, and the objection would not hold. What is pointed to is rather the partial platonist's refusal to distinguish as separate the ideal solid and the physical solid, which then become competitors for the same place at the same time. The obvious retort is that the ideal solid is misconceived if thought of as space-occupying; but Aristotle could reply that the partial platonist lacks the equipment to sort out space-occupying from non-space-occupying solids. (ii) 998ᵃ12-13: On this argument the Forms also should be in perceptible objects. This argument in *B* is importantly different from the one in *M*, and it is careless of Aristotle to conflate them. In *B* the argument merely applies to people who accept both Forms and intermediates: if both types of entity are accepted, on the same sort of grounds, then if the intermediates are taken to be in physical objects, why not Forms? The *M* argument is quite distinct. It mentions not Forms but 'powers and characteristics', and points rather to Aristotle's standing complaint (cf. 1059 ᵇ2 ff., 1077ᵃ1 ff.) that the Academy treat the subject-matter of mathematics in a way different from that of the empirical sciences, on no good grounds. If mathematics must have ideal objects, so should the empirical sciences, and if the former are none the less to be identified with features of physical objects, so should the latter; but the Platonists are firm that health, for example, the object of medicine, is not to be literally found in any particular man. (Eudoxus thought it was, but Aristotle finds his version of the theory of Forms not very philosophically acute–991ᵃ15-19 (= 1079ᵇ18-23).)

The two arguments in *B* not in *M* are

(iii) 998ᵃ14-15: Mathematical objects cannot be unmoving if they are in perceptible objects which move.

(iv) 998ᵃ15-19: What is the point of postulating intermediates, with all their problems, if they are then to be in physical objects? Not only will there be another heaven separate from the physical one, but it will be in the same place, which is even 'more impossible'.

It is easy to see why Aristotle drops (iv), which specifically concerns intermediates. Perhaps he drops (iii) because it is a type of argument he frequently brings against Eudoxus' theory of Forms that are in things (cf. the arguments referred to at 991ᵃ15-19 (= 1079ᵇ18-23), and he may have come to think that it had no special application to mathematical objects.

The argument with which he replaces (iii) and (iv) is not limited to intermediates but applies to any type of ideal mathematical object, and, unlike (i) and (ii), does exploit the absurdities springing from the idea that ideal objects are *in* physical objects. A solid must be divided along a plane, and a plane along a line, a line at a point. But if a physical solid actually contains an ideal solid and thus ideal planes, lines, and points, it can never be divided, for it would have to be divided at a point, and ideal points are not divisible (cf. 1002^{b}3-4). So either physical objects cannot be divided, or ideal points (and so the other ideal objects) *are* divisible after all; both of which are absurd.

This is not a good argument. Aristotle only obtains his conclusions by foisting implausibly crude conceptions on to his opponent, making him think of mathematical operations as if they were precisely analogous to physical operations, the sole difference being that they are performed on more rarified subject-matter. Just as the physical operation of splitting a length of some substance involves dividing some extent of it, so the geometer's division of a line at a point is thought of as splitting the point at which the division is made, taking the point to be a minimal extension. This leads to absurdity because the mathematician's points are not taken to be divisible. But this is a quite unacceptable way of thinking of a geometer's division of a line at a point, and one which Aristotle himself does not accept. To divide a line at a point is simply to treat that point as the end of one stretch and the beginning of the other. This means that boundaries of the two stretches exist, which did not exist before, but it does not mean that there has been a process of dividing a minimal stretch which brought them into being (1002^{a}28-^{b}11). Aristotle provides no argument to show why the platonist must think of dividing the mathematical point as though it were a minimal extended stretch. His strategy here, however, is analogous to that of better arguments later in the chapter; see the notes on 1076^{b}11-39.

These arguments are meant to show the partial platonist that there is no consistent position short of full platonism for someone who accepts that mathematics does not describe the world directly, if he wants to explain the nature of mathematical truth by the nature of its objects. In chapter 3 Aristotle will try to differentiate mathematics by its method rather than its subject-matter.

1076^{b}11 ff: Against platonism proper Aristotle has three types of argument:
(i) 1076^{b}11-39. The way platonists conceive mathematical objects is crude and leads to absurdities.
(ii) 1076^{b}39–1077^{a}14. Platonism rests on an 'argument from objectivity' which is fallacious.
(iii) 1077^{a}14-^{b}11. Aristotle's own theory of *ousia* shows that platonists are wrong to take the existence of abstract objects to be more basic than that of concrete particulars.

The arguments of types (i) and (ii) have more force than those of type (iii); not only do the latter presuppose an acceptance of Aristotle's own philosophical ideas, they misconceive the platonist position in some respects (see notes).

1076^b12-39: This is meant to be a single argument applied to geometry (1076 ^b12-33, plus corollary ^b33-6) and arithmetic (^b36-9), but the arguments are better treated as distinct.

1076^b12-36. Geometry: The thrust of this argument is to show that the platonist's ideal objects are nothing but an absurd and idle reduplication of ordinary objects. While Aristotle does also argue that the Forms reduplicate the world (see note on 1078^b32 ff.) the present objection is directed specifically to the nature of mathematical objects, platonistically conceived. Interesting in this regard is a comment of Wittgenstein's in *Remarks on the Foundations of Mathematics* IV. 5, where he points out the dangers of 'The symbol "a" stands for an ideal object.' The use of the expression is meant to be similar to that of a sign that has an object, and Wittgenstein clearly thinks that we can be badly misled; while we do not intend to think of the mathematical sphere as being a sphere, the idioms we employ lead us to do so, and to ask, e.g. whether there is one such sphere, or several. Wittgenstein calls this, perhaps not very fairly, 'a Fregean sort of question', no doubt because of Frege's extremely platonist ways of expression.

In similar vein, Aristotle here systematically works out the consequences of treating the ideal solid as though it were itself a solid. His argument produces splendid absurdities, but it demands that the platonist make two perhaps dubious assumptions: firstly, that he think of ideal mathematical objects as though they had the logical behaviour of the corresponding physical objects, and secondly, that he refuse to identify mathematical objects of the same type if they are introduced in different ways.

For example, a platonist will demand that theorems about lines be not about marks on paper but about ideal lines over and above these. Aristotle at once points out that the platonist accepts ideal solids and ideal planes, by analogous argument. What about the lines bounding the ideal planes, and the lines bounding the planes of the ideal solid? Presumably they are ideal lines too. But if so, there are three different sorts of ideal lines, which with the physical drawn lines makes four kinds of lines. Similarly there will be five kinds of points: points in ideal solids, points in ideal planes, points in ideal lines, ideal points, physical dots.

The platonist would presumably retort that he is not committed to three different kinds of ideal line. In the first place, it is not necessary to treat the ideal solid as a solid containing planes and lines the way a physical solid contains planes and lines. But even if one does, then if these lines are ideal lines, they are identical with the ideal lines reached by the different argument showing that truths about lines are not about drawn marks. The platonist could therefore challenge Aristotle's argument at two points.

How could Aristotle defend his argument? The first assumption is less defensible: a platonist could just refrain from talking as though the ideal solid were a solid, or, if he did, at least from drawing either mathematically obnoxious or ontologically prodigal consequences. The weakness of Aristotle's position here comes out in his treatment of planes, where in contrast with his straightforward treatment of lines and points he tries to squeeze an extra absurdity from the platonist position. He insists that not only are the ideal planes (introduced as distinct from physical surfaces) distinct from planes in the ideal solid, they are both distinct from a third type of plane, a type 'over and above' the planes in the ideal solid. In other words, the original argument to distinguish ideal planes from physical surfaces is reapplied at the level of the ideal solid. But a platonist would surely just reject this, for none of the arguments from the insufficiency of physical surfaces as the bearers of mathematical truth could be held to apply to the surfaces of the *ideal* solid. One suspects that Aristotle may be foisting a crudity on to the platonist here. It is noteworthy that he does not apply this argument to lines and points, but contents himself with premises which a platonist might well accept. (The difference in the treatment of planes leads Ross to comment that Aristotle begins with a geometric progression in his 'piling-up', but then tires of it and turns it into an arithmetic one. This seems pointless, however. The type of argument applied is the same in either case; it is just that with planes Aristotle makes an extra and dubious application of it.) The most that could be said for Aristotle's strategy here is that he takes himself to be justified in applying a crude conception of ideal mathematical objects, and reducing it to absurdity, in the absence of any explicit indications that such language must not be understood this way. This argument could be regarded as putting the onus on the platonist: if it is wrong to treat the ideal solid like a solid, then there must be some clear and explicit explanation of why and how it is wrong to do so, and what the alternative is.

What of Aristotle's second move—his insistence that the ideal planes introduced one way (via the ideal solid) are not identical with those reached another way (via the inadequacy of physical surfaces)? What is wrong with a platonist reply that *if* we are to talk about ideal planes in the ideal solid in any mathematically consequential way, there is no problem, because they are simply to be identified with ideal planes as originally introduced? It is not clear what Aristotle could reply. He might object that entities defined in such different ways could reasonably be assumed to be distinct. The platonist could retort, however, that the different ways of introducing the ideal planes are not meant to be definitions: the same items can be introduced and described in different ways. In reply Aristotle could only reiterate his point that in default of a *proof* that ideal planes in an ideal solid are identical with ideal planes over and above physical surfaces, the platonist is not entitled to *assume* that they are identical. This move would already display anti-platonist assumptions: what is true of a mathematical object is not independent of the way it is introduced. Thus Aristotle's dispute with the platonist here comes down to a difference of outlook which it is not clear could be resolved by argument. Aristotle's objection does, however, have force in so far as the platonist is shown up as making assumptions about the identity of different mathematical objects which could be taken to indicate lack of rigour.

One corollary (ᵇ33-6) is that none of these sets of objects has an undisputed claim to be the subject-matter of the appropriate branch of mathematics. Aristotle notes that some have a better claim because 'prior', presumably because incomposite (cf. 1. 18-9), but it is not clear why this sense of 'prior' should be relevant for knowledge. All ideal objects were said to be 'prior' to physical objects in a different sense at 1.14 (At 1.21 they are called 'unchanging'; Aristotle never explicitly lays out the platonist position he attacks here, but assumes it as well-known, introducing various features from time to time.) In spite of the unclarity about 'prior', Aristotle has a good point here: the ideal objects were introduced to give mathematics a satisfactory subject-matter, meeting higher conditions of definiteness and clarity than the physical world, and it is ironical that these objects turn out, according to Aristotle, to be unclear too.

1076ᵇ36-9. Numbers: The argument is now applied to numbers. By the last argument there turned out to be five different kinds of points. Counting, for a platonist, involves correlating what is to be counted with units, which for him are items that exist already and are what make our counting possible. The five different types of point would not be genuinely distinct unless correlated with different types of unit, so a platonist should be led by the results so far achieved to recognize different types of mathematical number (ordinary number used in counting); and this although according to him what distinguishes mathematical number is the fact that the units are *not* specifically different. The force of this is of course lost if the platonist has rejected the conclusion of the last argument.

The argument is thus complete even without Jaeger's insertion of 'infinitely many' before 'types'. This insertion is probably right, however, since Aristotle extends the argument beyond different types of points to difference in type of any object counted; and this move is independent of the last argument, and does not show anything absurd in the platonist's position, unless 'infinitely many' is added.

This argument is parallel to the last one: the platonist introduces an ideal number in different ways, yet assumes it to be identical, and Aristotle refuses to allow this identification.

1076ᵇ39–1077ᵃ14: These two arguments attack the 'argument from objectivity', namely: mathematics is objectively true, but its truth is not ensured by its correspondence with physical objects; so there must be other, non-physical objects which do this. Aristotle rightly regards it as wrong to characterize mathematics in terms of its objects rather than its method, and points out that this argument fails to characterize mathematics as opposed to other subjects.

1076ᵇ39–1077ᵃ9: The reference to *Metaphysics B* (997ᵇ12-34) is again to an argument which in *B* applies to the intermediates (and is argued again in this form at 1059ᵇ2 ff.), but is here tacitly generalized over all ideal mathematical objects. The argument is stronger in its original form, against intermediates, for most people would baulk at intermediate objects for other sciences. It has less force in *M* as applied to any ideal objects, for a member of the Academy might well just accept analogous ideal objects for the other sciences, taking them to be Forms. (The Academy actually argued for Forms from the existence of the sciences; see note on 1079^{a}8-9.) And even a platonist rejecting Forms might not object to saying that all sciences had ideal objects analogously to mathematics; whether or not this is objectionable depends on how such statements are to be interpreted.

Perhaps Aristotle is aware of this reaction, because he at once goes on to exhibit absurdities produced by the claim that non-mathematical sciences have ideal objects. Harmonics will study not actual sounds, token utterances by people, but ideal sounds. But where do ideal sounds come from? They should come from ideal throats of ideal people. So harmonics will study not only ideal 'separate' sounds, but 'separate' organs of utterance and 'separate' organisms that have them. Aristotle likes this argument; it appears also at 997^{b}23-4.

Aristotle's platonist here is a straw man. No doubt a teacher of harmonics might say that he was not concerned with the properties of people's actual, always faulty token sounds, but their ideal competence. And if he were unwary he might put this by saying that he never studied actual sounds but only the ideal sound. But he would certainly not think of 'the ideal sound' as a sound, or give it the logical behaviour of one, as Aristotle tries to force him to do. There is nothing of this in the use he makes of the notion within his field. The temptation to think of the ideal sound as a sound does not lead into real philosophical problems, as does the temptation to think of the ideal circle as a circle.

1077^{a}9-14: A new and better objection. The argument from objectivity manufactures objects irresponsibly, and at different levels, making it mysterious how two sciences can share the same subject-matter. This problem becomes acute if they share their methodology and the only difference is that the results of one are of greater generality. Aristotle's example is a good one, and recurs in chapter 3 to develop the idea that it is method and not object that characterizes a science.

At 1026^{a}23 ff. (*E* 1) Aristotle refers to this line of thought apparently to show that metaphysics does not deal with a special class of things merely because its treatment is more general than that of physics, for example.

1077^{a}14–1077^{b}11: Objections of type (iii) distinguished on p.139. Aristotle's term *ousia*, which is traditionally translated 'substance', is used by him to pick out individuals and especially living things as the most basic type of particular, things to which 'to be' (or 'to exist') applies in the basic sense (it is argued in *Metaphysics* Γ that the verb applies to other items in a derivative sense). In these arguments Aristotle is concerned to prove that the platonists' abstract entities, mathematical objects, have less claim to existence in the proper, underivative sense, than his own examples of living individuals. He argues that contrary to the platonists' claim, the latter items are in fact prior to the former. ('Prior' is explained at 1077ᵇ2-3: A is prior to B if A can exist without B but not vice versa.) In *B*, the book listing outstanding philosophical puzzles, Aristotle says that if body has the best claim to be reality (*ousia*) then the claim that mathematical objects have an even better claim puts one at a loss as to what reality can be (1002ᵃ26-8). It is probably this way of seeing the problem that dominates Aristotle's treatment here.

The weakness of these arguments lies partly in the fact that so many of Aristotle's own ideas are presupposed that sometimes the questions are begged by the terms of the debate; but partly also in the fact that Aristotle seems to misidentify his opposition. In arguing for the superior claim to reality of physical objects, he sees his opponent as claiming that numbers are more real than tables, have a better claim to the proper sense of 'exist'. But the claim that numbers are what really exist is no part of the position of a platonist, or at least not an essential part. What the platonist needs to deny is not that physical objects really exist but that they are adequate as a subject-matter for mathematics; numbers are needed to guarantee the truth of theorems, not to be exalted entities. So Aristotle's vindication of the reality of physical objects misses the point of platonism rather strikingly. It is, however, possible that he has in mind people who did make, implicitly or explicitly, some such claims about the unsatisfactoriness of claiming that physical objects are what really exist; there may have been people like this in the Academy, who were over-impressed by some things that Plato says about physical objects in the *Timaeus*. (We shall see that Aristotle overestimates the importance for the theory of Forms of the idea that the physical world is in certain ways radically unsatisfactory.) Such people may have made, or been taken by Aristotle to have made, assumptions about numbers like those Aristotle takes Plato to have made about Forms.

1077ᵃ14-20: 'Ordinary beliefs'. Aristotle thinks it important that philosophical elucidation of a concept should answer recognizably to our ordinary use of it. For him it is a prima facie objection to the Academy's theories that they would lead us to say counter-intuitive things about the reality of numbers and tables.

This argument claims that physical objects have ontological priority over the abstract objects that are the objects of mathematics, and not vice versa, and appeals to the notion of 'completeness'. A complete object may be temporally later than an incomplete one, but is none the less prior in reality; his example is that of living things. According to Aristotle (and common Greek thought) living things come from lifeless things and so are a temporally later stage of them; cf. 1049ᵃ1 ff.: earth becomes seed and seed becomes man. Still, it is the final stage, the fully formed individual, which can be explained as being what it is in its own right, whereas the earlier stages can only be explained as being what they are by reference to the later possessor of the form. The point is made at 989ᵃ15-16, 1050ᵃ4, *Physics* 261ᵃ13.

The application of this point to mathematical platonism is unclear. Aristotle seems to be arguing that although the platonists claim that their mathematical objects are prior to physical objects, in fact they are subsequent, because incomplete; the incomplete may be temporally prior but is ontologically inferior to the complete item to which it contributes. The trouble is that we lack a plausible sense here for 'incomplete'. The following arguments suggest that Aristotle is thinking of a physical object as a solid object made up of planes, lines, etc., so the latter are 'incomplete' in that although there have to be planes, etc. to make up a solid, the solid is that via which the planes must be identified and not vice versa. The relation of planes, etc. to solids is compared with that of the earth that becomes a man. But if this is Aristotle's argument he is confusing a mathematician's solid with a physical object; the latter is not made up of planes in the way the former is. That Aristotle is confused in this way is unfortunately all too likely, in view of some of the succeeding arguments, and also in view of the fact that the arguments in this section all seem to confuse the platonist's objection to the physical object *per se* with his objection to it as object of mathematical truth.

1077^a20-4: Aristotle now demands to know what makes mathematical objects one. He compares them, clearly to their disadvantage, with items which he takes to be uncontroversially 'ones'. An organic physical unity like a human being is one in virtue of soul or characteristic organization of behaviour. A plant or very primitive animal is one in virtue of part of soul, e.g. the nutritive capacity or ability to grow and maintain itself even without the higher capacities possessed by most animals. There are also non-organic unities held together with string, glue, etc. (cf. Δ 6, 1015^b34–1016^a4).

The strangeness of this argument is partly due to the fact that Aristotle has not distinguished two questions which are in fact rather assimilated by the Greek, 'is this thing one (*hen*)?' This can mean, 'Is this thing unitary?' or it can mean, 'Is it a unit (one in number)?' This argument runs together both these types of consideration. Aristotle points out that with physical objects we clearly know when we have one and when we have two, but that this is not the case with abstract objects of mathematics, although there is talk of 'dividing' them; and this looks like a complaint that the conditions for *individuating* them are obscure. This is a standing complaint of modern anti-platonists; cf. Quine's slogan, 'No entity without identity'. If we cannot individuate objects clearly, we have no reason to say that there are such things; clearly this will favour concrete over abstract objects. But the form of Aristotle's demands for the principle that holds mathematical objects together suggests rather that he is talking about what makes such objects *unities*, and complaining that there is nothing analogous to soul for physical objects. This objection appears somewhat more naïve, though no doubt has force as a ground-floor refusal to take anything on trust without proof which the platonist assumes about mathematical objects. A platonist would say in irritation that the triangles he is talking about are not the sort of things that can fall apart, as though they were bundles of sticks tied together with string. However, if Aristotle were to press him on how he knows this, he cannot appeal to the fact that in mathematics this is not allowed, that proofs just are not held liable to overthrow by the possibility of the triangle's collapsing. For Aristotle could object that a platonist claims not to allow or disallow things about the objects he deals with, but to *discover* facts about them.

1077ᵃ24-31: In this argument 'generation' is used of mathematical construction, specifically of objects in dimension *n* from objects in dimension *n* − 1, as well as of processes in nature. Since solids are constructed from planes, planes from lines, etc., and what comes later in generation is prior in reality, bodies have more claim to reality than planes, and so on.

As in the argument at ᵃ14-20, Aristotle is thinking of developing series in nature, e.g. babies to men, tadpoles to frogs, and assuming that one will end up with the fully formed individual. But this can hardly be applied without qualification to mathematical constructions. There might be many alternative ways of constructing such objects, not all of which involve regarding the dimensions in this way. (At *de Caelo* 268ᵃ7-24 Aristotle similarly remarks on the 'completeness' of a three-dimensional system, in rather an anthropocentric fashion: we live in three-dimensional space and presumably for Aristotle we only make sense of other-dimensional systems by 'abstracting' from the one familiar to us.) What the argument here seems to be pointing to is the fact that we cannot draw a plane without drawing lines, cannot construct a solid without putting planes together. But the platonist would regard this as begging the question; for him mathematics has nothing to do with the way we can or cannot draw things.

This argument, like the one at ᵃ14-20, confuses the physical object with the mathematical solid, and this emerges forcefully in the appeal to the fact that bodies but not lines, etc. can become animate. This misses the platonist's point that it is not the animate body he objects to but its status as object of mathematics. Even on Aristotle's own theory in chapter 3, the mathematician will, in thinking of a physical body as a three-dimensional object, have abstracted from features like that of being animate.

Aristotle himself recognizes elsewhere (1002ᵃ28-ᵇ5) that 'generation' of mathematical objects has a different meaning from its sense in application to physical objects; lines and surfaces 'come to be' (the word cognate with 'generation' here) without there being anything for them to come from, as is necessary with physical objects.

1077ᵃ31-6: Aristotle here qualifies slightly the claim that *bodies* are primary existents: the body is only matter, while its soul is the form. This, the theory of the *de Anima*, is irrelevant to mathematical solids in the same way as the other arguments.

1077ᵃ36–1077ᵇ11: Aristotle grants the platonists that their objects are prior in definition, but holds that this does not affect his own thesis that they have less claim to be primary existents.

There are two possible points that Aristotle might be making.
(i) He may still be thinking of the generation of solids from planes, lines, etc. as in the last two arguments. Then his point would be that even if solids are defined in terms of constructibility out of planes, etc., this does not mean that they are not ontologically prior, since they have other, better claims (argued for). This involves the same confusion of solid with physical object as in these arguments.
(ii) He may be making a distinct point about the ontological priority of ideal mathematical objects to physical objects as counted, measured, etc. The former would be prior in definition in something like the following sense: to define something as x inches long is to employ the concept of length, and this is already defined independently of particular exemplifications. But to define the concept of length is not correspondingly to employ the notion of anything's being x inches long. Aristotle is willing to grant this, since it does not threaten the ontological priority of the individual measured, etc.

Aristotle's example of 'priority' in definition is disappointingly simplistic, but 'white man' seems to be his standard example; cf. *Z* chapters 4 and 5. (At 1018^{b}34-7 the present point is made with the example of 'musical' and 'musical man'.) A is prior in definition to B if 'A' occurs in the definition of B. An interesting point is made by this simple example, however. 'White' is a constituent of 'white man', which as a whole stands for an independent item, while 'white' on its own does not stand for an independent item. This raises the possibility that in general an expression might fail to stand for an independent item and yet be capable of forming part of a larger expression which as a whole does. This is especially interesting in view of the introduction of 'abstraction' at ^{b}10. This is brought in without explanation as the opposite of 'addition', where the latter seems to mean: making a whole expression by adding to a word or expression that does not on its own stand for an independent item. (The Greek says 'adding to white', which gives the above sense, and should be retained, although some have proposed altering it to the more conventional Greek 'adding white'.) This use of 'abstraction' would provide a suitable backing for some of the things Aristotle wants to say in chapter 3. Numbers, for example, could be regarded as products of abstraction in the sense that 'number' was to be regarded as a word which, while capable of use within larger composite expressions standing for something, did not on its own stand for an independent item. Aristotle, however, does not make this move himself; in fact the word 'abstraction' does not occur in chapter 3, though it is used frequently elsewhere to refer to that theory.

1077^{b}11-17: A summing-up of the chapter. Aristotle notes cautiously that he has not disproved the existence of mathematical objects but rather established that they exist in a special sense; it is not so much false as misleading to say baldly that mathematical objects exist.

'We use "exist" in several senses.' Aristotle is clearly talking about the expression here. The idea that *einai*, 'be' or 'exist', has several senses occurs frequently in Aristotle (e.g. 1042^b25 ff.; cf. Bonitz, *Index Aristotelicus*, 220-1.)

CHAPTER 3

This chapter gives Aristotle's own alternative account of the way in which mathematical truth is to be explained. It is straightforward and the sense needs little elucidation, but it is extremely sketchy, and Aristotle appears quite unaware of the many difficulties arising when the ideas here are worked out more closely. See the Introduction, p. 29-33, for the ways in which this theory of 'abstraction' was developed, and its main problems.

1077^b17–1078^a9: Aristotle began (1077^a9-14) from his most plausible case against the platonist in order to show that the distinctive nature of mathematical truth cannot be based on what is distinctive about its subject-matter, but must lie rather in its way of treating a subject-matter which it may share with other disciplines. While he is of course right to insist that you cannot explain what mathematics is by citing special objects for it, he is not very precise about his alternative, namely that mathematics is actually about physical objects. He now explains it in two ways, by the 'as' locution (^b17-34) and by the contrast of incidental and non-incidental properties (^b34-1078^a9). No attempt is made to show that these two approaches must lead to the same result: Aristotle simply assumes that the two are equivalent, and there is considerable overlap between the two sections.

The mathematician is said to study physical objects, only not *as* (*hei, qua*) physical. What does this come down to? Some obvious uses of the 'as' locution suggest that what is in mind is the studying of one part or aspect of the object rather than another. But the 'as' locution can often be taken another way, indicating that there is a difference of approach to what is the same subject-matter. For example, 'I like him as a friend but not as a doctor' does not mean that I like certain parts or aspects of him but not others; rather, that I have different attitudes as I stand in different relations to him. It is not very clear which way we are to take the locution here. Aristotle's words suggest both. The geometer studies a physical object, but only certain aspects of it, for example its shape. On the other hand, when Aristotle is talking about the science as a whole, his words suggest that what distinguishes mathematics from other studies like physics is a general difference of approach to their shared subject-matter.

Aristotle's analogy with the study of moving objects suggests the former idea: studying physical objects in motion is simply studying one aspect of physical objects, not studying something completely distinct over and above physical objects. The example of general mathematical theorems and theorems in a specific area, however, implies that the subject-matter is the same, and what differs is the approach. This idea is less clear as an explanation of 'studying the physical but not as physical' than the notion of studying only certain aspects of physical objects. We know already that mathematics and physics differ in approach, and Aristotle's words here do not explain what this difference is. The analogy from within mathematics itself is not very convincing as an analogy for the different approaches of mathematics and physics. The development outside *M* 3 (see Introduction, p. 32-3) of abstraction as a psychological doctrine supports the idea that Aristotle predominantly thinks of 'studying the physical but not as physical' as studying certain aspects of physical objects—their shape, size, countability, etc.

The second line of explanation is that the mathematician studies his subject-matter ignoring what is merely incidental to it as so studied. The doctor in treating a man is concerned with his health but not with his colour; similarly the geometer studies merely the extension, shape, etc. of a man, not his colour or his health. Non-quantitative properties of a man are irrelevant to his study, and so are merely incidental to his object of study. None the less, it remains true that what he is studying is a man, not something distinct from a man. Thus, it is implied, the standard platonist moves are quite unnecessary; the subject-matter of mathematics is nothing distinct from the physical objects we are familiar with already.

Aristotle's use here of the distinction between incidental and non-incidental properties is interesting, for it involves relativizing the distinction to the description under which an object is considered. Normally for Aristotle properties which are incidental to a man are those which he could fail to have without thereby not being a man, which are therefore not necessary for his being the kind of thing he is. Thus it is incidental to man to be healthy or pale, but essential to be rational or two-legged (or however man is defined). Two-leggedness and rationality *are*, however, incidental to men-as-the-objects-of-the-geometer's-study; the only properties essential to them under this description are quantitative ones. This point comes out clearly at 1078^a26-8, where Aristotle is talking about men-as-the-objects-of-the-arithmetician's-study, to whom it is essential only to be indivisible (for purposes of counting). Aristotle says that properties which a man could have had even if he had not been indivisible (sc. *qua* man) clearly belong to him even without it. Thus there are properties which are only incidental to men considered as indivisible. (Aristotle puts this point less clearly than he might by writing 'them' rather than 'it' in line 28, thus making it sound as though being a man and being indivisible are two co-ordinate properties which a man (?) has. Clearly, however, what Aristotle has in mind is being indivisible *qua* man.)

This relativization of the distinction between a thing's essential and its incidental properties to the way it is described is congenial to modern views of necessity which place necessity in the way we talk about things rather than in the things themselves (a thing's essential properties being those that are necessarily true of it, and its incidental properties those that are not necessarily true of it). Aristotle, however, does not think of necessity in this way, and his statements here have implications which, if worked out, must have caused him discomfort. Unlike men, men-as-the-objects-of-the-geometer's-study do not form a basic kind, and seem to be just the sort of item of which Aristotle says elsewhere that they do not have essences at all (*Z* chapters 4-6).

1078a9-13: It does not seem true to equate accuracy with simplicity. Surely Aristotle does not believe that solid geometry must be less accurate than plane geometry. It may be that he is linking 'accuracy' here with certainty, and making the more modest and defensible point that the simpler things are, the less room there is for error, and so the greater the chance of precise and certain knowledge.

As Ross in his note points out, 'primary movement' probably means both circular movement among types of movement and movement among types of change.

1078a14-21: Aristotle repeats his point for harmonics and optics, and tries to meet the objection that mathematics cannot be about the actual world, because, notoriously, objects fail sometimes to measure up to the precision of mathematical concepts. His reply is that to apply mathematics to the world is not to falsify it, for it applies on condition that we abstract from the individual deviations of actual objects. It seems to us that Aristotle here fails to see an obvious objection: what is a deviation? Surely we do not know beforehand what must be described as a deviation in the object rather than as a mistake in the calculation. Aristotle seems to miss the point that there is often an element of stipulation involved: whatever the circumstances, nothing is to count as falsifying an arithmetical statement. Abstraction cannot account for this, nor for our tendency in general to stick to mathematical statements rather than let empirical happenings provide counter-examples to them.

This passage suggests that Aristotle is basically thinking of applied mathematics, and taking the necessity attaching to a mathematical theorem to be no different in principle from the 'natural necessity' attaching to scientific laws. But if so, his quarrel with Plato is not clear, for Plato is always emphatic that he is talking about pure mathematics.

1078a21-31: Aristotle now introduces the idea that the mathematician 'posits' mathematical objects. But it is not clear what force this has. If it means merely that he 'separates' them in thought from irrelevant properties, then there is no positing about it, in the sense of postulating; for an abstractionist the object is already there to be studied, not stipulated. If Aristotle does mean that stipulation plays a part, then this comment is unreconciled with the theory of abstraction.

The parallel of geometer and arithmetician brings out the way in which abstraction produces less convincing results for arithmetic than for geometry. The geometer studies man as a solid object, the arithmetician studies him as a unit, i.e. as indivisible for counting. But the arithmetician does not spend time studying properties of his units, as the geometer studies properties of solid objects.

ᵃ29-30: Aristotle may have *Euthydemus* 290b-c in mind, where Plato insists that mathematicians are talking about things that really exist. Aristotle does not want to appear to be denying anything but the unacceptable claims of the platonist.

The final phrase gives a new and startlingly unconnected way of accounting for the way mathematical objects can be truly said to exist even if platonism is denied. Aristotle here says that numbers, etc. do not *actually* exist, but exist in a different sense. We would expect 'potentially*', the usual contrast with 'actually'. At *Physics* 262ᵃ8–263ᵇ9 Aristotle accounts for the existence of the infinite in this way; it is thus plausible to take the phrase here 'as matter' to mean simply 'potentially'. Probably, however, there is a point in retaining the reference to materials. There may be here the germ of an idea which is found in more developed form in Proclus' Commentary on the First Book of Euclid, 78, and resembles (on a rather high level of generality) modern constructivist ideas. The mathematician's activity, when thinking of mathematical objects, is taken to be genuinely constructive and to be a kind of working on materials. Mathematical objects do not exist already for him to find, but neither does he create them *ex nihilo*; his thinking is constructive but has something to work on. This might be expressed by saying that the mathematical objects themselves have only the kind of existence appropriate to matter. Independently of the mathematician they exist only as the statue may be said to exist in the block of marble before the sculptor gets to work on it. However, this idea is thrown out by Aristotle without elucidation, and is not integrated into the rest of chapter 3.

1078ᵃ31-ᵇ6: The 'since' clause does not in fact give a reason for what follows. Aristotle elsewhere says that final causes are irrelevant to mathematical proofs (996ᵃ26 ff.) and that it is not the geometer's business to decide whether a straight line is the most beautiful one (*Posterior Analytics* 75ᵇ17). Here he does not take this back, but typically suggests that the right answer can only be reached by making distinctions. Teleological explanations are inappropriate in mathematics, but nevertheless mathematicians can and do prefer one proof to another on grounds of simplicity and elegance, which seem to be purely aesthetic grounds. Aristotle is not expansive enough here for us to be sure whether he is merely acknowledging the fact that mathematicians do recognize elegance as a desirable factor in proofs, or whether he thinks that elegance is a legitimate mathematical virtue.

Aristotle says here that he will take the subject up again elsewhere; this is not done in any surviving work, but an early marginal comment refers us to his discussion and transcription of Plato's *On the Good*. This provides an intriguing link with another passage, *Eudemian Ethics* 1218ᵃ15-32, which also has links with *On the Good*, and where Aristotle criticizes the Platonists for arguing from the goodness of unchanging objects like numbers to the goodness of health and strength. For Aristotle this is the wrong way round; one should start from things agreed to be good, like health and strength, and show that mathematical objects are good, if they are, by showing that they exhibit order and stability in a high degree, the goodness of things like health and strength consisting in order and stability. Aristotle leaves it open whether or not he himself accepts this last vital premise, but it is not very likely that he did. The *Ethics* passage does not make the present distinction between the spheres of the good and the beautiful; Aristotle seems to have changed his mind on the subject, and it would be interesting to know which passage is the earlier. (The relation of these three passages is discussed by Brunschwig.)

CHAPTER 4

In accordance with the programme of *M* 1, Aristotle now discusses the theory of Forms, the other type of platonism current in the Academy. He does not give it a new treatment, but presents a recast version of material used already. 1078^{b}12-34 is an altered version of part of *A* chapter 6 (987^{a}29-^{b}10) and 1078^{b}34–1080^{a}11 is a recast version of part of *A* chapter 9 (990^{a}34–991^{b}9). The relation between *M* 4-5 and *A* 6 has been extensively discussed; see Jaeger (1), pp. 38-45, (2), pp. 171-93, von Ivánka. Wilpert (3), pp. 15-26, Cherniss (1), pp. 177-98 and App. II. It is generally accepted that the *A* version is the earlier. This is supported by the minor changes in the *M* version (see p. 131-2, 154-5). There is the further point that the present passage is followed in *A* 9 by a long section (991^{b}9–993^{a}10) containing many arguments which seem to be embryonic forms of discussions in *M-N*. (Compare 991^{b}21-7 with 1080^{a}12; 992^{a}1-10 and 992^{b}9-13 with 1084^{b}13-32 and 1089^{b}33–1088^{a}14; 992^{b}18-24 with *N* chapters 1 and 2; 992^{a}10-19 and 992^{b}13-18 with 1085^{a}7-^{b}4). The whole lecture-course *M-N* seems to be a development of *A* 9, but with a change of emphasis; Aristotle is in the present context more interested in the philosophical basis of platonism, in the case of Forms and mathematical objects alike, than in Platonism in the narrower sense, restricted to the theory of Forms. 1078^{b}12-32: This passage is obviously related to *A* 6, 987^{a}29-^{b}10, but the emphasis is very different. In *A* 6 Aristotle is purporting to give a historical account of the theory of Forms; Plato is named, and said to have followed on from the Pythagoreans, just discussed. All the features of Plato's thought which resemble Pythagoreanism are stressed, and the theory of Forms appears almost as an aside. Plato's ideas are all made to fit (rather uncomfortably) into the *A* 6 discussion of first principles. In *M* 4, on the other hand, Aristotle gives only the material relevant to Plato's platonism, namely the theory of Forms; Pythagorean influence and the rest of Plato's thought are not appropriate here.

According to Aristotle, Plato was led to believe in Forms because he thought that knowledge must have stable objects, but that no physical objects will serve because they are always in flux ('the flux argument'). He was also, according to Aristotle, influenced by Socrates, who in his search for general definitions was on the way to universals; Plato took the further, disastrous step of giving these 'separate' independent existence, and so turning them into a kind of individual.

Aristotle's account of the theory of Forms can be questioned. It is true that in the dialogues Plato does often talk about Forms in a way which emphasizes their stability and fixed nature in contrast with the changeable and therefore unsatisfactory nature of physical objects (for example, *Symposium* 207c–208b, *Phaedo* 78e–79d, *Republic* 485b, 508d, 534a). But the flux argument as Aristotle presents it is nowhere to be found explicitly in the dialogues. Indeed, some parts of the dialogues suggest that Plato could not have accepted it. In the *Theaetetus*, which Aristotle knew (cf. 1010^b11 ff.), Plato refutes the Heracleitean theory that physical things are always in flux in every way, and does so without reference to Forms. *Republic* 523-4 and *Parmenides* 130b exploit the contrast between terms which have to be taken to refer to Forms and terms which refer quite adequately to physical objects; this argument could not get off the ground if *all* physical objects were in flux.

However, elements of the flux argument are to be found in different places in the dialogues. *Philebus* 59-62 argues that objects of knowledge must have the features of stability, etc. possessed by the classical Forms, but there seems to be no room for the latter in the *Philebus*' difficult metaphysics. *Cratylus* 439c–440c has Socrates saying that instead of believing that the world is in flux he prefers to believe that there are utterly unchanging Forms, but this is in no sense an argument for Forms on the basis of flux in the physical world. The nearest Plato comes to accepting something like the flux argument is at *Timaeus* 51-2, where he does accept that the physical world is in flux and that therefore objects of knowledge cannot be found in it. But the *Timaeus* assumes, and does not argue, that the latter are Forms.

Aristotle is then at best giving what he takes to be the leading idea behind Plato's theory, rather than pointing to what Plato himself argues. It is possible that he is thinking mainly of the *Timaeus* argument (the *Timaeus* is the dialogue he most frequently cites) and that this leads him to ignore the fact that the argument most prominent in the middle dialogues is in fact quite different from the flux argument, though it could be quite easy to confuse them. The line of thought stressed at *Phaedo* 74-5 and *Republic* 479-80, and referred to at *Parmenides* 128-9, depends on features of predicates of which 'equal' and 'just' are examples, and whose striking aspect is that one can, in the case of any particular to which it is applied, also apply the contrary with equal justification (what is just from one point of view is unjust from another, and so on). By contrast, the Form of Justice is that to which only 'just', and never 'unjust', can be applied. Forms must be distinct from particulars because only to the latter, never to the former, can one of these predicates be applied together with its opposite. Aristotle may have carelessly assimilated this 'argument from opposites' to the flux argument, which involves the succession of opposites and thus provides a support for the other argument, but is clearly different from it and not implied by it. Unless Aristotle has made this assimilation it is hard to see why he ignores a line of thought which is much more prominent as serious backing for Forms in the middle dialogues than considerations of flux and change. It is perhaps worth noticing that the arguments for Forms that he will mention are not those in the dialogues, but more technical Academy discussions. He may have thought of the arguments in the dialogues as too informal to merit close analysis, and so assimilated them all to the flux argument under the influence of the *Timaeus.*

Socrates' desire to provide definitions is mentioned not only in *A* 6 but later at 1086^{a}31-^{b}13. Aristotle's remarks here are supported by the dialogues. He does, however, ascribe the beginnings of scientific definition to different people elsewhere: Empedocles (*Physics* 194^{a}20 ff.), Democritus (1078^{b}17 ff., *Physics* 194^{a}20 ff., *de Partibus Animalium* 642^{a}24 ff.) and the Pythagoreans (987^{a}19 ff.).

Minor points:

^{b}13: 'truth'. In English 'true' applies properly to propositional items, whereas in Greek it can be applies to objects which 'really (truly)' are what they are. Some people in the Academy exploited this to argue for Forms; Aristotle regarded their arguments as too bad to need refutation (see Alexander, 78.13-15, 89.2-6).

^{b}19: 'natural scientists'. This is intended to sound vague, since Aristotle does not mean anything as methodologically specialized as modern science. The Presocratic cosmologists were philosophers as much as scientists.

^{b}22: 'reduced'. The word has the basic meaning of linking or fastening on, and is used of a reductive analysis of some kind or other; cf. Theophrastus, *Metaphysics*, 6^{a}15 ff.

^{b}24: 'reason formally' translates *syllogizesthai*, which passes from the informal 'discuss, reason' to the specialized 'syllogize' as a result of Aristotle's own work in logic.

^{b}28: 'arguments from particular to general'. This translates the adjective from *epagogē*, often translated 'induction', which is not, however, the same as modern induction, but more like a generalization from one or more convincing examples. (See *Protagoras* 350, *Laches* 193, *Gorgias* 514, *Euthydemus* 288-9.)

1078^{b}32–1080^{a}11: This section corresponds almost verbally to *A* 9, 990 ^{a}34–991^{b}9. There are, however, some puzzling minor differences (listed in order on p. 131–2).

(a)The opening passage in *A* 9 (990^{b}4 ff.) gives the argument there a weaker conclusion than does the *M* version (1078^{b}34–1079^{a}4).

(b) A new argument has been inserted at 1079^{b}3-11.

(c) The *M* version three times has a shorter expression than the *A* 9 version (990^{b}26–1079^{a}23; 991^{a}24–1079^{b}28; 991^{b}5–1080^{a}4).

(d) The *M* version seven times expands an *A* expression: 990^{b}20-1–1079^{a}17; 991^{a}4–1079^{a}35; 991^{a}17–1079^{b}21; 991^{a}30-1–1079^{b}34; 991^{b}3–1080^{a}2; 991^{b}7–1080^{a}6; 991^{b}9–1080^{a}8.

(e) In three places the neuter plural expression *ta eidē* ('the Forms') has a normal singular verb in *A* 9 and a plural verb in *M*: 990^{b}24–1079^{a}20; 990^{b}31–1079^{a}28; 991^{a}9–1079^{b}12.

(f) In some places a third person plural in *M* replaces a first person plural in *A* 9. In the 'common part' there are 6 first person plurals in *A* 9 replaced in *M* (990^{b}9, 11, 16, 18, 23, 991^{b}7). Jaeger and Merlan (Merlan (3)) propose an emendation at 991^{b}3 (which I do not accept), which would make the total 7.

The unimportant changes suggest that Aristotle did some stylistic retouching when writing out his old material. The only important difference is (f), which is usually taken as showing that *A* 9 was written when Aristotle was a member of the Academy, and *M* 4-5 later, when he thought it inappropriate to use 'we' of Academy ideas. (See Jaeger (2), pp. 171-93. But this can be exaggerated; see the Introduction, p. 83-4.)

1078^{b}32–1079^{a}4: Cf. 990^{a}34-^{b}8 (where there is a similar textual problem). The Academy are accused of trying to solve conceptual problems about physical objects by the introduction of Forms; but since they treat Forms as just another kind of object the problems are not solved but aggravated. There are three main problems with this section:

(a) Does Aristotle mean that there are more Forms than individuals, or more than types of individuals? The former seems to be generally accepted, but has the difficulty that there seems no possible way of calculating the relative numbers of Forms and objects. Besides, Aristotle knew Academy proofs for Forms which began from the infinite number of particulars and showed that definite number applied only to Forms (Alexander, 78.16-17; 89.2-6). Aristotle thought these arguments bad, but they would at least prevent his ascribing this view to the Academy; so it must be types of particular that are in mind here. However the sentence at a 2-4 is read there must be a reference to the idea that there is a Form for every general term applicable to many things (cf. *Republic* 596a). 'The same name': for Aristotle the word means 'with *merely* the name in common' but Plato uses it to express the idea that things are 'named after' the Form whose 'name' they share—cf. *Parmenides* 130e, 133d, *Timaeus* 52a, *Phaedo* 78e.

(b) In the corresponding passage in *A* 9, Aristotle says that there are 'about as many, certainly not less' Forms than types of object. Here he claims that there are more. This has been taken as an indication of different degrees of politeness towards the Academy, but is better regarded as a correction of the statement of the argument's conclusion. Perhaps Aristotle is noting that the One over Many argument (i.e. there is a Form for every general term) applies not only to terms for objects but to terms for the qualities, etc. of those objects; so that there are not just as many Forms as types of object, but more, since there are Forms for qualities, etc. of those objects. This would certainly be supported by the fact that Aristotle will shortly (1079^{a}19-^{b}3) argue that the Platonists want to have Forms only for objects, but are committed by their ideas to having them also for qualities, etc. Another explanation is possible, however (suggested to me by Professor G.E.L. Owen). One of the arguments Aristotle will mention is the Third Man, according to which any Form answering to a general term will generate an infinite number of Forms. So however many types of object there are, there are not only as many Forms corresponding, but infinitely many more. This interpretation would be strengthened if the 'eternal things' are taken to be Forms and not (as usually) the heavenly bodies (cf. 1040ª17).

(c) Jaeger's version of the text gives the thought: there is a Form over and above things called by the same name, and also a Form in other cases where there is a One over Many. That is, there is no explicit claim that there is a Form in *all* cases of words for qualities, etc. But, as Aristotle always seems to assume that the One over Many has unrestricted application, I follow Ross's text and translate accordingly: the One over Many will apply not only to all types of object but to all types of quality, etc.

1079ª4-19: Aristotle here refers to, without giving, a number of arguments. Presumably they were familiar to his audience from his earlier work *On the Forms*. Alexander gives some of them in his commentary on the corresponding part of *A* 9. Unfortunately they cannot be given or discussed here because of their length and complexity. They can be found translated as fragments 3 and 4 of *On the Forms* in Ross's translation of *Selected Fragments* of Aristotle (vol. 12 of *The Works of Aristotle translated into English*). They are discussed by Robin (pp. 15-24, 127-30, 173-90, 603-12); Cherniss (1), pp. 226-305, Appendices 2,3,4,6; Wilpert (3), chapter 1. Cf. also Owen, 'A proof in the *Peri Ideōn*', *Journal of Hellenic Studies* 1957, and my article 'Forms and first principles', *Phronesis* 1975.

1079ª19-ᵇ3: In this difficult argument Aristotle tries to show up a contradiction in Platonist beliefs. On the one hand, the Platonists want to say that there are Forms not only of objects but also of qualities, etc. of objects. (This is uncontroversial; Aristotle refers to formal Academic arguments proving the existence of such Forms—the 'argument from the object of thought' and the 'arguments from the branches of knowledge'—but he could equally well have indicated the Forms of Beauty, Equal, Just, and the like, which are prominent in the middle dialogues.) On the other hand, the Platonists are, according to Aristotle, committed to the belief that there are Forms only of objects. He tries to prove this here in two stages:

(1) ª25-31. Forms must *be* objects, as opposed to qualities, etc. of objects.

(2) ª31-ᵇ3. Given (1), there can be Forms only *for* objects. This argument is puzzling, and no interpretation has general acceptance. There are recent discussions by Owen (p. 122 of 'Dialectic and Eristic in the treatment of the Forms', in *Aristotle on Dialectic*) and Vlastos ('The "two-level paradoxes" in Aristotle', in *Platonic Studies*). My interpretation differs from theirs in making Arisotle's argument valid, though weaker than necessary for the conclusion Aristotle claims. For a detailed discussion, see my article 'Aristotle on Substance, Accident and Plato's Forms', *Phronesis* 1977.

(1) ª25-31. Aristotle appears here to attempt to argue as far as possible

from premises acceptable to a Platonist. Thus he grants the Platonists that Forms must be of such a nature as to be participated in, and grants them their understanding of '*a* (a particular) has the character F' as '*a* participates in the Form of F'. (Elsewhere he dismisses 'participation' as a useless metaphor (cf. 1079b24-6), but here it is not the Platonists' premises he is attacking but the consistency of their use of them.) The example he gives of an object or substance is the Form of Double ('the original Double'), which shows that here Aristotle is not insisting on his own notion of object, but using an example which both he and the Platonist can agree is an object in the weak sense of being a subject of which qualities, etc. are predicated. The argument depends not on Aristotle's metaphysical distinction between object and quality, but on the linguistic distinction between subject and predicate, which was recognised not only by Aristotle but also (in a more rudimentary form) by the Academy.

The argument goes: Suppose a particular, *a*, participates in the Form of Double. The Form of Double is eternal. Then it follows that *a* participates in something eternal—but only accidentally. The force of 'accidentally' here seems to derive from Aristotle's distinction between substance and accident. Crudely, a substance term predicated of an item tells us what it is, gives its essence or what it could not lose while still remaining that item. Aristotle's argument here depends on the claim (controversial, but defended by him elsewhere) that being eternal is not part of the nature of Plato's Forms, but is merely a characteristic that they could conceivably come to lose.

The argument here consists in pointing out that participation in a Form is different from participation in an accident of a Form. Whatever participates in the Form of Double will in a sense participate in whatever is an accident of that Form—but only in a sense. This fact is marked by describing the latter sort of participation as 'accidental participation'. It is possible that 'accidentally' here has the force of 'in a strained or derivative sense' (cf. *Categories* 5a39). But it is more likely that 'accidentally participates' is introduced to signal an ambiguity in the notion of participation, depending on whether a particular item participates (in the proper, straightforward sense) in a Form, or participates ('accidentally') in the accident of a Form. Since to participate in what is the accident of a Form is not the same as to participate (in the proper sense) in a Form, the Platonists are wrong to infer from the fact that 'participates' picks out a relation between the individual item and the Form of Double, that it also picks out a relation between that individual and the Form of Eternal. In other words, to predicate 'eternal' of the Form of Double is not yet to introduce another Form. Accidental participation is not participation, or at least is participation in a different sense.

Aristotle's point is reflected to some extent in Greek grammar. 'Participates in eternal' is odd, and would probably be heard by a Greek as 'participates in something that is in fact eternal (viz. the Form of Double)' rather than as 'participates in Eternality.'

Aristotle's argument here relies to some extent on ordinary language; the distinction between subject and predicate is important for Aristotle's concept of an object or substance, but is not one that Plato pays much attention to. Aristotle has shown, however, that if a term purportedly standing for a Form can be used to predicate an accident of a substance, then an ambiguity is generated in 'participates'; and if that term must be used unequivocally in the theory of Forms, the argument does show that substance and non-substance terms cannot both pick out Forms, at any rate not Forms of the same kind.

(2) ª31-ᵇ3. If Forms are objects (there being, by (1), no Forms answering to terms predicated of objects), then participants in Forms must also be objects. This produces the required conclusion that there can be Forms only for objects.

Aristotle is here again making his argument acceptable to a Platonist by appealing to the principle that the word or 'name' applied to both Form and participants must have the same sense in its application to both. It is assumed that a general term has meaning by virtue of corresponding to a single form possessed by the different things to which the word is applied. See *Republic* 596a for the One over Many principle: there is a Form for every collection of things to which the same word or 'name' is applied. Aristotle's acceptance of it here does not commit him to Platonic Forms, separate from the things they are the Forms of, merely to some common form possessed by the things to which a general term applies; hence in the translation I have put 'form' rather than 'Form'.

Aristotle sets up a dilemma: either Forms and participants have a common form, or they do not. (i) If they do, then they will have something in common. 'Two', then, will have the same sense when applied to a physical pair and when applied to the perfect pair which is the Form of Two, just as it preserves the same sense when applied to any two selected pairs, physical or non-physical. (ii) If they do not, then 'F' as applied to the Form will have a different sense from 'F' as applied to particulars. Form and particulars will be 'homonymous'; as explained in *Categories* chapter 1, two items are homonymous if the same word applies to both, but not the same definition or explanation of meaning.

Aristotle expects the Platonist to reject (ii), for the arguments for Forms would lose their interest if 'F' changed sense between Form and particulars; many ways of describing Forms imply that they have perfectly the characteristics which ordinary things have imperfectly. Thus the Platonist is expected to choose (i), and Aristotle's argument is complete: if 'F' applies in the same sense to Forms and to particulars, and Forms are objects only, then particulars are objects only.

This part of the argument is open to objection on two counts. Firstly, the Platonist might reject (i), but deny that the Form was F in a different and unrelated sense of 'F' from that in which particulars are F. Elsewhere Aristotle shows himself aware of Platonist arguments which exploit other possibilities. However, he is probably justified in ignoring them here, since they would involve a rejection of the One over Many principle in the rather crude form espoused here. Even so, there remains the second objection, that Aristotle's argument here commits him to the implausible principle that a difference of categorial application of a word amounts to a difference of sense. Elsewhere he holds the more plausible view that this is only true of the very general concepts *being, one,* and *good.*

1079^b3-11: In the dialogues Plato sometimes links the study of Forms with activities of defining and classifying, but the discussion is always on a very high level of generality (as for example at *Republic* 534a-c), and Aristotle complains with some justification at 1040^b2-4 that no believer in Forms had ever actually produced a definition of one. The present argument (which is not in *A* 9) should be compared with *Z* chapters 10, 11, and 15.

In this argument prominence is given to the phrases *ho esti* (1.6) and *auto* (1.10), used to characterize Forms. The phrases cannot be translated on their own; I have translated *auto to X* or *ho estin X* as 'the original X'. They are frequent in the dialogues—cf. *Republic* 507b5-7, *Parmenides* 135a1-3, *Phaedo* 65d12-e4. Aristotle elsewhere criticizes the use of these phrases very sharply, taking them to be mystifications serving only to hide the fact that Forms are just eternal examples of the concepts they represent (997^b8-12, 1040^b30-4, *Nicomachean Ethics* 1096^a34-^b4, *Eudemian Ethics* 1218^a10-14). Here his objection is rather that the use of *auto* will not serve the desired purpose in defining a Form.

Aristotle is sympathetic to the project of defining *circle* or *man*, objecting only to the attempt to produce a definition which will ensure that what is defined is a Form. He argues that *being a Form* cannot be added to a definition to ensure this, for it would be redundant. He asks rhetorically whether it would be added to some of the elements in the definition, or to all of them, adding a reason for thinking that it must be to all of them, namely that all the elements used to define a Form must themselves be Forms. (The example he gives presumably makes the point that the Form of Man must be defined by the Form of Animal and the Form of Two-footed.) However, if all the elements in a definition of a Form are already Forms, any addition of *being a Form* would seem to be redundant. Aristotle adds a further absurd result (introduced by 'Besides', as though it were a further argument, but probably to be taken with what precedes it): if *being a Form* applies to absolutely any Form used to define a Form, then it will have the logical role of a generic element in the definition of a Form; but this is absurd. Aristotle makes the absurdity sound striking by using the phrase *auto* (translated 'original'), which is used in phrases referring to Forms but cannot normally stand on its own.

Aristotle's arguments are good as far as they go, but they do not prove that Forms cannot be objects of definition, only that the notion of *being a Form* cannot ensure that a definition is a definition of a Form.

CHAPTER 5

These arguments criticize the relation of Forms to particulars. Aristotle examines possible ways in which Forms could contribute to, or be causes of, particulars, and finds that none applies, Logically this material should go into N, because it is part of the 'third inquiry' promised in M 1, but Aristotle puts it here, retaining the A 9 order, so as to get the whole of the theory of Forms out of the way. The options are not treated in a very logical order, and the whole chapter is a scrappy collection of separate arguments.

1079^{b}12-15: Forms cannot be efficient causes, i.e. they cannot originate change. This charge is also made at 988^{b}3-4, 1075^{b}27-8, 1071^{b}14-17. It may appear strange that Aristotle makes this charge when he is so sure elsewhere that Forms are only *formal* causes, and that Plato recognized only formal and material causes, in his own terminology (988^{a}7-11, ^{a}32-^{b}6). Aristotle seems to be doing less than justice to Plato in complaining both that the Forms do not provide efficient causation and that they do unsuccessfully try to provide it. However, Aristotle's own theory of the four causes rest on careful distinctions of the various types of explanation that can be given, and he could justly complain that Plato had not made these distinctions. (See below, on 1080^{a}2-8.)

1079^{b}15-23: Forms cannot contribute to knowledge of things, because they are not their substance or reality. For Aristotle definitions of what a thing is, which define its reality, are the first principles of scientific knowledge. The only reason why Forms cannot be the reality of things is that they are not 'in' them: Aristotle's point seems to be that Platonic Forms cannot fulfil the useful role of Aristotelian formal causes, because they are 'separate' and not, like Aristotelian forms, inherent in certain kinds of matter. This is more a confrontation of two philosophical positions than an argument. Aristotle adds that if Forms were literally in things they would make a real contribution to the natures of things, but that this is not a real option, for the theory of Forms it presupposes is impossible. The theory was never held by Plato and was due to Eudoxus; here Aristotle refers to his arguments against it in the second book of *On the Forms*, of which ten arguments survive (for a discussion of them see Cherniss (1), App. VII).

1079^{b}23-4: Aristotle is very sensitive to the use and misuse of 'from' which he discusses at 994^{a}22 ff., 1092^{a}21 ff., and which gets a whole chapter in his philosophical lexicon Δ (chapter 24). His own account of how many senses or uses it has varies, but he is constant in his irritation at its use to sketch a connection which cannot be spelled out precisely.

1079^{b}24-7: The first of five arguments against Forms as 'paradigms' or models. A paradigm is some kind of guide for change, so this is a different claim from the one that Forms are themselves supposed to initiate change.

Aristotle attacks 'participation' elsewhere as a mere empty metaphor (987^{b}13-14, 992^{a}26-8, 1045^{b}7-9). It is used to make important statements about Forms, yet never given a clear cash value.

^b26-7. Aristotle may have either or both of two things in mind here. He may be objecting to the way the Craftsman in the *Timaeus* is said to make the universe on the model of the Form of Living Creature, implying that this is mere unclear metaphor. However, Aristotle seems to exclude the *Timaeus* from his discussion of Plato's use of causes, probably because of its mythical form; otherwise he could hardly say, as he does at 988^a7-11, that Plato never makes use of final or efficient causes. More probably Aristotle is thinking of passages in the dialogues where craftsmen are said to make their products 'looking towards' the Forms: *Cratylus* 389a-b, *Republic* 596b, *Laws* 965b-c. As usual Aristotle is pitilessly literal with Plato's metaphor. It is not clear, however, that this is reasonable here, since the passages do not require Forms to be 'separate', only that they have something of the role of organizing principles to be realized in materials; not very far from Aristotle's own conception of productive activity. The criticism at *Nicomachean Ethics* 1097^a3-13 is more to the point: the Form of Good is too remote and abstract to serve as a paradigm for any particular craft.

1079^b27-30: Particulars can *resemble* Forms, as the Platonists want to say, without the relation being one of model to copy.

1079^b31-3: An individual like Socrates participates in more than one Form; merely by participating in the Form of Man he participates in the Form of Animal and the Form of Two-footed. So he will have not one but many paradigms. It is not clear why this should be absurd, unless Aristotle is assuming that the same thing cannot have more than one paradigm, which is surely false. Aristotle's example, however, suggests a more plausible point which he may be making (though if he is it is not explicit). If the Form of Man can be analysed into the Form of Animal and the Form of Two-footed, and if *all* Forms are paradigms, then the Forms of Animal and of Two-footed will import *redundant* paradigms for Socrates, not needed since he already has the Form of Man.

1079^b33-5: If there can be Forms for Forms (not just for physical objects), and if all Forms are paradigms, then a Form which is a paradigm will have a paradigm, and so be a likeness. So the same Form will be both paradigm and likeness. Again it is not clear just why this should be absurd. It is probable that Aristotle is combining in a deliberately inappropriate way different lines of Platonic thought about Forms. The Form of Man, say, is the paradigm for all earthly men. But various things can be said about Man, e.g. that Man is an animal. If the One over Many argument applies, then this is to predicate a Form of a Form, and so a Form will have a Form and thus a paradigm. This seems a total confusion of (i) the role of Forms as paradigms in the middle dialogues, (ii) their role in genus--species divisions in the late dialogues, (iii) Forms as produced by the One over Many argument. We should probably not accuse Aristotle of confusion, however; the argument is like other arguments of his on the same lines, designed to force Plato to separate these lines of thought and admit that Forms as produced by each of them have little to do with Forms as produced by the others, since absurdity results from treating them together.

161

1079ᵇ35–1080ᵃ2: This is essentially the same point as that at 1079ᵇ15-17.
1080ᵃ2-8: Aristotle mentions the *Phaedo* passage (95-105) again at *de Generatione et Corruptione* 335ᵇ9-24, and though the discussion and the examples are different the criticism is the same in both places:
(a) it is not explained how Forms can act intermittently; the Forms are always there, but things do not come into being without an acting efficient cause.
(b) Some things at any rate come into being without Forms but with ordinary visible causes; so there is no reason to postulate Forms in *any* case.

So Forms are neither sufficient (a) nor necessary (b) for coming into being. Aristotle thus clearly takes the *Phaedo* to claim that Forms are necessary and sufficient, or necessary, or sufficient, conditions for coming into being, i.e. causally operative in the modern sense.

Is this a fair interpretation of Plato? At *Phaedo* 101c Plato says that Forms are the only satisfactory causes or *aitiai*, and that a Form of F has to be brought into any account of why a particular becomes F, as well as any account of why it is F. Unless this is to be vacuous, Plato must be saying that Forms are at least necessary for a thing's coming to be or ceasing to be F, and in the absence of any explanation to the contrary, Aristotle is surely justified in taking Plato to be committed to some kind of efficient causation on the part of Forms. As often, Aristotle's criticism of Plato is based on Plato's failure to make distinctions which Aristotle himself is careful to make (in this case, at *Physics* Book II chapter 3). It could be said that Plato's discussion in the *Phaedo* does in fact anticipate some of Aristotle's distinctions, e.g. that between the final and formal causes; Socrates desires, but cannot provide, teleological explanations, and insists on the use of Forms as a second-best way. But the *Phaedo* does fail to distinguish Aristotle's efficient cause from the final cause. Plato rejects examples of efficient causation as being mere necessary conditions and not truly causes (98-9), and Aristotle is surely right in thinking that Forms are meant to replace them, rather than to provide a quite different sort of explanation.

Aristotle's arguments here do not imply that he thought that Plato put forward in so many words the absurd idea that Forms interfere in the course of what happens in the world (hence they are not inconsistent with the objection at 1079ᵇ12-15.) Rather, Aristotle takes Plato to be committed to this by his failure to distinguish senses of 'cause', and hence his failure to see that Forms do not provide an improvement on efficient causes, but an answer to a different sense of the question, 'why is x F?'

CHAPTER 6–CHAPTER 8, 1083ᵇ23

The 'third inquiry' to follow the discussion of Forms does not in fact begin until *N*; the rest of *M* consists of various arguments against platonist theories of mathematical objects, not challenging the basic principles, as in chapter 2, but pointing out weaknesses in existing theories. From now on, chapter divisions are misleading; I have bracketed them where they do not mark a genuine break, and have indicated the actual divisions of the argument by introducing sub-headings and by numbering arguments.

This section is, unlike the next, a planned unity. The main part consists of a refutation ($1080^b37-1083^a17$) of the Platonic conception of unique Form numbers each of which is a collection of units of a special type. The introduction (chapter 6) incorporates this into a wider attack on all platonist theories of mathematical objects by classifying these on various principles, only one of which is covered by the main argument, the rest being dealt with very perfunctorily in the conclusion ($1083^a17^{-b}23$). It seems as if Aristotle is re-using an earlier essay against one specific theory by fitting it rather artificially into the anti-platonist argument of *M*. While Aristotle is not very successful in extending the scope of his original broadside, the polemic itself is impressive and of great interest.

1080^a15-37: Given the received text, this long and grammatically chaotic sentence produces a classification which is internally incoherent and also fails to answer to Aristotle's actual argument which follows. On the traditional interpretation Aristotle is making a division of numbers into three classes:

I. Numbers in an ordered series, each specifically different, either (a) each unit being likewise specifically different, and non-combinable with any other, or (b) all units being combinable, or (c) units being combinable within a number, but non-combinable with units in other numbers.

II. Mathematical number.

III. 'That named last'.

This produces confusion. I(b) has already (1080^a21-3) been said to be like mathematical number, so II seems to be identical with I(b); but this cannot be the case, since there are infinitely many instances of each mathematical number, whereas in any variant of I each number is specifically different. Further, it is not clear how II and III can be alternatives to I, if they have already been introduced as variants within I. And what Aristotle goes on to discuss is not a variety of options about numbers, but a variety of options about units.

These difficulties are all cured by excising 'or' (*ē*) at $^a18$, supposing it to be a mistake by a scribe understandably confused by the tortuous long sentence. This produces the text I have translated. What Aristotle says is now quite clear. His first classification of platonist theories of number is:

I (17-20). Each number is a specifically different member of an ordered series, and so is each unit, so no unit is combinable with any other.

II (20-3). Units succeed one another directly, and any unit is combinable with any other, as with mathematical number, where no unit is different from any other.

III (23-35). Each number is unique of its kind and non-combinable with any other, and units in any number are combinable with units in that number, but

163

non-combinable with units in any other number.

IV (35-7). All three of the above types are possible.

This now corresponds with what Aristotle proves. He does not deal with IV, but does not need to, since he proves that none of I-III is possible. He deals with them in the order II, I, III, showing in each case that the conception of units involved is inconsistent with the conception of number.

In I numbers are said to be in an ordered series, each specifically different. In III they are said to come in an ordered series and not to be produced by addition; and 2 is called 'the first two' and 'the original two'. It is reasonable to suppose that in I and III we have the same concept, that of Form number. This will be borne out by the actual arguments and the use they make of 'combinability' (see notes on 1080ᵇ37 ff.).

Aristotle does not proceed to the arguments, but instead produces more principles of classification (see above).

1080ª37-ᵇ4: Numbers are classified as 'in' objects or separate from them. The last sentence is obscure, and the view it describes peculiar. Some commentators have understandably bracketed it. Aristotle here insists that he is not talking about partial platonism but the view that numbers are literally in things, i.e. the Pythagorean view. He has trouble fitting the Pythagoreans into his classifications here since they are like platonists in one way, viz. believing in the reality of numbers, but unlike them in another, viz. not taking numbers to be distinct and separate from things.

1080ᵇ4-23: In limiting himself to people who treat one as a principle of number Aristotle is in fact including all theories of interest to him, i.e. Pythagoreans and all the Academy theories. The theory accepting both Form numbers and mathematical numbers belongs to Plato, the one accepting only mathematical numbers belongs to Speusippus, and the one identifying the two belongs to Xenocrates. Aristotle never names the person believing only in Form numbers, and this view quietly disappears (in the summing-up it is Xenocrates' theory which is called 'the third view' (1083ᵇ2)). It is certainly an odd view, for what account could it give of mathematical statements? There is some temptation to follow Jaeger in excising it as a textual mistake.

1080ᵇ23-36: Aristotle points out that the same classification applies to geometry as well as to arithmetic. However, since the main argument concerns only numbers, this section is not relevant to it, and serves only to point out, as an aside, that all the theories of number have objectionable analogues for geometry. Plato accepts two kinds of ideal geometrical object, Speusippus only one, and Xenocrates accepts Plato's two but identifies them. Speusippus accepts only geometrical objects, i.e. ideal circles, lines, etc. We would expect that the other class which Plato and Xenocrates accept would be geometrical Forms, especially if the geometrical case is to be parallel to the case of number, where the two classes concerned are mathematical numbers and Form numbers. But in fact the class in question is called 'the objects after the Forms'. This is another indication that the role of the geometrical Forms was rather unclear in Plato's later thought. (See the Introduction, p. 24-26.)

Xenocrates is criticized for saying mathematically objectionable things about mathematical objects (cf. 1090ᵇ27-30) because of identifying them with Forms. Aristotle mentions two such beliefs, one geometrical, the belief in indivisible lines (attacked in a polemic possibly by Aristotle), and the other a belief about numbers, namely that not every two ones or units make up two. The latter point appears as a fault in Plato's theory (1082ᵇ16-19), but presumably Aristotle regards the error as more gross in Xenocrates, who insisted that this number was none the less mathematical number.

This comprehensive introduction gives little warning that by far the largest part of the discussion will be devoted to the problems Plato's theory has with units, and that the other theories will not be touched on until the final summing-up.

1080ᵇ37–1081ᵃ5: The arguments in this section use the notion of 'combinability'. For Aristotle *sumblētos* normally means 'comparable, i.e. measureable by the same unit of quantity' (or more loosely, 'comparable as items of the same kind',), but this cannot be its sense here where it is applied to units. From the way non-combinability of units is introduced at 1080ᵃ18-20 it seems as though it is extended from its application to numbers, which are Form numbers (see notes). Since Form numbers do not have mathematical operations defined for them and are thus not addible, and since they are all specifically different, each being unique of its kind, we can formalize non-combinability for Form numbers as follows:

(C = combinable, SS = specifically the same, A = addible):

(a) $- C(x,y) \leftrightarrow [- SS(x,y) \,\&\, - A(x,y)]$.

But this is not how Aristotle understands non-combinability for the *units* in Form numbers. For his arguments at 1081ᵃ17 ff. all presuppose that units are non-combinable with one another and yet can be added in some way to make up numbers. For units he thus assumes something weaker than (a). Here it is worth noticing that he argues first against the option he listed second, namely that all units are combinable. This suggests that he wants to begin with combinability and understand non-combinability in terms of it. Now the assumptions of the first argument (1081ᵃ5-7) are that if units are combinable they are undifferentiated (i.e. specifically the same) and addible to make up numbers. So Aristotle is assuming here for units.

(b) $C(x,y) \rightarrow [SS(x,y) \,\&\, A(x,y)]$.

Aristotle does not argue for this; it probably seems obvious to him from the concept of a unit, which is precisely what can be counted and has no differentiating feature. However, if (b) defines combinability, non-combinability will be defined by

(c) $- C(x,y) \rightarrow [- SS(x,y) \vee - A(x,y)]$,

which is obviously weaker than (a). In many of the following arguments Aristotle ignores addibility and concentrates solely on specific difference when considering non-combinable units. Often he uses 'differentiated' as though it

165

simply meant 'non-combinable' (e.g. 1082^b1 ff., 1083^a1-17). Although he does not justify this, the arguments provide the material for a justification. At 1081^a19-20, combinable units are characterized as undifferentiated $(C(x,y) \rightarrow SS(x,y))$ and this would entitle him to the contrapositive: if units are differentiated then they are not combinable $(-SS(x,y) \rightarrow -C(x,y))$. At 1081^b12-17 he says explicitly that whether units are differentiated or not, number must be counted by adding one more each time (taken as adding a unit). So if he thinks that units are addible whether they are differentiated or not, he may well feel entitled to drop the $-A(x,y)$ from (c). He several times thereafter assumes that if units are non-combinable then they are specifically different (e.g. 1081^b33-7, 1082^a4-9, $^b1$ ff.). This gives us: $-C(x,y) \rightarrow -SS(x,y)$. This together with the contrapositive of 1081^a19-20 gives us the biconditional
(d) $-C(x,y) \leftrightarrow -SS(x,y)$.
(Inaddibility is not excluded; it comes in at 1082^b16-19, in a rather weak argument. But the bulk of the arguments rely on (d), not on (c).)

Aristotle is thus justified in understanding non-combinability in terms of (d) rather than (c). But this leaves the question whether he is justified in understanding it in terms of (c) rather than (a). If the Platonists did understand non-combinability of units wholly as an extension of the notion as applied to numbers, they may have required (a), in which case a great many of Aristotle's arguments would simply misfire. Unfortunately, we have no way of knowing whether these arguments are in fact based on fundamental misapprehensions. However, this is unlikely, in view of the precision of the arguments. Besides, it is even harder to make sense of units that cannot be added than numbers that cannot be added, and even if the Platonists began with (a) they probably lapsed into (c) for units, if not for numbers.

If the above is right, the following arguments prove that Plato's Form numbers, each unique of its kind, cannot be made up of (non-)combinable units, however (non-)combinability is to be understood. Most of the argument is devoted to the third option, namely that a Form number is made up of units combinable in the number but non-combinable with units in other numbers. See the Introduction, p. 16-19, for the suggestion that Plato probably did put forward this view in response to Aristotle's criticisms of the idea that Form numbers are made up of units. These criticisms showed that if a Form number is unique of its kind, the units cannot be undifferentiated; but any way of differentiating them leads to unintelligibility or infinite regress. The counter-suggestion is that the units in a number can be characterized non-circularly and non-vacuously as combinable in that number but non-combinable with other units. Aristotle's criticism is systematic. If (non-)combinability has application to units at all, there are three possible interpretations: they are all combinable, or all non-combinable, or they are combinable 'within the number' in the way demanded by Plato's theory. On the first option Form number is not possible. On the other two, contradictions are produced with the concept of Form number held by the Platonists. So none of the options is compatible with belief in Form number. The conclusion is that the Platonists must avoid this attempt to patch up their theory; it is fundamentally unsalvageable. While the arguments are uneven, the organized ruthlessness of the whole polemic is impressive, and it is this that challenges comparison with Frege's *Foundations of Arithmetic*, chapters 2 and 3.

1081ª5-17. The second option: If all units are combinable, then since any two units make two, there will be many twos and two will no longer be unique. But the Form number Two is unique; so on this option numbers cannot be Forms. What is at stake in this argument is the uniqueness of the Form number. Unfortunately Aristotle has not been able to resist the opportunity to draw more striking absurdities from the attempt to identify repeatable numbers with non-repeatable Forms, and he assumes that not only are all numbers Forms but all Forms numbers. But the absurdity wrung from this supposed identification of all Forms with numbers follows just as well from the weaker assumption that numbers are Forms. It is clear that this is a polemical move on Aristotle's part and not a report of actual Platonic doctrine, both because Aristotle has to make up his own examples (compare 1084ª14 and 25) and because he produces an argument that Forms *must* be numbers, inept if Plato did in fact say that they were. (See the Introduction, pp. 62-8).

For a suggestion as to why Aristotle treats the second option first, see notes on 1080ᵇ37–1081ª5.

1081ª17-ᵇ35. The first option: Although Aristotle says that nobody held this option, he seems at ᵇ6-8 to be referring to what someone actually said. Probably he is referring to informal discussions which did not reach the stage of a full-blown theory. In any case, treatment of this option is necessary for the strategy of the whole section.

In these arguments Aristotle assumes that units, although non-combinable, are addible; all that needs to be assumed about non-combinability here is that a unit is uniquely differentiated by its position in the series of units. There is an interesting parallel here with Jevons (*The Principles of Science*, pp.153-72, cf. p. 72), who actually espouses the view sketched here, namely that a unit is, though addible, specifically differentiated by its position in a series. Jevons reasons that units are countable, and that counting two exactly similar things is counting the same thing twice; so units must be differentiated by their position in a series, marked notationally by strokes (1, 1′, 1″, 1‴ etc.). Frege ((1), pp. 46-8, 54-7) refutes Jevons on the ground that this conception of units is inconsistent with the uniqueness of each natural number; which is strikingly like the way Aristotle refutes this option here. His strategy throughout is to show that if numbers are Form numbers, a series of unique objects each specifically differentiated by its position in a series, then the units making them up cannot also form such a series. If units are non-combinable in this way, then Form numbers cannot be unique and non-combinable.

1081ª17-21: Aristotle may be trying to show that this conception of units will not fit the intermediates; he does not complete the argument in this way in the case of the third option, probably because it seems clearly analogous to the present argument.

1081ᵃ21-ᵇ35:

(a) In this and the next argument Aristotle appeals to the fact that the natural numbers form a sequence, in which 2 is the direct successor of 1, 3 of 2, and so on (= NS). (This is independent of their derivation from the Platonist principles.) He shows that this is incompatible with the premise that all units are non-combinable (= NC). Here Aristotle states that NS is incompatible with simultaneous generation of units in a number, using the example of 2 in order to appeal to Plato's own words. It is not easy, however, to see how this is to be connected with NC.

It is tempting at first to suppose that Aristotle means that the units in a number are generated *simultaneously with each other* (= S'). But while this is incompatible with their being generated in an ordered series, it is not necessarily incompatible with NC, which might still hold if they were differentiated some other way. If Aristotle means S', there is no real argument. Ross tries to remedy this by turning (a) and (b) into a single argument, altering 'Besides' to 'since'; but the resulting sentence is implausibly clumsy Greek, and Aristotle would be given a very bad argument: he would grant the Platonists that units in a number are produced simultaneously, and then argue against them on the assumption that they are *not* produced simultaneously.

A complete argument can be found for (a) if we take the point to be rather that the units in a number are, for the Platonists, produced *simultaneously with that number* (= S''). Aristotle does not say so, but this seems to be entailed by NC; if NC is true, units cannot be put together to form a number, on the assumption that non-combinability implies inaddibility. (This is one passage which makes one slightly unhappy about Aristotle's dropping of inaddibility as a requirement for non-combinable units, especially as there is a definite reference to Plato.) A number cannot be produced out of units; they have to be created along with the number, not one by one before the numbers are produced. So NC → S''. But S'' → – (NS), because if S'' holds, the place of the generated units in the number sequence is undetermined. But – (NS) is absurd, so by *reductio ad absurdum* NC is proved to be false. The step from S'' to – (NS) depends on Aristotle's assumption that the sequence of natural numbers is one into which the units enter—i.e. we get 1, then 2 by adding a unit, 3 by adding another unit, and so on. Aristotle is thus confusing adding a unit with adding 1. Unless he is making some such assumption it is hard to see why the sequence of *numbers* should be upset by the simultaneous production of two *units*.

The obvious objection to (a) is that it depends on the confusion of 1 and unit, but even without tracking down this specific error a Platonist might object that Aristotle is wrong to conclude that the sequence of numbers is upset by the production of units; units and numbers could form separate series which do not compete. Against this objection Aristotle could invoke (b) (though it is not its explicit target).

(b) Aristotle now lets the Platonist drop the assumption that NC → S″. Even so, NC implies the absurd − (NS). If the units are not generated simultaneously with their numbers, they are generated one after another in a series. But then Aristotle invokes a general principle not confined to units, namely that any compound of two things one of which is prior to the other, is prior to the second but subsequent to the first. This is, to say the least, not obviously true as a general principle, nor is the sense of 'prior' apparent. Aristotle is probably thinking of the compound of form and matter, which is prior to matter but subsequent to form (1029^{a}5-7). (But even this is not quite analogous, for there Aristotle says only that since form is prior to matter it is by the same argument prior to the compound of form and matter, and does not seem to think that the same argument proves that the compound of form and matter must be prior to matter, which is assumed here.) Aristotle applies the form/matter analysis to numbers elsewhere (e.g. 1084^{b}28-9); it seems rather artificial, but he would perhaps defend it as a way to make intelligible the idea that numbers are produced out of units. Here it gives rise to the strikingly absurd result that the number sequence will go: 1, first unit in 2, 2, second unit in 2, and so on. so denying NS and thus by *reductio* implying the falsity of NC.

(c) A further problem even if the series of numbers and that of units are kept distinct. If we start with 1, then 2 will correspond to the next unit after 1, 3 to the next unit, and so on. There is thus a sense in which 2 is correlated with two units and 3 with three units, whether or not one is prepared to say that the number-series is actually produced by addition. But this contradicts the original assumption about the series of Form numbers. For if the series of units really begins with 1 and continues, we have:

numbers	1	2		
units	1	1′	1″	1‴
number of units	1	2	3	4

There are thus two units before we have 2, and similarly three units before we have 3, and so on. But the idea that things are 'named after' Forms is almost a commonplace of the classical theory of Forms, one of the purposes of which was to give an intelligible account of our use of general terms. (Cf. *Phaedo* 78e, *Timaeus* 52a, *Parmenides* 130e, 133d.) So here things come the wrong way round; the originals come after what is supposed to be named after them, and there is a conflict with the concept of Form number.

(d) On the traditional interpretation of this argument, Aristotle is unfairly pressing the Platonic use of 'the first one'; Plato meant by this something like 'original' and Aristotle is being unfair in taking it to mean 'first in a series' and arguing that there must therefore be a second and a third in the same series.

There is, however, a more interesting way to take it. Aristotle is explicitly drawing an implicit consequence of (c). If there is another 2 before the original 2, then not only are there other twos not named after the original Two, but the original Two is not unique of its kind. So here Aristotle points out that if there is a series of different and distinct ones there will also be series of different and distinct twos and threes and so on; and this of course contradicts the assumption of the uniqueness of the Form numbers. We get

ones	1	1′	1″	1‴	1⁗
alternative twos	2	2′	2″	2‴	
alternative threes	3	3′	3″		

ᵇ6-8 forms a parenthesis. One cannot have it both ways, and say *both* that 2 comes first after 1 *and* that there is a first and second unit after 1. i.e. given

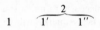

one has to choose between 2 and 1′ as the successor of 1. Aristotle seems to be meeting the Platonist who might insist that units and numbers come in different series and do not compete, by showing that on his premises there is at least one case where they do. This is in effect to assume that non-combinability has the same force when applied to units as to numbers. This is rather unsafe ground for Aristotle, since most of his arguments depend on the assumption that this is not the case.

(e) This argument is not very clear, and its relevance to differentiated units is obscured by a long digression criticizing the Platonist method of producing Form numbers. Ross makes the section from 1.27 a separate piece of argument, but it is hard to see what it is supposed to prove. The course of the argument seems to be as follows: if units are differentiated, then numbers cannot be Form numbers. Numbers are counted by adding on one every time: this is presented as a fundamental common-sense truth. But if so, each number will merely be differentiated by its extra one or unit; 2 will be 'part of' 3 in containing two of the ones or units needed to count to 3, and so on. But then numbers cannot be distinct, unique, and non-combinable (cf. 1082ᵇ34-7). The Platonist retorts to this that Form numbers are not produced by adding one every time; they are produced by doubling, from one and the indefinite two. Aristotle blocks this move by pointing out that even so he will be committed to distinct twos and threes, so that the peculiar mode of generation cannot save the unique and non-combinable nature of the Form numbers. It is no good saying that 4 is produced by doubling from the indefinite two, and so is reached by a quite distinct process from that producing 3 or 5. According to the Platonists' own account, 4 is produced from 2 by the indefinite two, so unless it actually contains the indefinite two (an obvious absurdity) it must consist of two 2s. The case is even clearer with 2 itself, which must contain two 1s, if it is not to contain the original principles, which would be absurd. So the special and bizarre nature of the number-production does not save the Platonist from having to say that numbers are made up of other numbers; so he will still have different and distinct twos and threes. And since they are not mathematical numbers they must be Form numbers and so made up of differentiated units. But the Platonists have no possible consistent account of this.

1081^{b}35–1083^{a}20. The third option: Since this was Plato's actual theory it receives most attention. I find eight arguments; Ross finds nine, but I follow Bonitz in taking 1082^{a}15-20 and 20-6 as a single unit of argument.

(i) 'Not just any' is Aristotle's somewhat scornful way of describing the Form number made up of units combinable only within that number. The argument runs: 10 is made up of two 5s; but since 10 is a special sort of number, so will be the numbers making up that number, and so these 5s also must be made up of units combinable only within the number. But this is fatal. For it follows that the 10 units fall apart into two differentiated 5s, each of which makes up a special 5; if they did not thus fall apart, there would not be two 5s in 10 (ll. 5-6). If there are two *different* 5s in 10 then there is some relevant difference between the two groups of 5 units (l. 7). But then there is no guarantee that this is the *only* relevant difference; given 10 units, there are many ways (252 in fact) of dividing them into two 5s. Merely picking out two groups of 5 does not entitle us to say that we have picked out *the* two fives in 10; we can always at least ask (l. 7-9) whether there are other 5s that can be put together from other combinations. But if this is possible (for it would be strange (l. 9) if there were some arbitrary restriction on the ways the units in 10 could be put together), then surely these 5s can be put together to form more than one 10? (l. 10). If there can be more than two special 5s in 10, they can make up more than one 10, and so the original special 10 cannot be the unique 10. But then what 10 do they make up? Or is there another 10 in the original 10? (ll. 10-11).

Lines 11-15 defend the ascription to the Platonists of the idea that special Form numbers can be made up of other special numbers. This is implied by what they avowedly hold about the indefinite two: it produces *two* twos to make four, so they do believe that there are two twos in four, so they might as well accept that there are two fives in ten. This points out that a Platonist has to be inconsistent even to accept the premises of this argument, which accepts from the start that some Form numbers are repeatable and made up of other numbers. The argument only works against someone who thought that in '5 + 5 = 10', '10' stood for the unique number 10, but had also not worried about the double appearance of '5'.

(ii) How can a number like 2 be a unity, on this option? It fails all the conditions Aristotle accepts for a thing's being a genuine unity. The Platonists just present us with a collection of units, and a collection is not an entity over and above its members. This is a simple anti-platonist point, and Aristotle adds examples to show that it is not limited to units. This general point is rather weak here; after all, the combinability of units was designed, among other things, to account for the unity of a number, and Aristotle is just denying this without argument. He returns more effectively to this problem in (iv) and (viii); all seem to be developments of a single elliptical sentence at 992ᵃ1-2: 'Why is a number, when taken all together, one?' Cf. the Introduction, p. 16-17.

(iii) This is a bafflingly bad argument. It seems to go as follows: if numbers are Forms then, since some numbers make up and so produce others, we will have to say that some Forms make up and so produce other Forms. Since the units in the numbers behave like the numbers, the same is true of them, so they will be Forms too. So Forms will be composed of other Forms; but this is absurd, if we consider that the things the Forms are Forms of will also be composed of other things. If the Form of Man is composed of the Form of Animal, a man will be partly composed of an animal.

Nearly every step here is dubious or plainly indefensible. Worse, the main line of thought has nothing to do with units. They enter the argument only by the dubious second step: units produce other units in the way the corresponding numbers produce other numbers, so since numbers are Forms units are Forms too. This is plainly a *non sequitur*. Besides, it is not a problem proprietary to the units of this option, i.e. differentiated units. Perhaps it was put in this section by mistake by an editor, and the argument itself has got garbled in the process.

(iv) It is clear from the fact that this objection occurs here (and is developed also in (ii) and (viii)) that Aristotle thinks that this option is more artificial in its differentiating of units than the first option. Whereas that merely required that units be differentiated by their position in a series in a fairly straightforward way, the present option demands that units be differentiated in a very obscure fashion.

The point here is treated more thoroughly under (viii); all that is peculiar to this argument is a rather dubious slide from talk of numbers being equal to talk of what is equal in numbers—i.e. a move from two numbers (sets of units) being equal to there being no difference between the units. (This does not follow—there might be some way of differentiating the units, which Aristotle has not ruled out.) Aristotle wants to show that difference between numbers cannot be a difference in the units, and tries to do so by showing that sameness of number entails sameness of units in the number. A Platonist might object that the question was simply being begged, since they did not accept this (and Aristotle knew this—cf. 1093ᵇ21-3).

(v) If any two things can be counted to make up a two (something we are supposed to take for granted as a common-sense assumption), then the Platonists cannot be right to posit a difference of kind between units in different numbers. Aristotle gives an example: Can you make 2 from one unit in 2 and one in 3?

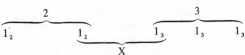

The units are tagged to show which number they are combinable within. If X is a number, as it ought to be since it is made up of two perfectly good units, it creates problems. It ought to come between 2 and 3, but there is no number between 2 and 3 (not in Aristotle's sense of 'number'). But to deny that there is any such number as X is to deny that any two units make up a number. Aristotle represents this as flying in the face of common sense; 'we say' appeals to what anyone would say, not to ideas of his own. Most people think that you can count two items, however heterogeneous, but the Platonists are committed to saying that not every two mathematical units make up a two. However, this is just what a Platonist would say, and would appear to be the whole point of the theory of non-combinable units; so is not the argument question-begging? Strictly, perhaps; but Aristotle succeeds in making the important point that a Platonist can give no account of why X is not a number. The theory of non-combinable units either allows numbers which are not proper Form numbers or rules them out, but can give no good reason for doing so.

(vi) If 2 and 3 are specifically different (which as Forms they have to be) then 3, being bigger by 1 than 2, will 'contain' a number equal to 2 and so not be differentiated from 2. But if there is a 'first and second number', i.e. if numbers are Forms and come in a series, there cannot be a number identical with 2 in 3. This seems superficial at first glance; one wants Aristotle to sort out what might be meant by 'contain' and 'part of' before deciding that the Platonist is committed to objectionable results. Worse, the argument seems to have nothing to do with units. There may, however, be a reference to the topic of this section in the use of the word 'equal', A Platonist accepting the third option would only be able to say of two numbers that they were or were not made up of units of the same kind. He could not say that two numbers were equal, or contained an equal number of units, without falling back on the circularity that the theory was designed to avoid: using number to define the units in number. All he could come out with would be the unhelpful statement that the numbers were different. But surely a good theory of number should save the intuitive statement that 3 is a larger number than 2. Aristotle is not being naïve here, as is often assumed; he is insisting, as does Frege, that a good philosophical analysis of number should answer to, or at least not fall foul of, our every-day use of the concept.

(vii) This argument is introduced by the 'heading' that Forms cannot be numbers. It is clear, however, from the argument that this is not what is proved at all. It is concerned only with the way numbers have to be Forms, for Plato, to be consistent with one view of units. It is not even an argument that numbers cannot be Forms, since it introduces a reason why the Platonists are *right* to say what they do, since they insist that numbers are different in kind. Perhaps the argument just has a wrong 'title'. There is certainly something wrong in the text, because the commentator pseudo-Alexander read some text which we do not possess, although the argument as we have it is not incomplete.

Aristotle points out that non-combinable units are required if numbers are to be Forms, and so unique; if units are all identical there will be many 2s, 3s, and so on, whereas one point of the theory of Form numbers was to preserve the uniqueness of each number. So Aristotle ironically praises Plato for his consistency in sticking to the consequences of his theory, but points out that these are flagrantly false. Plato has to deny that we count by means of a single repeated operation—about as fundamental a fact as one could deny. But to admit this means giving up the generation from one and the indefinite two. In fact it is not clear that Plato regarded this mode of generation as having anything to do with the way we *count*. Aristotle is on surer ground in criticizing the Platonists for manufacturing ideal numbers to account for our ability to count, since they take adding one to be a different process from that of reaching a different number. Aristotle is surely right to be contemptuous of this: we can give an intelligible account of how we can be doing the same thing in two different ways, or under different descriptions, without appealing to distinct objects for the different descriptions.

(viii) The last and best version of the point treated in (ii) and (iv). This time Aristotle demolishes systematically the idea that a unit can have a differentia. Numbers cannot differ qualitatively, only in quantity, i.e. by being bigger or smaller than or equal to one another. But this difference in quantity cannot apply to units, for if units could be bigger or smaller than other units, then two numbers whose units were in 1:1 correlation could still differ in that one had bigger units than the other. Aristotle regards this as self-evidently absurd; the difference of combinability that the Platonists appeal to (cf. 1093ᵇ21-3) was meant to avoid such an absurdity. The only alternative is that units differ qualitatively. Aristotle rules this out in two stages:

(a) they cannot differ qualitatively as this notion applies to numbers. I take it that Aristotle is saying here that differences of quality between numbers, like being prime as opposed to being composite, are merely shorthand for differences in quantitative relations between numbers (being or not being divisible by other numbers). If units differed in this way, the qualitative difference would always be translatable out into a quantitative difference; but this has already been shown to be impossible (cf. 1020ᵇ2-8).

(b) If the Platonist is driven back to saying that units have an ultimate, *sui generis* differentiation, this is not intelligible. He can give no reasonable account of how this can be so on his own principles. Aristotle does not deny outright the possibility of such a difference, like that between red and yellow; he merely insists that it must be rationally accounted for. It is no good just saying that units *are* ineffably different, without being able to give a coherent account on one's principles of how they are. Otherwise no real claim has been put forward, merely an implausible assertion.

Aristotle's treatment of the third option is less satisfactory than his treatment of the other two; some of the arguments are obscure or of doubtful relevance. But they do make the essential point: the theory has not been saved by the sophistication of the theory of non-combinable units. The notion of combinability offers no way between the Scylla of circularity and the Charybdis of vacuity.

1083ª17-20: In his summing-up Aristotle again says that 'Forms are numbers', but the context makes it clear that this is a mistake or not to be taken seriously, since it is the theory that numbers are Forms that has been the subject of criticism.

1083ª20-b1: Aristotle now gives a lightning refutation of Speusippus' theory of mathematical number, which gives him his conclusion: if separate numbers must be either Form numbers (Plato) or mathematical numbers (Speusippus) and both are impossible, then numbers cannot be separate at all. Formally there is nothing wrong with the construction of the argument as a whole, but some awkwardness in Aristotle's adaptation of his original material to serve the needs of a wider argument shows clearly in the vast disproportion between the pages just devoted to Plato and the few lines given to Speusippus.

Both theory and criticism confuse one and unit. Speusippus in accepting only mathematical number takes there to be infinitely many units which combine into infinitely many twos and threes, etc. Aristotle's objection is usually understood to be that since all the ones or units derive from an original one, so should the many twos and threes derive from an original two and three, since a 'first' should have a second and third. This is rather weak: why should what applies to one apply to two and the other numbers? Units are what numbers are made up of, not themselves numbers. It is more probable that Aristotle's argument is that Speusippus is inconsistent to reject Form numbers and yet retain the derivation of numbers from one and the indefinite two. These principles are supposed to produce Form numbers, and these are the 'originals' of the many twos, threes, etc. Speusippus, by clinging to a line of thought which gives him the original one as head of a series of units, is committed without realizing it to an original two, three, etc., and this is inconsistent with his rejection of Forms. There is some indication that Xenocrates used this argument too (cf. 1086ª5-9), but used it to support his identification of Form number with mathematical number.

1083b1-8: Xenocrates gets even less space, but this is more reasonable, since his theory, identifying Form numbers and methematical numbers, inherits the problems of both theories and does not require a separate critique.

1083^b8-19: The Pythagoreans are dealt with briefly, because their refusal to separate number from things puts them outside the line of thought just discussed. It is interesting that Aristotle does not here attribute to them an outright explicit identification of things with numbers, but infers this from the fact that they treat mathematics as directly descriptive of the world (this is also Plato's complaint about them in *Republic* Book VII). Hence they confuse the indivisibility of units, which is a conceptual demand, with physical indivisibily of objects counted or measured.

1083^b19-23: This is the conclusion of Aristotle's whole argument. In fact only one of the alternatives has been argued with any thoroughness; see notes to the beginning of chapter 6.

CHAPTER 8, 1083^b23—CHAPTER 9, 1086^a21

This section contrasts sharply with the last; it is an unconnected string of arguments beginning and ending abruptly and with no connecting topic. The arguments are in a rougher state than the preceding ones, and more of them are weak, crabbed, or baffling. Some seem to be preliminary versions of arguments which are given a more satisfactory form elsewhere in *M-N*. All this suggests that this section is a collection of notes for lectures, at different stages of polishing, probably put together and perhaps even inserted here by an editor (the first arguments appear to continue the theme of the last section, units, but this is a superficial link only). However, whether or not Aristotle meant them to stand here and in this form, they are appropriate to *M*, continuing the attacks on platonist theories of mathematical objects. Many of them appear mysterious because they are directed against specific targets which are now lost, and, for the same reason, it is sometimes impossible to know whether Aristotle's criticism is quite fair to the opponent.

1083^b23-36: This draws out difficulties in combining two Platonist ideas, namely the concept of numbers as sets of units and the derivation of numbers from one and the indefinite two. Aristotle asks how the units in the numbers are to be produced from these principles, in particular the units in 2 and 3, and sets up a dilemma.

(a) ^b25-30. Suppose some units come from the great and some from the small. But if the work of producing units in the numbers generated is to be divided between the two factors of the great and the small then (i) each unit will not come from all the elements, and, further, there will be a gratuitious difference of type between the units: 2, for example, will be made up of two units of different (indeed opposed) types. This argument applies to the second principle only under the description 'the great and small', and would not apply to it as described as, for example, 'the indefinite two'. The notes on *N* chapter 1 (especially the notes on 1087^b4-12 and ^b12-33) discuss further the fact that many of Aristotle's arguments apply to the Platonist second principle only under one of its descriptions. The present argument raises a further point: is it not a misunderstanding to talk about 'the great and the small' as though they were two separable factors? Plato's 'great and small' was meant to be a single factor. Aristotle's move here (which he makes elsewhere) has frequently been criticized as sheer misconception. Aristotle could defend himself by claiming that the idea of a single principle which is great *and* small is incoherent, and that the only sensible way to understand Plato's words is to take his principle to be a conjunction of the great and the small (see notes on 1087^b4-12).

(ii) There is an extra problem with odd numbers like 3. Even if one unit is produced by each of the great and the small, there is an extra unit left over, making the number odd. What produces it? Aristotle suggests that the original one, the first principle, has to step in here. Actually this seems to have been something like the way the Platonists themselves thought of it (see Introduction, p. 49-51). So Aristotle's point is not a successful point against the Platonist account (unless he is claiming that it is absurd for the two principles to work separately; but that is not the announced topic of the argument). It would be attractive if Aristotle's point here were an objection to the confusion of one and unit that results in the idea of an 'odd unit'; a unit which when added makes a group odd-membered is not *itself* odd (we cannot ask, 'Which is the odd unit?'). But Aristotle subscribes to this confusion himself (cf. (b) (ii) below), so unfortunately it is not his target here.

(b) ^b30-6. Suppose, on the other hand, that each unit comes from *both* the great and the small. Then we still get objectionable results. (i) The first unit produced will be the first unitary determinate product of the great and small. But this should define the number 2, the first definite product of the infinitely doubling element. So the Platonists have no way of distinguishing 2 from the first of its units.

(ii) But in fact the first unit in 2 is prior to 2. (This is the common-sense point that 2 minus 1 is 1, with the confusion of one and unit already seen.) So since 2 is a Form, its first unit, being prior to it, must be its Form, and so be 'the Form of a Form'. (On the assumption that if A is prior to B, A must be the Form of B, see 1082^a32 and my article mentioned in the notes on 1079^a14-19. A Platonist might well reject this part of the argument; but the rest does not depend on it.) Also, since the first unit in 2 is prior to 2, it must be produced before 2, but where from? The indefinite two only doubles, so it can produce only twos, so it cannot produce a unit or one. If the Platonists are going to maintain that units in numbers, as well as numbers, are produced from their principles, then there will be the awkward result that the units have to be produced before the numbers are. A Platonist might object that the production of units is supposed to be part of the production of numbers, not something in competition with it, but in default of a precise account Aristotle is surely justified in trying to pin the theory down exactly and in finding an incoherence here.

These arguments may seem at first sight inept, since the Platonist principles were supposed to produce numbers, not units in numbers, and Aristotle's complaint looks rather like a complaint that a machine cannot properly be said to produce boxes of eggs if there is no answer to the question of how it produces the eggs. But Aristotle has in fact shown that the Academy's derivation of numbers from their principles has no obvious connection with their concept of numbers as sets of units, and that the most obvious ways of connecting them lead to absurdity.

1083ᵇ36–1084ᵇ2: Aristotle now sets up a dilemma which faces the platonist who takes numbers to be 'separate' from the items they are the numbers of. According to Aristotle, he is committed either to (a) the existence of an infinite number, of which he can give no account, or to (b) an arbitrary and absurd limitation of the number-series. (a) is dealt with in 1084ᵃ2-10, and (b) from ᵃ10 to ᵇ2.

Aristotle here wants to force the platonist to agree that either the number-series is infinite, in which case there must be an actual infinite plurality of numbers, or it is finite, and therefore stops at some arbitrary n, both alternatives being absurd. Aristotle's dilemma may seem to be a false one, even without the benefit of the work on infinity of nineteenth-century mathematicians. Surely one can accept that there are infinitely many numbers without accepting that this infinity actually has a number that could be given; one could insist that the number-series does not end with any n, even an infinite n, but continues for ever. Aristotle himself adopts this approach to the question in his treatment of the infinite in *Physics* Book 3 (especially 207ᵃ33-ᵇ15): number goes on to infinity in the sense that you *can* always go on adding to any number you reach, not in the sense that there already exists a number which is the number of the infinitely many additions that can be made. Aristotle would probably say, however, that the Platonists could not deal with the problem in this way, because they are committed to an actual, not a potential infinite. That this was Plato's view appears clearly from the *Physics* discussion and the care Aristotle takes to insist that on his interpretation the numbers that go on for ever are *not* 'separate' from the process of adding. Presumably this is why he takes care here to insist that the dilemma holds against those who do make number 'separate'. Because of their platonism, the Academy can only understand the infinite continuation of the number-series as the existence of an actual infinity of numbers, and so they have either to answer the question what sort of number this infinity has, or to accept that the number series is finite.

(a) ᵃ2-7. If the platonist accepts the existence of an actual infinity of numbers, then he faces two problems in claiming that there is a number of that infinity, i.e. an infinite number.

(i) Any number is odd or even, but the infinite number is neither. Why? Aristotle does not give a reason for this, but he adds, presumably as support, the fact that the Platonist generation of numbers is always the generation of an odd or even number. (See Introduction, pp. 52-3.) He thus shows that the

Platonists have no way of showing that the infinite number is either odd or even. However, is this not to assume the point at issue, namely that the infinite number is neither? Why should we not identify the infinite number with one of the odd or even numbers produced? Aristotle does not say, but he would probably think himself entitled to refuse to do this in the absence of a Platonist proof that any number produced was the number of all the numbers. Of course a Platonist could insist that if there is an actual infinity of numbers then there is an infinite number of that plurality, whether or not *we* can show it to be odd or even. Aristotle would probably reject the notion of a number that we could never construct as unintelligible. This is to some extent a matter of temperament; other philosophers have been convinced that there is an infinite number, and that our inability to make sense of it (since we could never show it to be odd or even, i.e. what we mean by 'number') should merely lead us to marvel at the ineffability of infinity (see Pascal, *Pensées*, Everyman ed., p. 343).

(ii) ª7-10. If numbers are Forms then the infinite number will be the Form of something. But whether it is taken to be the Form of perceptible items or items of another kind, this contradicts the Platonists' understanding of the theory of Forms as well as what is reasonable. (This is clearly the general drift, though the last sentence, and the reference to arranging Forms, are unclear to me.) Presumably what is unfortunate for a Platonist is the fact that such a Form would be a Form of an infinite plurality; but the idea of a Form of what is infinite conflicts with the notion that a Form is essentially a principle of limit and finitude. At *Philebus* 16d-e Plato apparently says that it is only when we cease to consider a thing as an instance of a Form, and attend to its individual peculiarities, that we are 'letting it go into the infinite'.

(b) ª10-b2. The idea that the number-series only goes as far as a certain point, and then stops, is obviously bizarre, and should figure only as an obviously unacceptable alternative to the assumption (a). Aristotle, however, uses the opportunity to list some objections to the claim that the Platonist number-series stopped at 10. These are not strictly appropriate (see the Introduction, pp. 54-5), and are disproportionately long.

(i) ª12-17. If Forms are to be identified with numbers, then there must be more than ten numbers because there are more than ten Forms. This argument is often produced as evidence that Plato did in fact identify Forms with numbers, but is surely rather a rudely debunking interpretation of what Plato said and omitted to say about numbers, expressly intended to produce absurdities (as is true of all the arguments in this set). If Aristotle were reporting Plato's own words, he would not have had to make up his own examples (contrast l. 14 with l. 25). There is a problem with 'in these' (l. 16). If this just means 'among the numbers 1-10' it is hard to see the force of 'but . . . still'. Ross suggests that Aristotle means also to refer to the numbers in the numbers 1-10 (e.g. the 2 and 3 in 4, the 2, 3, and 4 in 5, etc.). The trouble with this is that it is incoherent to suppose that there are only ten numbers, but that these numbers, which are all that there are, also contain more numbers. However, Aristotle is probably scrutinizing all possibilities, whether or not they are absurd on the Platonist premises; so he probably is suggesting that the numbers 1-10 will soon run out, even if we stretch the list a bit by adding the numbers that these numbers contain.

(ii) ª18-21. Aristotle here argues: If Three is Man (the Form of Man), then every three is Man, for all threes are similar—that is, there is no relevant difference which would make it reasonable for one (or more) three to be Man while the others are not. (This interpretation of the words in brackets seems to me more plausible than the idea that Aristotle is still talking about the numbers in the numbers 1-10, for there are not infinitely many of these. This does have the consequence that this argument does not really address itself to the limitation of numbers to 10). If every three is Man, then there are infinitely many men (since there are infinitely many threes). Further, if every three is Man, then each man will be Man, i.e. the Form of Man. If not, there will still be infinitely many men. This argument shows ingenuity, which is somewhat misplaced, since a Platonist would simply refuse to admit that the Form of Man, which is unique, could be identified with a three which was repeatable. He would accuse Aristotle of confusing the unique Form number Three with repeatable mathematical threes.

(iii) ª21-5. Another absurdity easily got from identifying Forms with numbers; the example is again Aristotle's own (cf. 1.14).

(iv) ª25-7. This is true enough, but does not imply that Plato explicitly denied that Form numbers went beyond 10, merely that he did not see the necessity for some kind of theoretical account of the fact that they did so.

(v) ª27-9. This is clearly out of place, and belongs in chapter 5. Displacement is not very surprising, considering the state of this section. Ross makes it relevant by taking 'Forms' to mean 'Form numbers', but this is surely wrong, for there is no warning of this, and the parallel at 1080ª2-8 tells against it.

(vi) ª29-b2. Aristotle here criticizes the way that the Platonists talk of 'the dekad' and its properties, thereby adding another objectionable item to their overcrowded supersensible universe. He also complains that although they claim that it is 'complete' they do not in fact have any rational grounds for treating it as a unitary object. He sketches their grounds for calling it complete in a way which seems designed to make them sound silly and arbitary, and clearly insufficient to establish the dekad as a genuinely interesting mathematical object. A long fragment of Speusippus (fr. 4 Lang) defends respect for the dekad because of the many interesting mathematical facts that are exemplified within it. Either Aristotle wrote this criticism before Speusippus wrote his fragment 4, or else he regards Speusippus' reasons as mere rationalizations—rightly, since this stress on the dekad is mathematically sterile and is surely due to pre-mathematical intuitions that make 10-based counting systems common and 'natural'.

Aristotle's references to the Platonists' grounds for the completeness of the dekad are tantalizingly half-informative, probably because they are designed to suggest mere silliness. The void seems to have been elucidated by the 'space' between numbers, or perhaps by the 'gap' in the middle of even numbers when these are represented as two rows of units with no unit in the middle to 'stop' the infinitely progressing series. (Cf. *Physics* 213^{b}27, where Aristotle is talking about the Pythagoreans.) Theophrastus (*Metaphysics* 6^{a}25-^{b}3) says that space, the void, and the infinite were derived from the indefinite two alone without one. One on its own produced, among other things, soul; this suggests that this is not a rational or even rationalized mathematical project, but more like a fanciful assignment of various things to the principles on a mystical basis. Proportion is introduced in a more sophisticated way: examples can be found within the dekad of the three most important types of proportion, arithmetic (1, 2, 3), geometric (2, 4, 8) and harmonic (2, 3, 6). Speusippus in his fragment 4 points out more of the same sort of fact. For the connection of one with the odd, see the Introduction, pp. 49-51. We have scrappy evidence for the identification of the principles with the contrasts of good/bad and rest/motion (change). (Cf. Eudemus (Gaiser(1), pp. 536-7, and 988^{a}14-15.) However, we know very little about the sort of 'derivation within the dekad' hinted at in this passage. From these remarks of Aristotle's it would seem that this is just as well.

The last sentence is obscure and textually difficult. The 'first indivisible line' seems to be Plato's way of describing the point (see Introduction, pp. 25-6). Aristotle appears to be referring to a further way of taking the dekad as complete: identification of the series 1-2-3-4 with that of point-line-plane-solid. This goes with representing the dekad in the form of a 'tetraktys', i.e.

```
        *
      *   *
    *   *   *
  *   *   *   *
```

a Pythagorean idea which figures in Speusippus' discussion of the dekad, but obviously has little to do with the ordinary use of the numbers 1-10. It is quite probable that Plato's ideas about the generation of numbers and geometrical objects made some contact with this kind of Pythagorean fantasy, but we have no good evidence that this contact was anything but incidental; Plato would naturally see here foreshadowings of the systematic ideas he was trying to present.

1084^{b}2-32: This is a long and comparatively well-worked-out criticism designed to show a basic error in the Academy's way of deriving number. By tracing the error to its roots, Aristotle hopes to remove the need to be puzzled by the apparent problems it engenders. The first question, whether one is prior to number or vice versa, leads naturally into a wider discussion of the way in which one can be said to be a principle of number. The discussion illustrates clearly the confusions in the Platonists' conception of their one. Since these are easy to make in Greek, where *to hen* covers 'one', 'the one', and 'unity', it is the more to Aristotle's credit that he distinguishes two logically different things the Platonists were trying to say by means of an expression which for him as well as for them was undifferentiated between them.

Aristotle begins by remarking that the ones or units of which a number is made up stand to the number, in his own terms, as matter to form. So, 'Which comes first?' cannot be answered as it stands; it depends on the point of view from which it is asked. In one sense the ones or units come first, because the number results from adding them. But in another sense the number comes first, since we can definitely identify a group of units only by knowing how many of them there are; it is their number that identifies a group of units as a group of so many *units*. Aristotle is thus saying that the Platonists went wrong through failing to distinguish two senses in which the question can be answered, and trying to make their one prior in both at once. The Platonist one has to be one in the sense of being the matter, the ones or units out of which a number is made, and also by being the form, the formal unity of a set of units. So it has to be form *and* matter in the same way at the same time; but this is an incoherent demand, and the concept of the Platonist one is built on a confusion.

Aristotle somewhat complicates this straightforward line of thought by developing, without clearly distinguishing it, the further idea that of these two senses one, that of form, has a *better* claim to be prior than the other. He uses the example of right and acute angles as a case where of two things A and B, A is prior in the sense of form and B in the sense of matter, and A is prior in a more basic sense than B. (The same example is used in *Z* chapters 10 and 11, where the form/matter distinction is used in a discussion of the ways in which the definitions of parts are parts of a definition of the whole.) Acute angles can be regarded as the matter of right angles, since they are what a right angle is 'made up of' and can be 'divided into'; they are prior in the way materials are prior to a finished object. A right angle, however, is presupposed in the definition of an acute angle, whereas its own definition is independent of that of an acute angle, and it is 'determinate' (a right angle is 90°, an acute angle is simply *any* angle between 0° and 90°); so it is prior in the sense of form. This example shows that the form/matter contrast does not apply particularly well to mathematical ideas. The characterization of angles as matter relies on a not very appropriate metaphor, and its weakness is shown even more clearly by the impossibility of applying this example with any clarity to the point that one is prior to number in the two senses of form and matter.

At ll. 20-3 Aristotle supports the claim of formal priority in another way. Form is actuality; a number does actually have a formal principle of unity. Matter is rather the range of a thing's potentialities; so to say that there are 3 units is just to say that we *can* count that unit three times. Units do not have actual existence; their existence is merely potential and is dependent on our actually counting. So, since for Aristotle what is actual is always prior to what is merely potential, the existence of the number as a unity is prior to the existence of the units in it. There has to be a number with the formal properties of 3 for us to be able to count up to 3 and so actualize 3 units. Here again Aristotle's philosophical terminology is somewhat unilluminating when applied to numbers and units.

^b15: Ross in his note argues convincingly that the ellipse should be supplied as in the translation. One would suppose at first reading that the point is that universal, particular, and element are *indivisible* in different ways. But, as Ross argues, no good sense can be given to 'indivisible in time', which this reading produces.

^b25-8: Aristotle may mean that the Platonists treated units as matter of numbers in the way they treated points as matter of lines; or he may mean that in thinking of units as the matter of number they were succumbing to the temptation to think of a number as made up of units in a crude way as though units were groups of mysteriously disembodied points. Either way he is implying that a platonist conception produces an inappropriate and misleading model.

^b24 ff.: Aristotle ought to be saying: (i) as mathematicians, the Platonists were concerned with units, and also (ii) as philosophers, with the formal unity of numbers, but since they combined the two viewpoints they produced a confused hybrid of both conceptions, namely their one. But in fact he complicates matters by putting a confusion into both arms, so that his point comes out in the following way: (i) as mathematicians, what they made prior was the unit (though looked at another way this is really not prior but the reverse, what is prior being the formal unity of the number), and (ii) as philosophers, they were interested in the formal unity of a number (but also treated it as if it were a part of the number, i.e. a unit). In both cases their one had to be both form and matter, though in fact it cannot be both. Aristotle has somewhat spoiled his point here, since what he is claiming is that the Academy were similarly confused from *both* viewpoints, whereas the 'cause of their error' as it appeared from l. 23, seemed to be the illicit combination of two independently unobjectionable viewpoints. Compare 992^a32 for Aristotle's complaint that philosophy in the Academy has become mathematics, which he regards as a serious confusion.

1084^b32–1085^a1: This and the following two arguments seem to be preliminary versions of arguments elsewhere, and are all crabbed and obscure. This one attempts to show that for the Academy the units in 2 must be prior to 2, thus creating embarrassment for their claim to have a rational theory of number, in which 2 should follow 1. The argument is obscure, however. If the first one differs from the other ones or units merely in being a first principle, then the units in 2, say, will be more like it than they are like 2, and so they will be prior to 2. What could be meant by 'more like' here is quite opaque. According to the MSS., what makes the original one different is that it is 'without position', but this makes the argument even more obscure. None of the proposed alterations is very convincing. It does not seem as though any emendation could redeem the argument, which looks like a vague and unsatisfactory version of the kind of argument at 1081ª17-ᵇ33, to the effect that, if units are produced in a series, this will interfere with the production of the number-series in the proper way. Cf. (a) and (d) in particular.

1085ª1-2: This looks like a sketch for the argument at 1082ᵇ11-16, which is framed more sharply and effectively.

1085ª3-7: Another sketch rather like the first of these three arguments; perhaps an embryonic form of the argument at 1081ᵇ6-8.

1085ª7-ᵇ4: A quite unconnected topic begins, that of the Academy's account of geometrical objects and the production of objects in each of the three dimensions. Most of these arguments have occurred already in the section of *A* 9 (991ᵇ9–993ª10) replaced by *M-N*. They show remarkable lack of development in comparison with the arguments about units, which have developed in precision and scope.

1085ª9-20: This answers to 992ª10-19, where, however, Aristotle talks not of producing objects from the principles but of reducing objects to the principles. This seems to make no important difference, suggesting that the distinction between the 'way up' and the 'way down' from the principles was perhaps not so important as some modern theories about the unwritten doctrines imply.

The objection is the same in both places: the Academy account of the generation of geometrical objects misrepresents the relation between dimensions. If lines, planes, and solids are produced from different versions of the great and small as their matter, there are two possibilities, both objectionable. If the matters for the different dimensions are themselves different, then objects in one dimension will be generically different from objects in another, and there will be no connection between them; but this is absurd in view of mathematical practice. But if they are merely more determinate specifications of what is one and the same matter, then lines, planes, and solids will all be the same sort of thing. The Academy cannot stop the relation between the dimensions from becoming too tight or too loose. This brings out well that the notions of form and matter (which are what are involved here, even if the Academy did not use the actual words) are completely unfitted to express the production of geometrical objects, and obscure the fact that the relation between dimensions is neither that of genus to species nor that of exclusive genera.

In the *A* 9 passage Aristotle adds the point that numbers are also supposed to come from the great and small, but do not seem to fit into the scheme at all. Here he omits this, because he is concentrating on geometrical objects, but adds the point that there is dispute over the formal principle as well as the material one (this is developed at 1085ª31 ff.), and that necessary details like angles are unprovided for in the Academy's unsuitable conceptual scheme.

1085ª20-3: This corresponds to 992ᵇ1-9, and Aristotle recurs to the point again at 1088ª17-21. He accuses the Academy of taking the various forms of the great and small to be what numbers and magnitudes are made from, whereas they are in fact attributes that numbers and magnitudes have. The Platonists, however, probably did not claim in so many words that numbers and magnitudes were made out of the various forms of the great and small. It is likely that Aristotle is taking this to be a consequence of their account in terms of 'generation' or production, and that he is, as usual, insisting on taking Platonist terms in their straightforward and literal sense.

1085ª23-31: An apparently intrusive point. If one believes in the real existence of universals, as platonists do, then one has to accept that the Form (assumed here to function as a universal) is present in its instances. But how can Animal, or One, be present in many instances? This point appears to have nothing to do with geometrical objects, or indeed with the topic of *M-N* at all, in spite of the example of one. It is possible that this argument is merely out of place (cf. 1084ª29-9). However, it is just possible that there is in fact a connection with the present context, though it is not actually drawn. For a platonist, the genus, 'great and small' will have to have actual existence in each of its kinds, 'broad and narrow', etc. That is, for a platonist 'broad and narrow' should directly imply 'great and small', which it obviously does not. This point would be linked with the previous point that the Academy can give no coherent account of the relation between the dimensions, and leave it conveniently unexplained. Aristotle himself avoids this problem by taking the genus to have merely potential existence in its species. This interpretation has difficulty with the example of one, for numbers are not species of the genus one; but the example of Animal supports it. It is probable, considering the state of this section, that the argument as we have it is not complete.

1085ª31-ᵇ4: This repeats the earlier argument at ª7-20, but with a different point, for Aristotle appeals not just to the unsatisfactory Academy relation between the matters of the different dimensions, but the more general principle that things which come from the same principles or elements and are not differentiated are identical. Aristotle uses this form of argument elsewhere, chiefly to prove that Plato must identify Forms and numbers (see Introduction, pp. 64-8). All that are added here are some remarks on the variant modes of generation. The person who tried to generate geometrical objects from the point and a sort of pseudo-plurality is generally thought to be Speusippus; the next few arguments are all directed against him.

1085ᵇ4-34: These arguments are all aimed at theories generally agreed to be those of Speusippus. They all claim to show that his variations on Plato's theories not only do not successfully evade the original problems, but actually add more of their own. One criticism surprisingly absent here, though it would have come in well after the last few arguments, is the complaint that Speusippus, in producing objects of different dimensions from quite separate matters, makes his universe a mere series of episodes, like a bad tragedy. This criticism appears later, in a less appropriate place (1090ᵇ19-20) as well as in Λ (1075 ᵇ37–1076ª3).

1085ᵇ4-12: Aristotle is not necessarily claiming that Speusippus said nothing on the subject, merely that he has no independent rationale for his theory, which is just a way of trying to avoid the problems attaching to the indefinite two. We do not know who 'some' are who generated number from 'a particular plurality'; probably the reference is to informal Academy discussions. Since two is the first example of plurality, this view clearly collapses into the original theory employing two. (Aristotle is simplifying matters by understanding the indefinite two as just a kind of two.) Plurality in general is Speusippus' own candidate to replace the indefinite two. Aristotle claims that this alternative inherits all the problems facing Plato, and in the next section adds an objection peculiar to Speusippus.

1085^{b}12-23: Here Aristotle claims that no coherent account is possible of how units come from one and plurality. He succeeds in proving this, but one can suspect that perhaps Speusippus did not claim to derive *units* from one and plurality, only *numbers*. It is a pity that we do not know what exactly Speusippus said, but in view of the arguments above, at 1083^{b}23-36, to show that Plato cannot coherently derive units from his principles, it seems unlikely that either Plato or Speusippus had said anything definite on this topic; otherwise Aristotle would hardly produce a priori arguments to show that it must be impossible.

The argument plays on the difficulty in seeing how plurality could contribute anything towards the formation of a unit, since a unit is precisely what cannot be pluralized; so it seems that plurality cannot be a factor in the production of units. One way out of this is to say that it can, in the sense that a unit is a definite and indivisible part of a plurality; so units can be analysed as one and *part* of plurality. Aristotle rejects this on two grounds. Firstly, it leaves out what we want to know, namely how plurality, not parts of it, can figure in the analysis of a unit. Secondly, since 'a plurality of indivisible parts' is just what is meant by number, the account imports 'another number', i.e. it is circular. This at first seems puzzling. What is circular in using number to define unit? Perhaps Aristotle has become confused about the object of his criticism. But the argument would have force if Speusippus had *defined* number in terms of units, as plurality of indivisible parts; for it *would* then be circular to define the units in terms of the plurality of indivisible parts which is the number. Unfortunately we do not know if Speusippus did this or not.

1085^{b}23-7: This is introduced as though parallel to the criticism of Plato's theory at 1083^{b}36 ff., but is in fact quite different. Aristotle is drawing a distinction probably not found in his opponent's account, and demanding that he commit himself to one or other of the alternatives. He does not here, however, add any arguments to show that the option of 'infinite plurality' is objectionable. By this is presumably meant 'bare plurality', the indeterminate possibility of taking more. 'Finite plurality' presumably refers to plurality in the sense of a determinate plurality of units, as in the last argument, which then serves to point out the objection to this option. If so, the status of this argument depends directly on that of the last, since if Speusippus did not accept such 'finite plurality' they are both ill-directed.

1085^{b}27-34: A problem proprietary to Speusippus' generation of the geometrical magnitudes. If the formal principle is the point, how it is legitimate to talk as though there were more than one point? Aristotle derisively suggests that points could be produced from the original point and a sort of indefinite distance; but anyway this would not be parallel to the production of units, because magnitudes are not made up of indivisible parts as numbers are. Aristotle here seems to be complaining that this theory of Speusippus violates mathematical usage; but since he has said that Speusippus treats mathematical objects in a way appropriate to mathematics this must be uncharacteristic. Perhaps Speusippus had made unfortunate remarks about 'the point'.

1085^{b}34–1086^{a}21: A summing-up, ending with a quotation as Aristotle's lectures often do. This conclusion is surprising at the end of a rough and untidy section, and may be an all-purpose summing-up used at the end of some versions of M or parts of it. It is quite a good conclusion to a course on the troubles that arise with the Academy's theories of number. Different members of the Academy are said to be right on some points, but Aristotle stresses his repeated theme that the Academy's theories are wrong in fundamentals, and that the right way to challenge them is to criticize their initial assumptions.

There is a problem about the points which Aristotle accepts as correct in the Academy. Plato is right to keep Forms and numbers separate; Speusippus is right to reject Forms; Xenocrates is right to identify Forms and numbers on the ground that both come from the same principles without differentiation. How can Plato and Xenocrates both be right? Either Aristotle is writing carelessly, or he means that both were right to accept their conclusions *given their premises*, since Xenocrates is thinking of Forms and numbers in the context of the principles, not in the context of Plato's original arguments.

CHAPTER 9, 1086^{a}21–end

There is a very abrupt break, and this section returns to the programme of chapter 1, but also effects the transition to the 'third inquiry' mentioned there. See the Introduction, p. 81-88, for a discussion of Jaeger's theories about the structure of M-N, based on the prominence of this break. The first sentence is abrupt and should be taken with the last sentence of the previous section; Aristotle, having finished with numbers (the second inquiry) now goes on to principles and causes (the third inquiry). The topic is not taken up at once, however, and the rest of M is something of a parenthesis before the third inquiry is taken up in N.

Chapter 9 harks back to chapter 1 in its terms of reference: thus the third inquiry is represented as being whether numbers and Forms are themselves the promised 'causes' (the formulation in chapter 1). Chapter 9, however, also mentions the principles of Forms and numbers, and it is these principles which in fact receive most attention in N. Because chapter 9 returns to the same ground as chapter 1, Jaeger took it to be an (earlier) doublet of chapter 1, and found evidence for this in the fact that, while both refer to the *Physics*, only chapter 1 refers to the (later) *Metaphysics* ZHΘ. But chapter 9 does not repeat what was said in chapter 1; chapter 1 classifies types of platonism, whereas chapter 9 begins by emphasizing the third inquiry, namely the inquiry into principles and elements. The references to the *Physics* are also in fact different. In chapter 1 Aristotle refers to the *Physics* and ZHΘ for a discussion of the matter and form of physical objects as opposed to abstract objects. In chapter 9 the reference is to the *Physics* discussion of principles and causes of physical objects, and ZHΘ is not relevant.

The reference to people who posit only mathematical numbers (and treat them as causes), i.e. to Speusippus, is taken up in *N* at 1090ᵃ2 ff., and 1092ᵇ8 ff. Aristotle does not deal with Forms as causes in *N*; his arguments against them in this role are to be found in *M* 5, no doubt because the material in *M* 4-5 has been taken over wholesale from *A* 9. This means that there is a gap here, and it is perhaps because of this that Aristotle here launches a short digression on Forms. It refers back to the *M* 4 discussion, but is not a doublet of it (the reference to Socrates, for example, could hardly be understood except as a reference to a previous discussion), and the whole argument is designed not, as before, to describe the theory of Forms, but rather to subject it to lethal criticism, by showing that its very formulation involves a contradiction. Drawing on the materials of his discussion in chapter 4, Aristotle claims that the two intellectual antecedents he there posited for the theory (the flux argument and Socrates' search for definitions) together lead to a self-contradictory search for items which are *both* universals *and* particulars. This short dismissal of Forms is characteristic of *M-N*, where Aristotle has little time for them. The faults in Aristotle's criticism here lie not in the form of his argument, but in the premise on which it is based, namely, that his discussion in chapter 4 gives a sound analysis of the intellectual motivation behind the theory of Forms.

CHAPTER 10

This chapter is a separate discussion. Aristotle examines a problem which confronts not only the Academy but also himself; he had discussed the difficulty (without offering a solution) in Book *B* (1003ᵃ5-17, the twelfth problem; cf. also the ninth problem, 999ᵇ24−1000ᵃ4). In the twelfth problem, the dilemma was as follows: if first principles and elements are universals, they will not be real objects, since a real object is always individual, a 'this' and not a 'such'. But if they are individuals, there can be no knowledge of them, for knowledge always requires a universal. The problem as stated here is not exactly the same; it is that if real objects are such as to have separate existence, their principles cannot, apparently, be either universal or individual. The two problems come down to the same difficulty; however: if a certain class of items is taken to be basic, and to have favoured ontological status, then if these basic items are particulars, there is a difficulty if they have to have principles or elements into which they can be analysed, and which are therefore in some sense more basic than they are. Aristotle here sets up the apparent dilemma arising when one tries to characterize the elements of one's basic particulars, whether the latter are Forms, as for Plato, or, as for him, living organic individuals.

If the elements are individuals (option (a)) then (i) each will be a mere 'this' and not a 'such' of any kind; being one in number it will not be the same in kind as anything else (it will not 'share its name'; cf. the ninth problem in *B*). They will thus be bare particulars; general terms will not properly apply to them, and (though Aristotle does not draw this conclusion) they will strictly be referents only of logically proper names. (This raises many interesting issues over the semantics of the theory of Forms and what Plato took them to be; but there is no scope to develop these here.) The sentence in brackets is odd, but probably refers to Forms, considered as the principles of the things they are Forms of; Aristotle points out that the Platonists do actually say that the Form is unique in each case, and this confirms his *a priori* argument that the principle or element in each case must be unique.

(ii) The elements will not be knowable. This is an obvious extension from the last point; knowledge involves more than just apprehension of an individual as an individual, but requires a universal. We might expect Aristotle to give as his example knowledge of general concepts, such as redness, as opposed to perception of red objects; but in fact he gives examples of connections between concepts, e.g. between being a triangle and having angles equal to two right angles. These examples suggest that by knowledge Aristotle has in mind predominantly what is (1) knowledge of what *must* be the case, not what contingently happens to be the case and (2) knowledge of connections or inferences. This raises problems with his solution of the problem of how individuals can after all be knowable (see below).

The second half of the dilemma (option (b)) is dealt with more quickly. If the principles of basic particulars are universals, then either universals will be more basic than particulars, or basic particulars will have principles that are less basic than they are. (cf. 1038^b34–1039^a3.) Aristotle regards both alternatives as obviously unacceptable both to himself and to a Platonist.

Aristotle sums up the problem at 1087^a4-7, and characteristically draws a distinction which enables us to see that the difficulty is only apparent and that the dilemma can thus be overcome. It is the first horn that he tries to break. According to him the trouble lies in accepting the platonist premise that over and above the individuals sharing a common form there is a separate extra entity, the Form. The Platonists assume that the only satisfactory way to explain the fact that things share a common form and common name is to posit another thing over and above them, the Form. But if one accepts that a separate Form is necessary to explain this fact, then one is in a dilemma: one's basic particulars cannot have principles or elements. This is true both for the Platonist, whose basic particulars are Forms, and for the Aristotelian, whose basic particulars are living organic individuals. (Hence the problem is carefully presented as one shared by Plato and Aristotle alike.) If one's basic particulars are Forms, then any attempt to give them principles will fail, because it can only result in manufacturing more Forms. For Forms to have principles they must have something in common; but then all we can bring in to account for this is another Form, and we never get beyond Forms. But on the other hand, even if one rejects Forms as ontologically basic, still, as long as one retains the platonist assumption that a shared common form of individuals implies a separate Form, one can give no coherent account of the principles or elements or one's basic particulars as being either universals or individuals.

Aristotle tries to show, though not in much detail, that this result is not inevitable; if we reject the platonist assumption then there can be elements of basic particulars without their being Forms.

(1) Things can be one in kind and share a common form without there being an extra entity over and above them to explain the fact of their sharing a common form. There can be many elements or letters of the same kind, e.g. many As, without this implying either that there is a Form of A or a mysterious universal A. Tokens can be tokens of the same type without this leading to the manufacture of an exalted status for the type over and above its tokens and separate and independent of them. It is wrong to assume that things cannot share a common form without there being another thing to explain this.

The ideas in this passage are of great interest as regards Aristotle's theory of form. Here he seems to agree that basic particulars (individual men, horses, etc.) can have forms, as long as these are not taken to be separate from the things they are the forms of, like Platonic Forms; and further, these forms can be regarded as first principles of the individuals they are the forms of, and are individuals. The first point is familiar from Aristotle's writings elsewhere, and the second is familiar also in the idea that forms provide a type of explanation or 'formal cause'. The claim that these non-separable forms are nevertheless individuals enables Aristotle to escape from the present dilemma, but it presents difficulties. Firstly, how can such non-separable individual forms be *elements* of their particulars? (Aristotle might avoid this problem, if we can take his words at a 4-5 to imply that it is wrong to think of forms as being elements at all; but as they stand his words apply only to Platonic Forms.) Secondly, how can this passage be reconciled with Aristotle's insistence elsewhere that what is individual has separate existence? The problems raised here go beyond the scope of this commentary, but it is at any rate clear that this passage is not a final and considered treatment of the difficulties facing Aristotle's theory of form.

(2) The problem that if the elements are individual they will not be knowable is solved in a way which is meant to establish that there can in a sense be

knowledge of individuals. Aristotle appeals to his distinction between actuality and potentiality: knowledge of the universal is merely potential, and is only actualized when individuals are brought into the picture. To have knowledge of A is to be able to recognize particular shapes as being examples of A; only when faced by some such shape is the grammarian *actually* knowing an A. Aristotle's discussion and examples are reminiscent of his discussion at *de Anima* 417^{a}21 ff.

Aristotle apparently wants to say that since there is a sense in which knowledge is of individuals, we do not have to say that the elements or first principles are unknowable if they are individuals. But it is not clear that establishing that individuals are knowable in this sense can solve the problem Aristotle has presented. I shall mention only two problems raised by this tantalizing passage.

(1) Aristotle has established that I can know an individual token A in that my recognition of it *as* an A is an actualization of my knowledge of the (type) A. But are we entitled to call this simple recognition an instance of *knowledge* at all? Aristotle's examples which indicated that knowledge must be of universals (1086^{b}34-7) involved reasoning and connections between concepts, not the mere recognition of instances of a single concept. Further, the paradigms of knowledge offered there seemed to be instances of necessary truth, whereas 'this is an A' is a simple matter of fact. The examples in terms of which Aristotle offers his solution are so different from those he employs in setting the problem that he seems unclear about what the conditions for knowledge are to be.

(2) It is not clear how Aristotle's answer to the problem of how the elements or first principles are knowable can be reconciled with his claim that they are individuals (though not with separate existence, like Platonic Forms). Aristotle has shown that there is *a* sense in which there is knowledge of individuals, namely, in the sense in which the individual is known by the actualization of the (merely potential) knowledge of the universal. But if we apply this to knowledge of the first principles or elements, we find that these do after all have universals prior to them in some way (since knowledge of them is necessary for there to be knowledge of the elements), and we seem to be back with the second horn of the original dilemma. Thus, although what Aristotle says here does not contradict his often-repeated claim that knowledge is of the universal, neither could it be said to solve the present problem.

Jaeger claims that in this argument Aristotle's use of the words 'reality as we want to describe it' show that Aristotle is speaking as a Platonist, that the argument applies only to Platonists who 'presuppose Plato's conception of substance', and that the result is to distinguish two kinds of Platonist, those who accept the theory of Forms and those like Aristotle who do not. Jaeger puts some weight on this conclusion in his dating of *M* 9-10. Neither of his claims holds, however. Aristotle's use of the first person does not prove that he is speaking as a Platonist; he might as well be arguing from his own independent standpoint. But in fact 'we' here must cover all parties to the discussion, Platonists and non-Platonists, or the argument loses all force. Jaeger also claims that 'reality' here must be suprasensible reality, or the following words, 'and in the way in which individual existing things are said to be separate' 'would be meaningless' (i.e., presumably, uselessly tautologous). However, 'and' in Greek (*kai*) has a well-established use not to introduce a new point but to amplify what goes before (that is why I have not translated it). What follows the 'and' cannot contrast with the platonist's view, or the argument would fall apart; but it might well amplify a notion of separate existence which Aristotle and Plato *share*. Only so does the argument do what it is supposed to do. Jaeger claims that if we do not understand the objects under discussion to be Platonic Forms, we shall miss the point of the dilemma, because only so will 'reality as we *Platonists* understand it' be destroyed. But Aristotle explicitly says that this argument applies both to those who accept Forms and to those who do not.

On elements and letters, see notes on 1088ᵇ14-35.

BOOK *N*

N contains many striking parallels with *Metaphysics* Λ. Many themes treated in *N* also turn up in Λ: rejection of two contraries as first principles, a theory of three first principles, and a discussion of the sense in which not-being is a principle (Λ chapter 2); insistence that the universal causes do not really exist in the way individuals do (chapter 5); discussion of first principles and the good (chapters 7 and 10). There are also parallels in detail: compare Λ 1072^{b}30–1073^{a}3 with *N* 1092^{a}11-17; Λ 1075^{b}13-14 with *N* 1088^{b}14-16; Λ 1075^{b}37–1076^{a}4 with *N* 1090^{b}13-20; Λ 1075^{a}34-6 with *N* 1091^{b}35-7; Λ 1075^{b}1-11 with *N* 1091^{b}11-12; Λ 1075^{a}28-34 with *N* 1087^{a}29-^{b}4.

I do not think however, that this suffices to show that *N* as it stands is an independent treatise, as has been claimed. Aristotle seems to be quarrying the same materials for criticisms of other (*N*) and for his own constructive account (Λ). Moreover, Λ contains one parallel with *M* also (compare Λ 1069^{a}33-6 with 1076^{a}19-22). And *N* contains parallels with, and affinities to, other treatises (*Categories, Metaphysics* I and Θ, *Physics* I, *de Caelo*).

CHAPTER 1

This chapter falls into three parts (each of which assumes acquaintance with other parts of Aristotle's work). Aristotle criticizes systematically first the Academy's account of the opposition between the first principles from which they derive mathematical objects, then their account of each of the principles in turn.

1087^{a}29-^{b}33. The opposition of the two principles

1087^{a}29-^{b}4: Aristotle's point here is not complicated, but it is made hard to follow by the broken course of the argument and the difficulty of grasping what is meant by key phrases, especially 'as being something else'. Greek permits a compression here which is inevitably cryptic in English, but to bring out the meaning more fully would involve paraphrase rather than translation.

The contrast drawn between just being ϕ and being ϕ as being something else is the contrast between being a subject of attributes and being attributed of a subject. 'White' does not pick out something which is a subject of attributes in its own right; there is not just white, but white *things*, so a thing is white as being something else (an object of some kind). Aristotle's point here is that the Platonists say that their principles are contraries, but this implies a contradiction, for contraries are attributed to a subject underlying them and are not themselves subjects, whereas principles have to be subjects not attributable to any further subject.

The course of the argument is broken up by the two points I have put in brackets. The first is illustrative, and is merely unfortunately placed; the second is a different argument and is out of place. Here I set out the stages of the argument with comments.

(a) ª29-31. The principles of unchanging as well as changing objects (and so of Forms and numbers) are taken to be contraries. By 'everybody' Aristotle means not the man in the street but previous philosophers who have put forward schemes of explanation of the nature of things. He implies that the Academy have come to give their principles a role like that of the fundamental opposites in Presocratic cosmologies.

(b) ª31-2. The principle of everything cannot have anything prior to it. The Academy's principles were designed to be the ultimate terms of explanation by which all kinds of existing items were to be explained.

(c) ª32-6. A subject of an attribute is prior to an attribute, so since there is nothing prior to the principle of everything it cannot be the attribute of any subject. An item like white presupposes *things* that are white; the fact that one can talk about white on its own without overtly mentioning things that are white does not remove the fact that the white things are prior to the white which is attributed to them.

(d)ª36-ᵇ2. Contraries, however, are prime examples of items which are attributes of a subject and not themselves subjects. Aristotle here appeals to his analysis of change in the *Physics*, book 1. Change is always between contraries: a thing changes from F to not-F or not-F to F, but this change implies an underlying subject which remains through the change. A change from being green to being red is properly to be spelt out as change from being a green *apple* (leaf, plum, etc.) to being a red *apple*, etc. There is always a *subject* of the change, and the contraries presuppose it because it is the subject which changes from one contrary to the other. Presumably Aristotle says that contraries are the best examples of items that presuppose an underlying subject which are not themselves subjects, because of his own lengthy demonstration in *Physics* book 1.

(e) ᵇ3-4. So whatever the principle of everything may be, it is not a contrary. So the supposed Academy principles cannot in fact be the ultimate principles of things, since they are contraries.

Two points about this argument:

(i) It applies to the Academy's principles only in so far as they were taken to be contraries, and so only under some of their descriptions—equal/unequal, same/other, etc. The argument does not apply to them when described as one and the indefinite two, for example. Aristotle will shortly complain that under some of their descriptions they are not proper contraries even for the Academy.

(ii) The argument might seem to be making an unjustified equation of logical and ontological priority. Surely the priority of subject to attribute is language-relative, whereas the Academy were concerned with substantial metaphysics? Aristotle, however, regards the subject/attribute distinction as itself a fact of some metaphysical importance, which language reflects and does not create.

194

The Academy are not just using unfortunate expressions but getting things ontologically backwards.

The short argument at 1087^{b}1-2 that breaks the line of thought has to be filled out by reference to the *Physics* at 189^{a}32-3 (perhaps that is why it is in its present unsuitable position, by attraction to the reference to the *Physics* in the main argument). A real object has no contrary (neither Socrates nor man has a contrary—cf. *Categories* 3^{b}24-7). So contraries cannot be real objects. So real objects cannot come from contraries, or real objects would come from objects with less claim than they to reality.

1087^{b}4-12: In claiming that the Academy make one of the principles matter (cf. 987^{b}18-20) Aristotle does not necessarily mean that the Academy explicitly used the terms 'form' and 'matter', but that he is judging them to have attempted unsuccessfully with their two principles to do the job that Aristotelian form and matter do successfully. Much of the criticism in the last third of this chapter, and chapter 2, consists of pointing this out in various ways. (cf. *Physics* 187^{a}12-20, 189^{b}8-16, 191^{b}35-192^{a}25, for more of this sort of criticism.)

Aristotle here distinguishes Plato, who derives numbers from 'the unequal' (a variant on 'the great and small'), from Speusippus, who derives them from 'plurality'. He claims that the two theories are not parallel, as they might seem to be, since while Speusippus' plurality is a single factor, Plato's unequal is really two numerically distinct factors, though defined as one. Aristotle often calls 'the great and small' 'the great and the small' and treats it as two factors. This is usually taken as misunderstanding of the fact that Plato's second principle was conceived of as indeterminate *duality*, progression towards the great *and* the small. But this argument shows that Aristotle is quite aware of this. His point is that while you can *define* any two things as one thing, you do not thereby make them numerically one thing. Nothing can *be* the great *and* the small; so to call one thing 'the great and small' is for Aristotle just a trivial verbal move which fails to establish that there can actually be any such single factor. (This passage does not conflict with *Physics* 192^{a}11-12, where Aristotle complains that Plato does not have two factors although he calls his factor a two. The point there is that the nominal distinctness of the great and small does not establish the required two logically different factors (like matter and privation) with different functions.)

In this passage equal is mysteriously equated with one. This may be a textual error (see notes on the text), but may be right—1092^{a}35-^{b}1 indicates that the Academy identified one and equal with a casualness Aristotle finds maddening. Cf. also 1056^{a}7-11.

1087^{b}12-33: Aristotle here claims that none of the Academy's way of characterizing the first principles gives a genuine contrariety. His point must be that although the Academy claim that their principles are contraries, none of the formulations of the theory adequately expresses this, and so no adequate theory has been formulated. His criticisms are all aimed at actual Academy descriptions of the principles. 'Great and small', 'many and few', and 'exceeding and exceeded' are all rejected because they oppose *two* factors, not a single factor, to one. Among the single candidates, Aristotle prefers 'plurality', as being the nearest to a contrary to one; but since the true contrary of plurality is fewness, there still results the absurdity that one will be a few. (The Greek *polus*, covering both 'much' and 'many', facilitates this step in Greek.)

Aristotle's arguments seem at first rather linguistic in nature. Surely the Platonists were not making a claim about the meanings of terms; their claim is much more likely to have been to the effect that the different terms employed did in fact refer to two principles which were opposed. Aristotle may well, therefore, be confusing a claim about reference with a claim about meaning in pointing out that the terms used are not contradictories. He does claim, however, that these terminological variations remove no real problems, only verbal ones (ll. 18-21). It is possible that changes of description had been employed as a means of avoiding difficulties, and that shifts between 'indefinite two', 'plurality', etc. represent attempts to meet difficulties. Aristotle's tactics here are recognizable also in his lengthy criticisms of the second principle in the last third of this chapter and in chapter 2, and frequently the same doubt arises: how relevant is Aristotle's criticism of a logically anomalous use of 'unequal', for example, to the actual Academy conception of the second principle? It is obviously open to a supporter of the Academy to point to the use made of the principle in the theory (even in the few fragments we possess) and claim that this is what Aristotle should be criticizing, not the names used for it. It is typical of Aristotle in general, however, to hold an opponent to his exact words and the plain meaning of them, without benefit of possible interpretations that are vaguer and more charitable. And in the present case he might well point out that the only way the Academy can show that their principles are contraries is to show that they are properly picked out by mutually contradictory expressions. Aristotle himself studies contraries with great care (see, for example, *Metaphysics I,* chapters 3-10.)

1087^{b}33–1088^{a}14. Criticism of one as a principle

Aristotle here curtly asserts that the Academy are wrong to take 'one' to refer to an actual existing thing. It is, of course, characteristic of platonism to accept the existence of numbers, but for the Academy one is not a number but a principle of number, so they are faced with the separate need to assert that 'one' refers to an item which really does exist. Aristotle does not offer any special argument against this, possibly regarding it as merely a natural part of the platonist assumptions attacked in M 2. (At *Sophistici Elenchi* 169^{a}33-7, however, Aristotle regards the idea that 'one' refers to an existing individual as a natural temptation offered by language.) Here he merely puts forward his own alternative account as obviously better. What he says here is cursory and not fully understandable without reference to the fuller account in *Metaphysics I,* chapters 1-3. See Introduction, pp. 36-39, and cf. especially 1052^{b}18-27, 35–1053^{a}30, 1053^{b}4-8, 1053^{b}24–1054^{a}19.

The way Aristotle approaches the problem of counting a man, white, and walking is instructive. Two of his frequently asserted doctrines are (i) that 'one' has as many senses as 'is', (ii) that, like 'is', 'one' does not mark out a genus. There is no genus of things that are (existing things), because 'is' applies in irreducibly different senses in different categories; and the same is true for 'one'. Consistently with this Aristotle should hold that we cannot count together items in different categories. Objects, qualities, relations, etc. do not form a group of things that all exist, in the same sense of 'exist'. So, since counting involves at least the ability to reidentify things as being of a certain kind, they do not form a group of things that can be counted either. Socrates and his whiteness do not add up to two of anything. Aristotle actually asserts this idea at *Physics* 248^{b}19-21: number-terms have different senses according to the category of the items counted. But this idea is hard to sustain and give content to apart from a technical theory of types like Russell's; in connection with a theory of categories like Aristotle's, which relies on tests of ordinary language for distinguishing different categories of items, it becomes rather bizarre. In this passage we find Aristotle sensibly conceding that we *can* count the items—there is some unit measurement that can be applied, if only 'categorially different item'.

1088ª15-^{b}13. Criticism of the second principle

Aristotle goes on to claim that his own logical distinctions likewise show that the Academy are wrong to think that the expression for their second principle refer to a real thing. His treatment is thus parallel to his treatment of 'one'. But his claims here do not hold for all the expressions used for the second principle, only for those which according to him pick out items in the category of relatives, that is, for 'unequal' and 'great and small', but not for 'the indefinite two' (though he refers to it at ll. 15-16.) So, even apart from doubts about the relevance of objecting to the names for the principles (see above), Aristotle's argument is incomplete here. It might be claimed that for Aristotle the indefinite two is just a kind of two, and numbers for him fall into the category of relatives. But in *M-N* he clearly takes the indefinite two to be a principle of number and not a number (cf. 1081ª16-17, 21-3, ^{b}17-18, 1090^{b}35–1091ª5). It could also be claimed that it was essential to the generation of mathematical objects from the principles that the second principle should be a relative (this looms large in the 'categorial reduction' of recent German reconstructions of the unwritten doctrines). I do not think that the evidence supports any connection of this with the derivation of mathematical objects, but the evidence is really too fragmentary for us to judge whether Aristotle's arguments here are relevant in this context.

1088ª17-21: This argument appears to rely on the fact that it is unnatural to take 'numbers are many and few' etc. to mean that this is how numbers etc. are constituted; it would normally be taken to mean that these are characteristics numbers etc. can possess. See notes on 1085ª20-3.

1088^{a}21–1088^{b}4: Aristotle claims that the Academy second principle, since it is, at least under some descriptions, an item in the category of relatives, cannot be said to exist in the primary or basic sense of 'exist'. It is misleading to translate the Greek phrase which I have translated 'relatives' by 'relations'. The modern idea of a relation, explained in terms of a function in two variables or a two-place predicate, is foreign to Aristotle. His relatives include relational properties, and sometimes, perhaps, even items like heads and hands. The insistence here on the ontological inferiority of relatives is a departure from the *Categories*, where there is merely one statement that if the 'primary substances' (individuals like Socrates) did not exist, no items would exist in the other categories (2^{b}5-6). It is not clear from the *Categories* why the converse should not also be true. In this passage Aristotle seems to be using the theory of categories to oppose the ontology of the Academy, who, by deriving objects from first principles which are 'relatives', get the priorities reversed.

The passage raises three points:

(i) Since what Aristotle says depends on the second principle being referred to as a relative, he must be thinking of 'great and small', along with 'unequal', as picking out a relative. But the arguments apply not to 'great and small' but to 'great' and 'small'; Aristotle is assuming that the former expression can only be understood as a conjunction of the latter two. Even so, however, he is ignoring his own suggestion (*Categories* 3^{b}30-2, 5^{b}11–6^{a}11) that the appropriate category may actually be that of quantity.

(ii) According to Aristotle, relatives come bottom of the category list (presumably only of the four categories mentioned) in ontological claim, because they are attributes of quantities. This is clearly false of most relatives, however (and cf. *Nicomachean Ethics* 1096^{a}18-21, where relatives are said to depend on objects). Aristotle can only be thinking of 'great', 'small' and the like.

(iii) For the 'change-test' cf. *Physics* 225^{b}11-13. Aristotle means, not that items in these categories themselves change, but that one item can change in respect of possessing different items from these categories. Socrates can change in quality by becoming musical, in quantity by becoming fatter, in place by going to Megara. But with change in respect of relatives, there are two differences. All such change depends on change in respect of some other item; and it can take place without any change in the subject. Socrates can cease to be a husband, for example, if his wife dies, without any change in him. (For this to apply to 'great' and 'small' the assumption must be made that correct application of these terms is always relative to some other object as standard of comparison.) It is not made clear why this fact about relatives should lead to the conclusion that relatives have inferior claim to existence.

1088^{b}4-13: Here the principles are called elements, but this argument is distinct from the following arguments about elements, and seems more analogous to 1088^{a}17-21: since the Academy predicate 'many' and 'few' of numbers, they should not consistently regard them as elements that make up numbers. Aristotle here adds another argument: the Academy apply both 'many' and 'few' to numbers, but while they do recognize a smallest number they fail to recognize a largest. Presumably Aristotle is taking a vague statement like 'numbers are many and few' and insisting that if it means anything precise it means that there is both a smallest and a largest number. The move from 'many' to 'large (number)' and from 'few' to 'small (number)' is Aristotle's own, and Greek; but the move to 'largest (and smallest) number' is Aristotle's own, and is of a familiar type: Aristotle insists on a literal sense, open to determinate criticisms, for an Academy statement put forward in confident obscurity.

CHAPTER 2 (to 1090^{a}2)

1088^{b}14-35: Aristotle argues here that eternal objects like numbers cannot have elements. This attacks an account of the first principles that makes them elements of mathematical objects. Here again we do not know whether or not Plato actually had such a view. It does figure in passages in later authors who are drawing on the unwritten doctrines, and we know that Plato was the first to use *stoicheion*, which had hitherto meant only 'letter of the alphabet', in the technical sense of 'element'. It is also possible, however, that Aristotle is criticizing as if it were a full-blown philosophical thesis an idea put forward more casually; his other criticisms deal with the role of the principles as elements in a rather superficial way (see notes on 1088^{b}4-13), and this suggests that there was no explicit argument on the Academy's part. Aristotle, however, who is characteristically careful about eternality, thinks it important to point out that the Platonists run into trouble with it as a result of thinking of the principles as elements, however casually the latter idea may have been put forward.

The argument has the following steps:
1. If a thing has elements it is a compound.
2. A compound is a compound of form and matter.
So
3. If a thing has elements it has matter.
1-3 are not all explicitly in the text, but Aristotle must be assuming 1 and 2 to think himself entitled to 3. However, how can he assume that a compound of elements in the Academy sense must be a compound of form and matter in his sense? We would like more independent knowledge of what exactly the Academy understood by 'element' in order to know whether Aristotle is in fact using an argument the Academy could reject on the grounds that it uses 'element' in a sense to which they are not committed.
4. If a thing has matter, it contains the possibility of existing.
5. A genuine possibility of existing is also a possibility of not existing.
6. No eternal object can contain the possibility of not existing.
So
7. No eternal object has matter.

Hence

8. No eternal object has elements.

The upshot of this argument (though it is not a conclusion explicitly drawn in the text) is that the Platonists do not really think of objects such as Forms and numbers as genuinely eternal, merely as lasting a very, very long time (cf. *Nicomachean Ethics* 1096ᵇ3-5).

Plato frequently refers to Forms as eternal, and clearly does not mean merely that they are long-lasting. Aristotle here is applying his own conceptual tools to the Platonist position, in order to claim that Plato's notion of eternity is defective, since he fails to distinguish what merely happens to last for ever from what *must* as a matter of necessity last for ever. For Aristotle a thing is only eternal if it *could not* fail to exist, i.e. if it excludes the possibility of failing to exist. The Academy's purportedly eternal objects fail this condition. Even though they are supposed to exist for ever, they do not exclude the possibility of failing to exist. Worse, by saying that they have elements, the Academy imply that they are such as to contain matter, and hence the possibility of failing to exist. So the Academy's supposedly eternal objects are actually *precluded* from being eternal.

Is Aristotle's argument fair? It is quite legitimate for him to apply distinctions of his own to show that the Academy have failed to make an important distinction. It is more questionable whether he is right to assume that they are actually prevented by their notion of Forms and numbers from saying that the latter last for ever necessarily and not just as a matter of contingent fact. To do this he has to interpret their statement that Forms and numbers have elements as meaning that they have matter. Once this step is granted, however, the argument follows: matter imports the possibility of existence, and hence of non-existence; so anything with matter can only last for ever *de facto*, and there is no guarantee that it *must* necessarily last for ever. So it cannot be properly said to be eternal. Aristotle is careful to exclude all possibility from his own eternal entities, leaving them pure 'actuality'.

The reference to 'another work' is probably to *Metaphysics* Θ chapter 8.

ᵇ28-35 is apparently Aristotle's only justification for the way he subsequently concentrates on the second principle under those of its descriptions which imply that it falls into the category of relatives. Since Aristotle is still talking about elements, the passage is not a doublet of 1087ᵇ4 ff., as has been supposed. This passage is one which suggests that under the description 'the indefinite two' the second principle or element was primarily thought of as a producer of numbers.

1088ᵇ35–1090ᵃ2: This long section is a criticism of the two Academy principles, but not in their role as producers of mathematical objects. Aristotle's target is rather the way they figure as the principles of Being and Not-being, from which all objects, not just mathematical objects, are in some way derived. He finds this theory fundamentally misguided, and claims that it is the product of a basic philosophical mistake.

This is the only section in *M-N* where this side of the principles is systematically treated. We are here faced by a problem over Aristotle's method of criticism. We know (from fragments of Plato's colleague Hermodorus and Aristotle's colleague Eudemus) that Plato did, in some way, identify his two opposite principles with Being and Not-being, but we know nothing of the reasoning behind this peculiar move, except that the opposition of the two principles seems to have become identified with other, wider, oppositions, e.g. those of good and bad, and rest and motion. In this chapter Aristotle professes to give the Academy's arguments, and then criticizes them in his own terms. But although Plato himself is clearly indicated, it is impossible for these to be Plato's arguments, as can be seen from his treatment of not-being in the *Sophist*. Nor can the problem be solved by a chronological hypothesis (the *Sophist* coming later than *N*) because Aristotle makes what look like two unmistakable references to the *Sophist*. Aristotle may be guilty of some misunderstanding here. The problem is discussed at the end of the notes on this chapter.

1088^b35–1089^a6: Aristotle's reference to Parmenides would naturally be taken to be a reference also to *Sophist* 237a and 258d, where the passage is quoted; and he is right in taking Plato's treatment of the problem to spring from a desire to overcome the apparent force of Parmenides' reasoning. But the argument he contemptuously dismisses as old-fashioned is not in the *Sophist*.

In the 'Way of Truth' Parmenides faces us with a dilemma: given any subject of thought or speech, there are only two paths we can take—it is, or it is not (fr. 2, fr. 6, fr. 8 l. 1). In fact there is only one path we can take, for the second is not really a possible path. You cannot really say of anything that it is not, for what is not cannot be known or spoken of (fr. 2 l. 6-7). Parmenides is appealing to the idea (to have a long and eventful philosophical history) that you cannot refer to or think about what is not there to be referred to or thought about (an object that does not exist, or a state of affairs that is not what you take it to be). He goes on to argue that since it is impossible to say of anything that it is not, we can only say of it that it is (fr. 3, fr. 6 ll. 1-2). For what can be spoken or thought of must be, or it would not have been possible to speak or think about it. Parmenides then goes on to claim that various things which we take to be self-evidently true are rationally unacceptable because they involve one in the impossibility of saying of something that it is not. Plurality, movement, and change are all shown to involve this impossibility. Here Aristotle deals only with the denial of plurality (for reasons which become clearer later in the chapter). If there were two subjects, this would involve saying of each of them that it was not the other; so there is only one genuine subject that can be spoken or thought of, and it cannot be divided either internally or externally, from anything else. So Parmenides reaches monism from a purely logical argument (and one appearing very difficult to deny).

Aristotle claims that the Academy accepted the force of Parmenides' reasoning but wished, reasonably enough, to deny his conclusion. In order to give a rational backing to the apparent facts of plurality and change, they insisted on the reality of not-being along with that of being. Parmenides had argued that it is impossible to refer to or think of what is not, so they insisted that what is not does have being in some way too, and so can be referred to as well as what is. So Not-being is rehabilitated, and since it is no longer impossible to say of anything that it is not, Parmenides' conclusions no longer follow, and plurality, movement, and change are vindicated. It is hard to see exactly what argument Aristotle ascribes to them here. Possibly he is vaguely gesturing to the *Sophist* as a whole (see notes at the end of the chapter). He represents it as an insistence that since it is not, as a matter of fact, impossible to speak of what is not, it follows that what is not has being in some way, and so can be referred to; so Not-being is a principle as basic as Being (cf. Sartre, *Being and Nothingness*, trans. H. Barnes, p. 5). This is reminiscent of the Atomists' insistence, against Parmenides, that not-being (equated with the void) exists just as much as being. But there is no reference to them here; Aristotle presents the Academy as working out Parmenides' problem for themselves.

1089ᵃ7-15: Instead of attacking the alleged arguments directly, Aristotle tries (in somewhat Austinian spirit) to attack the theory at its base by showing it to result, at least in part, from insensitivity to the use of words.

It is a frequently repeated doctrine of Aristotle's that 'be' (or 'exist') has as many different senses as it has application in different categories; in many works he sees this as a useful tool against other philosophers' theories (see *Soph. Elench.* 182ᵇ23 ff.; *Physics* 1 chapter 3). Here he uses it to reduce to absurdity the claim that any genuine subject to which 'it is' applies is not distinct from any other subject to which 'it is' applies in the same sense. If 'is' has ten senses (the maximum number of categories is ten) then we get not monism but 'decadism', which is absurd.

At. ll. 10-11 Aristotle concedes that the opponent might not accept the previous argument, but would maintain that Parmenides had shown that everything—individuals, qualities, etc.—made up one single unity of everything to which 'is' applies at all. This is in effect to reject the idea that 'is' applies in different senses in different categories. Aristotle points out that the opponent has in that case no factor except the second principle to explain how individuals are different from qualities, etc. But it is absurd for a single factor to have to account for the many differences between items in different categories. Presumably Aristotle means us to understand that it is more plausible to accept his own solution in terms of the multivocity of 'is'.

1089ᵃ15-19: Aristotle says elsewhere that 'not being' has many senses (1067ᵇ25, 1069ᵇ27, *Physics* 225ᵃ20) and distinguishes 'not being' from 'not being something' (*Physics* 186ᵇ9-10, 187ᵃ4-6, *Topics* 167ᵃ1-7).

1089ª19-31: Aristotle argues three points here:

(i) Plato means falsity 'and that kind of thing' by not-being. This is rather vague. Plato says at *Sophist* 237a and 260b ff. that not-being makes falsity possible, but he is committed only to saying that he can give a reasonable account of false statement because of his theory of not-being. At 263b he says that a false statement says things other than the things that are. It says things that are not as things that are, but things other than the things that are about the subject of the sentence.

(ii) One argument (presumably in the Academy) went as follows:

Geometers make false assumptions in order to prove truths, so falsity is necessary for truth. The 'false assumption' is not a sceptical point about the impossibility of exact measurement; a geometer can draw a line 2 inches long and say, 'let this be 1 foot long'. Aristotle might well have attacked the ir-relevance of this point to the problem of not-being, but in fact he confines his criticism to the idea that geometers reason from false premises. (Cf. *Prior Analytics* 49ᵇ35 and *Posterior Analytics* 76ᵇ41.) What the geometer is doing is to set up an initial postulate, and the proof is conditional on this, but does not itself assert the truth of the postulate.

(iii) In any case, although 'is not' can mean 'is not true' (cf. 1026ª33 ff.), this is not relevant to contexts involving coming into being. If an X comes into being from what *is not* an X this has nothing to do with falsity, but refers to the potentiality for being X. Aristotle is again accusing Plato of confusing the different senses of a word.

1089ª31-ᵇ4: Aristotle now turns his attention to the second principle con-sidered as what makes plurality possible. Regarded as an answer to Parmenides' arguments for monism, it has to be the factor that accounts for the fact that there are many things and not just one; it is the source of plurality in general. This is a breathtakingly general idea, and again we do not know whether the Academy consciously maintained it, or whether it is an interpretation of their second principle by Aristotle. The course of the arguments rather suggests the latter, because Aristotle's main point is that the Academy do *not* in fact provide a principle of plurality in general although they should do so; this rather suggests that they did not in fact try to do so.

Here the argument is that since the Academy use their principles to pro-duce individuals of various kinds, their second principle is not really a principle of plurality in general, but only of plurality among individuals. He claims that they should have provided for plurality in the other categories too— qualities, relatives, etc. Aristotle has pointed to a gap in the Academy account —*if* their second principle was meant to have the role of a principle of plurality in general.

The cryptic remark at the end alludes to Aristotle's own solution to what he takes to be the salvageable part of the Academy's problem. For him what makes individuals of the same kind different is difference of matter; matter (in one of its many roles) serves as the principle of individuation within a kind. He makes scattered remarks (1029ᵇ22-7, 1070ᵇ16-27; cf. 1089ᵇ27 below) to the effect that matter has this function in every category, but that it is the same only 'by analogy'. For Aristotle there is no such thing as a principle of plurality in general. Matter is what accounts for there being a plurality of individuals of any given kind, but there is nothing which is the same matter in all kinds (or categories). What is the same in all cases is the relation of matter to form. Matter in two different categories is only analogically the same–i.e. whatever the matter is in each category it bears the same relation to the form, whatever that is in either case. But it is a mistake to look for anything which is independently identifiable as the same matter in all categories. (This is quite different from the problem of 'prime matter', which applies only in one category.) Arguments from silence are always weak, but I suspect that if the Academy had put forward an explicit argument for the second principle as the principle of plurality in general, Aristotle would have argued against it on something like the above lines, instead of arguing, as he does here, that they *ought* to have put forward such a principle.

1089ᵇ4-8: 'The same aberration' is probably the desire to provide a principle of plurality in general; this principle would also have to be the opposite of being and of one.

1089ᵇ8-15: The Academy are charged wtih failure to provide a principle of plurality for relatives. This is especially striking because their own second principle is (under some descriptions) a relative, and the Academy seem to assume without question that it comes in various versions (depending on what is to be produced from it) and so in some sense forms a plurality.

1089ᵇ15-24: Here the point about the need for a principle of plurality in general is repeated. Aristotle's expressions here do not imply that Plato in fact used the word 'relative' of the second principle (though he may have done) any more than that he used the typically Aristotelian concept of potentiality (see notes on 1089ª20 ff.).

1089ᵇ24-8: On the mention of matter here, see notes on 1089ª31-ᵇ4. Aristotle does not pursue the topic of non-substantial matter further, except to say that matter in each category is only the same by analogy (see notes on 1089ª31-ᵇ4). If he had developed this passage further, what he said might have helped to clear up a vexed problem about the nature of non-substantial individuals (which appear only in the *Categories*). The alternatives are, very roughly, that individual qualities, for example, are either items unique to the individual they are in (the red of a particular apple, which will perish when it does) or items which cannot be predicated of any further items but which can nevertheless turn up in many individuals (the red of an apple which it may share with other apples). Aristotle's words here are unfortunately compatible with either conception and do not help to decide between them; indeed the unclarity of the suggested solution in terms of matter indicates that he had perhaps not clearly distinguished between the alternatives. This is in any case the only discussion of the question of non-substantial individuals outside the *Categories*.

1089^b28-32: This passage is rather cryptic, and it is hard to be confident of any interpretation. Aristotle is saying that, in contrast to the other categories, the first category (that of substance or objects) does not present a real problem if one considers how there can be many items in it. Presumably we are meant to think that the concept of matter has its surest application within this category, so that the question, 'How can there by many men and not just one?', for example, gets a satisfactory answer in the availability of matter as well as form. Aristotle then adds a puzzling exception and a puzzling final comment.

The exception seems to indicate the fact that 'this' can serve not only to pick out concrete individuals as distinct from other concrete individuals, but to refer to types of thing, so that in a sense not only the individual but the form can be said to be a 'this' in Aristotle's sense. Aristotle does sometimes refer to the form as a 'this', and in such cases it is no longer true that matter provides an uncontroversial answer to the question of how there can be many thises.

The final remark seems to say that there is a real problem left over even when one admits that one can understand how there can be many individuals. Perhaps Aristotle means that the solution offered by himself (and according to him by the Academy also) is in terms of potentiality, matter being the source of a thing's potentialities. So there is still a sense in which the question, 'How can there be many men and not one?' is still unanswered. What accounts for there *actually* being many men here and now? Aristotle does not indicate what form would be taken by an answer in terms of something other than matter, but perhaps he intends something like *de Generatione* II ch. 10: coming into being is brought about by the motion of the sun in the ecliptic.

1089^b32–1090^a2: Compare 1089^a31-3. Aristotle takes the Platonists to confuse the mathematical objects produced from their principles with physical bodies. Typically, he tries to force a precise interpretation on to the Platonists: either they accept that bodies are identical with magnitudes, which is absurd, or they do not, in which case, since their principles produce only magnitudes, they are irrelevant to the plurality of objects.

*   *   *

There is good evidence that the Academy did hold the view here criticized —that their two basic principles were in some way also principles of being and not-being. And it is clear from the way Aristotle connects this idea with their wish to answer the question, 'Why are there many beings?' that their system did have its origin in their desire to answer Parmenides and meet the problem he had posed. What is more puzzling is that Aristotle takes himself to be attacking not only the Plato of the Academy, but also the Plato of the *Sophist* —for there are two surely unmistakable references to the *Sophist*, and Aristotle is apparently appealing to that dialogue to support his claim that the arguments he describes here are Plato's arguments for the rehabilitation of not-being as a principle as basic as being. Yet the arguments here have nothing in common with Plato's complex and beautiful (and considerably more interesting) arguments in the *Sophist*. Has Aristotle just failed to understand the *Sophist*?

Even if Aristotle *has* misunderstood the *Sophist*, it does not vitiate his argument here, which is mainly directed towards the *Academy's* arguments. But the question of misunderstanding is still of interest because of the light it sheds on Aristotle's relation to Plato.

In the *Sophist*, Plato is quite sure that not-being somehow is (and therefore that the sophist can be tracked down) even before the main arguments. At 240c and 254c-d it is stressed that not-being must be in some way, since we presuppose it in what we say; the problem is that we can give no coherent account of this, and get into paradox when we try to speak of it. The point of the central arguments is to show that it is not paradoxical to talk of not-being. In fact it turns out to be necessary. Aristotle is thus right if he thinks that the *Sophist* does affirm (as was done already at *Parmenides* 161e–162b) that not-being must be, just as much as being, since we can and do make true statements which presuppose it. What is surprising is that he seems to take this to be the *Sophist*'s sole contribution to the topic, and so can appeal to it as confirmation of the Academy arguments, which he could hardly do if he were thinking of the way in which not-being is actually rehabilitated in the central arguments.

So Aristotle is here not so much twisting the significance of what is said in the *Sophist* as apparently failing to grasp what is most interesting in the dialogue. There are, however, reasons why this may have come about. Firstly, it is not uncommon for one philosopher to fail to understand another, even massively, if they are working in the same area and both are powerfully original minds. (Russell's misunderstanding of the *Tractatus* is a good example of this.) Secondly, the central arguments of the *Sophist* employ the notions of the Greatest Kinds 'blending', 'mixing', and so forth, and their relationships are never spelled out unmetaphorically. Aristotle greatly dislikes metaphor in philosophy; at *Posterior Analytics* 97^b37 ff. he protests that defining in terms of metaphor leads to the disaster of arguing in terms of metaphor. He may well have found the central part of the *Sophist* a cloudy mass of unexplained metaphor, with no indication as to how the metaphors could be cashed out. If so, it is easier to understand how he might have extracted from the whole dialogue only the vague idea that Plato retained Parmenides' terms of reference but attempted some kind of rehabilitation of not-being. Thirdly, Aristotle's failure here is part of a more general failure to recognize the achievements in the philosophy of language in Plato's later dialogues. Again, it is plausible that he was put off by a presentation and methodology that he finds inappropriate to the subject. Finally, Aristotle's focus here is distorted by his solution to these problems in terms of his theory of categories. He takes himself to have exposed a philosophical pseudo-problem and to have got to the root of a mistake on which a whole pretentious theory is based, by the method of paying careful attention to the different senses of words. In the whole of this passage he is somewhat obsessed by the categories as providing a solution to these problems and a way of entangling the Academy's large and vague pronouncements in absurdities. This seems to have prevented him from seeing that Plato may have conceived of the problems rather differently. Because Aristotle thinks Plato guilty of a serious mistake here he does not bother to pay attention to the details of how it was made.

This passage is the only one in *M-N* where Aristotle unquestionably distorts his presentation of Plato's ideas because of some failure in understanding. There are, however, reasons for this, and it does not follow that he is always, or even usually, unreliable in his reports of Plato, or unsuccessful in his attempts to understand him.

CHAPTER 2, 1090ª2–CHAPTER 4, 1091ª29

There is an abrupt change from discussion of the principles to this section, where the subject is numbers and Forms, and the principles are discussed only in connection with the latter. Since the next section returns to discussion of the principles in their own right, the present section seems rather out of place. Because of this, and because some of the points here have already been dealt with in *M*, Ross says that this section 'cover[s] much the same ground as that covered in *M* 2-3', arguing from this that '*M* and *N* cannot have been meant to form parts of a single treatise; they were originally independent essays.' There are, however, two important differences between this section and *M* 2-3. In *M* 2-3 the argument is systematic and decisive; Aristotle is concerned solely with platonism as a theory about mathematical objects, and with giving an alternative when it is refuted. The present passage is an unsystematic set of arguments in which Aristotle deals, often indecisively, with various different people, and develops criticisms of their ideas, rather than directly attacking a specific theory; further, there is no hint of any alternative account, like that of *M* 3. Secondly, *M* 2-3 is limited to the problem of the existence of mathematical objects, whereas in this section this question is throughout combined (often confusingly) wih the question of whether mathematical objects can be 'causes' of things. So it seems that we do not have a doublet of *M* 2-3, since the present section does belong to the 'third inquiry' announced in *M* 1: whether Forms and numbers can be causes. (We have seen that this inquiry is not well distinguished from discussion of the principles and the type of explanation provided by derivation from them, and this section provides an example of the way in which the two questions tend to come together.)

The actual points of contact do not support Ross's thesis either. 1090ª13-15 refers to *M* 3, but in a way which presupposes that *M* 3 has already been read

as an earlier part of the same treatise; so it can hardly be a doublet. The same
is true of 1090ᵃ28-9. Other points of contact are not as impressive as they
might appear at first glance. The initial distinction between Plato and Speusippus recalls 1076ᵃ19 ff., but it is bound up with the new discussion of numbers
as causes. The Pythagoreans are discussed quite fully (1090ᵃ20-5) in a way
that might suggest the references to them at 1080ᵇ16-21 and 1083ᵇ8-19; but
the present passage seems rather to echo the whole passage in *A*, 985ᵇ23–986
ᵃ13. There is some repetition of minor points capable of use in different
contexts, which prove nothing about the nature of the context—e.g. the
reference to the indefinite two generating only the powers of two, or to
Xenocrates' falsification of mathematics (1090ᵇ27-30; cf. 1083ᵇ5-6 and
1086ᵃ9-11) and to his long-windedness (1090ᵇ30; 1091ᵃ7-9; cf. 1083ᵇ6).

Aristotle's main complaint about mathematical objects as 'causes' here is
that the Academy leave it quite obscure what kind of explanation they provide. The discussion slides easily into discussion of the inherent obscurities of
these entities. This is in contrast with Aristotle's attitude to numbers as causes
in the final section of *N*, and to Forms as causes in *M* 5, where his complaint
is rather that the Academy do have a precise, but wrong, claim about the way
in which numbers and Forms explain things. There is no contradiction here;
Aristotle, as we have already seen, often attacks an opponent for making a
'claim which is either too vague to be useful, or, if interpreted precisely, false.

1090ᵃ2-15: This is a forceful expression of Aristotle's specifically mathematical anti-platonism. He is more hostile to Speusippus, who believes that
only numbers, but not Forms, exist, than he is to Plato, although Plato believes
in both Forms and numbers and therefore would *a priori* seem more objectionable. Aristotle's reason is that for Plato numbers are a kind of Form, and
he at least has independent reasons for accepting the existence of Forms. Here
in an extreme form is Aristotle's preference for the argued over the unargued,
even if he thinks the arguments invalid; and also his tendency to identify a
theory with the arguments put forward for it. It seems from this that Speusippus put forward no more explicit arguments for mathematical platonism than
Plato did. (Aristotle is wrong, however, in assuming that Plato insists on the
reality of number simply because numbers are Forms; see the Introduction,
pp. 3-13.) It is worth noting here that the question whether numbers exist is
treated together with the question whether they are a kind of cause, whereas
in *M* they are sharply separated.

1090ᵃ16-20: It is the Platonists who 'set out' one Form over and above the
many particulars of a single kind. After the last argument, a serious identification of Forms and numbers cannot be in mind here. The point can only be
that since the Platonists thjnk of numbers as Forms, some Forms are numbers,
so it is relevant to show that an argument to establish Forms does not work.

1090ᵃ20-ᵇ5: In this argument the Pythagoreans, who believe in the reality of
numbers but do not distinguish them from physical objects, are contrasted
with people who believe in the reality of numbers as separate objects. (Lines

25-6 limit these to people who accept *only* mathematical number, i.e. Speusippus, but this is misleading, for the Pythagorean position is contrasted with that of anyone who accepts that numbers exist and are distinct from physical objects—and that certainly includes Plato.)

The two theories are contrasted so as to show that each reveals a fatal problem in the other. The Pythagoreans are rightly impressed by the way mathematical statements are true of the world and have application to the way things actually behave. (The classical example is the Pythagorean discovery that simple numerical ratios underlie the musical intervals of octave, fourth, and fifth.) But they are led by this to say that numbers are actually identical with the substance of the world, and this leads on to absurdities—e.g. producing bodies (with weight) from numbers (without weight). These absurdities are avoided by the Academy's move of taking numbers to have existence in complete independence of physical objects. But in so doing they fall back on the problem that the Pythagoreans did have an answer for: how properties of numbers apply to the behaviour of physical objects.

In connection with the idea that the truth of mathematical axioms is irresistible to the soul, it is interesting to compare a similar argument for platonism from Gödel: 'Despite their remoteness from sense experience, we do have something like a perception also of the objects of set theory, as is seen from *the fact that the axioms force themselves upon us as being true*. I do not see any reason why we should have less confidence in this kind of perception, i.e. in mathematical intuition, than in sense perception . . .' (p. 271 in Benacerraf and Putnam, italics mine).

1090ᵇ5-13: This is indeed a feeble argument, though we know that the Academy accepted it, or at least its conclusion (1028ᵇ16-18). It may come here, rather than in *M* 2, because it involves the sequence of dimensions, which is important for the following argument.

1090ᵇ13–1091ᵃ5: This passage has raised a great deal of controversy in recent Platonic scholarship. Aristotle is clearly complaining about the way the Academy produce geometrical objects in one, two, and three dimensions. What, if anything, do the earlier productions contribute to the later? If points are produced before lines, lines before planes, and so on, Aristotle demands a rational account of the way in which points are supposed to contribute to the production of lines, and so on. Presumably the lines are not just made up out of the points, or there would be no need to produce lines separately, out of a different version of the second principle. As often, Aristotle's criticisms suggest that the Academy had not in fact said anything very definite. One theory is criticized on the grounds that all the mathematical objects are produced disconnectedly, i.e. there is no rational way in which the earlier contribute to the later. This is generally agreed to be Speusippus' theory (the reference to 'a series of episodes like a bad tragedy' occurs also at Λ, 1076ᵃ1). Then this is contrasted (ll. 20-4) with another theory that does try to unite the objects of different dimensions by the expedient of producing them all from different numbers. (This is a pathetically crude way to produce a connection between them, but at least it attempts to meet the point.) There follow criticisms (ll. 24-32) which seem to refer to Xenocrates (cf. 1083^b5-6 and 1086^a9-11). What follows is a criticism of Plato's theory of intermediate number. The controversy centres on the second theory (ll. 20-4). It is ascribed to 'the people who posit Forms'. Does Aristotle mean Plato or Xenocrates?

The answer to this has important implications for the reconstruction of Plato's unwritten doctrines, because if this theory can definitely be ascribed to Plato, there would then be good grounds for also ascribing to him another disputed passage, *de Anima* 404^b16-30, in which objects of different dimensions are correlated with the numbers 1-4 and also with different mental faculties; and if both these passages can be ascribed to him, the unwritten doctrines seem to have contained fantastic developments far beyond anything suggested in the Introduction. It is on the basis of the *de Anima* passage in particular that modern German scholars have ascribed to Plato a theory of the correspondence of the real and the mental.

The interpretations of this passage (especially those of Saffrey and Cherniss) are discussed by Gaiser (the interested reader should consult Gaiser (2), pp. 39-49). Gaiser claims that three formal features of this passage make ascription to Plato certain, but I think that room for doubt remains. (i) If Speusippus is dealt with in ll. 16-20, Xenocrates in 20-32, and Plato only then, then Plato's view on the main problem is not discussed. But it is by no means the case that Aristotle solemnly reviews the opinions of all three on every important matter. (ii) ll. 31-2 clearly refer to Xenocrates; Gaiser takes this to refer back to ll. 27 ff., not to ll. 20 ff. To Cherniss, however ((3), pp. 83-4), the Greek demands the opposite reading. (iii) According to Gaiser, 'the people who posit Forms' must refer to Plato. But in the context it refers to anyone who accepts the existence of Forms, in contrast with Speusippus. The fact that Plato is then distinguished at l. 32 suggests if anything that the phrase referred to Xenocrates before. The evidence outside the passage is equally confused and inconclusive; the Greek commentators disagree over whether Plato used only one as first principle, or also used the other numbers up to 4. The difficulty in judging between these accounts is increased by the difficulties over the *de Anima* passage.

However, these problems do not much affect the philosophical interpretation of the passage. Aristotle's complaint is that the geometrical objects are not connected in any logical way; the Academy are in effect defining points, lines, etc. in independence from one another (this complaint has arisen before). What he demands is a rational account of how objects in one dimension are related to those in others, and it is clear that a fanciful expedient like that of deriving them all from number, but from different numbers, does nothing to solve the problem. (It is only fair to add that recent scholars have produced elaborate non-fanciful ways of relating the numbers 1-4 with the different dimensions, but there is no basis for this in the evidence, and probably the most we are entitled to see here is the ancient way of representing numbers by pebbles or dots, two being necessary to form a line, three a plane and four a solid).

Aristotle adds an attack on Plato's intermediate number. It is not obvious why it comes here; it is not a special case of what has gone before (as Gaiser claims), because that concerned geometrical objects. Aristotle is passing, somewhat carelessly, from one type of objectionable 'intermediary entity' in Academy theories to another. There are two arguments:

(i) The two types of number will be identical if they come from the same elements (Aristotle relies on this principle elsewhere; see the Introduction, p. 64-8.) If the elements are different, there will be rather a lot of primitive elements. This is a valid objection, since the project of deriving number from two primitives was surely meant to be one of simplification and unification.

(ii) If the two types have different elements, there will be different types of formal principle as well as different kinds of second principle. But the formal principle is *one*, and so supposed to be unique. How then can there be two ones? There will have to be a one common to them. Plato seems to have thought that the formal principle was *the* one, and obviously unique, and so failed to see this problem. Why does Aristotle not raise this problem for geometrical objects? Perhaps he raises it only for numbers because only in their case had Plato explicitly stated that 'number can only be produced from one and an indefinite two'. It is certainly hard to square with the doctrine of intermediate number, and Plato seems never to have faced the problem of reconciling them.

1091^{a}5-12: Cf. the end of the long untidy section in *M* (at 1086^{a}14-18). The gibe about the indefinite two is not attached to anything in the context, and further suggests that this section is not in finally polished form.

1091^{a}12-29: Aristotle returns to the claim that mathematical objects are 'generated' from the principles, and tries to specify precisely what the Academy mean by it. He contrasts them with the Pythagoreans, who explicitly treat the derivation of number as a temporal process. In contrast, he claims, the Academy are really committed to such a temporal process but do not admit it. There are some dubious points in Aristotle's claims here. Firstly, he does not in fact relegate the Pythagoreans to his discussions of natural science; there are many more references to them in the *Metaphysics* than in the *Physics* (and one of the *Physics* references, 213^{b}22 ff., discusses the same theory as is found here). They have frequently been mentioned in *M-N*, even though Aristotle finds them difficult to fit into his framework of discussion. Secondly, his claim that the Academy are committed to a temporal derivation is shaky. His statements that they use tensed language, and deny that the odd was generated, do not support his conclusion, that they are speaking of a time-taking process. The Academy seem not to have distinguished between a historical account and a logical analysis, and Aristotle is merely taking what they say at face value and insisting, not altogether appropriately, on a literal interpretation. He does, however, have serious arguments elsewhere against the claim that Plato's account of the creation of the world can be taken in a non-literal sense, as a mere 'logical analysis' (*de Caelo* 279ᵇ32–280ª11, ª28-32, 283ª4 ff., *Physics* 251ᵇ17-18.) Aristotle's literalism was opposed by Xenocrates, who did think that the generation of numbers was a 'theoretical construction', and identified it with the construction of the soul in the *Timaeus*. Aristotle's insistence on giving the plainest of sense to Plato's statements may well be the result of a reaction against fancies like those of Xenocrates.

CHAPTER 4, 1091ª29–CHAPTER 5, 1092ª17

This is another independent discussion of the principles, this time of their relation to the good. Here Aristotle provisionally accepts the idea of good or the good in general, and shows that even on the Academy's own terms neither theory about it current in the Academy is adequate. He criticizes first Speusippus, who denies that the good is a basic principle, then Plato, who identifies it with one, the principle of numbers (see notes on 1091ᵇ20–1092ª5). He concludes that neither account is satisfactory because both rest on wrong assumptions. We would expect this to be followed by an account of his own designed to supersede the two accounts he finds faulty while preserving what he finds salvageable in them. In fact there is no such account here, and it is impossible to tell whether he would here subscribe to the account he offers in the similar passage Λ chapter 10: 'we must consider also in which of two ways the nature of the universe contains the good and the highest good, whether as something separate and by itself, or as the order of the parts. Probably in both ways, as an army does, for its good is found both in its order and in its leader, and more in the latter; for he does not depend on the order but it depends on him' (Ross's translation). Elsewhere, however, Aristotle mostly rejects the idea of good in general as vacuous and unhelpful, and insists that what is good is always specific to a certain type of thing (as is the related notion of a thing's 'end'). In *Nicomachean Ethics* 1 chapter 6 and *Eudemian Ethics* 1 chapter 8 he attacks Plato's Form of Good and the notion of good in general, even saying that 'good' has different (though related) senses in the different categories within which it has application. In the present passage Aristotle's own ideas are not to the fore and he attacks the Academy in their own terms.

1091ª29-33: The beautiful at once drops out; Aristotle assumes that the Academy treat it as part of their very general discussion of good. Cf. 1078ª31 ff. where Aristotle distinguishes good from beautiful in the context of unchangeable items.

Jaeger ((2), p. 190) takes it that Aristotle's use of 'we' here serves to identify himself as a Platonist. This certainly does not follow. Throughout this section Aristotle relentlessly attacks both forms of the Academy's position, and even if he is referring to the Academy's concept of good he is not committing himself to it. (Cf. Cherniss (1), p. 493-4).

1091^a33-^b20: These are the arguments against Speusippus (though there is another later- out of place- at 1092^a11-17). He seems to have rejected the idea that goodness is a basic or ultimate principle, presumably saying that it did not apply to mathematical objects but only to items produced 'later'. His positive argument is criticized later; here the reason ascribed is merely negative, namely desire to avoid the absurdities involved in Plato's view identifying goodness with the principle of being or one. (Aristotle has a tendency to treat Speusippus' views as merely attempted solutions to difficulties with Plato's views). Here he claims that Speusippus should have abandoned the premises he continued to share with Plato (b2-3) rather than the premise that goodness is an ultimate principle. It is the Academy's metaphysics that are suspect, not their desire for teleological explanations. In Aristotle's own terms, Speusippus is right not to identify formal and final causes, but wrong to deny that the latter provide just as valid a type of explanation as the former.

1091^a33-^b15: Presumably Speusippus had made an appeal to tradition to support his view that goodness is not an original principle, by pointing out that the ancient myths do not make their first creator and original principle of cosmogony a principle of goodness: the source of justice is Zeus, who comes later. Aristotle himself is capable of appealing to myth and tradition in this way (for example, to support his theories about the stars having life, 1074^a28-^b14), and his objection here is not to the appeal itself but merely to its inaccuracy.

Aristotle's references are primarily to Homer and Hesiod mediated by Plato. Hesiod (*Theogony* 116, also quoted at 984^b26-8) makes Chaos the first principle. Homer has some slightly peculiar references to Oceanus and Tethys as a cosmological origin (*Iliad* xiv, 201, 302, cf. 246); this was not a common account, but Plato had mentioned it (*Cratylus* 402a-b, *Theaetetus* 152e), and Aristotle gives it a half-serious rationalizing account at 983^b27. The references to Night and Heaven have been thought 'Orphic', but are more likely to be later elaborations on Homer and Hesiod (see Kirk and Raven, *The Presocratic Philosophers,* pp. 20-4).

Aristotle claims that the poets only say things like this because they have to reconcile their belief in the justice of Zeus, the present world-ruler, with their narrative which says that the rulers of the universe have changed. Since they do not want to make Zeus an unjust usurper, they have to deny that his predecessors were good; but this does not amount to a philosophical point. Aristotle backs up his claim by appealing to writers who are not bound by such exigencies of form, and who do claim both that Zeus is good and that he is the original creator of the world.

Pherecydes of Syros is an odd figure whose book is a naïve combination of narrative and account of how the world is now. His work began, 'There always were Zas, Time, and Chthonie; but Chthonie got the name Ge (Earth)', putting Zas (Zeus) firmly at the beginning of things. See Kirk and Raven, pp. 46-72, West, *Early Greek Philosophy and the Orient,* chs. 1 and 2. (West, however, thinks that Time is meant here, which is clearly not in Aristotle's mind.) It should be noted that Pherecydes is Aristotle's only real counter-example to the appeal to tradition. The Magi were a priestly Persian caste who taught Zoroastrian dualism: the principles of good and of evil are equally basic. Aristotle discussed them in Book 1 of his lost work *On Philosophy* (fr. 6 Ross). The reference to Empedocles and Anaxagoras is very odd and untypical (though paralleled in the similar passage Λ 1075^b1-11). Elsewhere, while Empedocles is said to have 'lispingly' grasped the final cause (985^a4-10), Anaxagoras is said by Aristotle (following Plato's complaints in the *Phaedo*) to have made Mind only an *efficient* cause and not to have recognized final causes at all.

1091^b16-20: This is rather a baffling passage. It is fairly clear that Aristotle is claiming that a first principle must be good, and that its goodness is in some way essential to it. He takes this much to be established by his refutation of Speusippus. But it is not made clear what the connection is between goodness and properties like being eternal and being self-sufficient. The second sentence rather suggests that these qualities are good-making qualities; but the third sentence says firmly that a first principle has these qualities because it is good.

1091^b20–1092^a5: Aristotle now turns, dialectically, to the opposite view, Plato's, which he represents as a simple identification of the good with the principle of mathematical objects, one. He points out that if this identification is made then numerous absurdities follow, and painstakingly works them out. But did Plato in fact make such a straightforward identification? It appears, as far as we can tell, that he did not and that Aristotle is (as often) interpreting vague statements literally for polemical purposes.

The importance of the good as a basic principle for Plato is apparent in the emphasis in the *Republic* on the Form of the Good, which is mysteriously said to be 'beyond being'. There has naturally been some temptation to link this up with Plato's lecture 'On the Good', which dealt with the basic principles of mathematics and so developed another theme of the *Republic*. Krämer (1) in particular has stressed the axiological aspect of Plato's metaphysics, and insists that we can find, in the fragments of *On the Good*, a theory of rational and ethical structure which underlies all of Plato's written works. (See also Gaiser, Ilting, Wippern, Gadamer and Schadewaldt.) Apart from the rather speculative constructions of these scholars, however, we know very little of the exact role of the good in *On the Good*. We know from a report of Aristoxenus, who got it from Aristotle, that the audience were finally baffled by 'the limit, that good is one'. This phrase, however, has been translated and interpreted in many ways, as identifying the good and one, as saying that goodness is unitary, that unity is good, and even that limit is one and so good. (See Cherniss (2), p. 87 n. 2, and Gaiser (1), pp. 452-3.) In the absence of more definite information we do not know that this was the sort of identification that Aristotle has in mind here. Moreover, Aristotle elsewhere writes as though Plato had in mind something different. At 988^b6-16 he complains that Plato makes goodness merely incidental to one and being; and at 1075^{a}38-^{b}1 he says that the people who oppose Speusippus on this fail to say whether the good is formal, efficient, or final cause. Further, there is an interesting passage at *Eudemian Ethics*, 1218^{a}16 ff., where Aristotle seems more concerned to present Plato's ideas (in order to criticize their method) than to attack them as here, and where we get a different picture: '. . . At present it is from things not admitted to possess goodness that they prove the things admitted to be good, for instance, they prove from numbers that justice and health are good, because they are arrangements and numbers—on the assumption that goodness is a property of numbers and monads because the Absolute Good is unity. But the proper method is to start from things admitted to be good, for instance health, strength . . . And it is a hazardous way of proving that the Absolute Good is unity to say that numbers aim at unity; for it is not clearly stated how they aim at it, but the expression is used in too unqualified a manner; and how can one suppose that things not possessing life can have appetition?' (Loeb translation). Here the Academy are said to prove that goodness is unity from the fact that numbers aim at unity, and so to commit the absurdity of inferring facts about what is good from the 'behaviour' of numbers (they must be making the assumption that what numbers aim at is what is good). Whatever the merits (or demerits) of this line of thought, it is clearly not a straightforward identification of goodness with one, the principle of mathematical objects, but an altogether more vague and metaphorical line of thought.

Aristotle's approach in the present passage is presumably another example of his insistence on taking metaphor in philosophy literally. He takes it that the Platonists intend to identify the good with one, quite literally, and then, rather heavy-handedly, draws out some consequences.

(i) All ones or units will then be types of good. But since there are a lot of units (infinitely many, in fact) there will be an unreasonable number of sorts of good.

(ii) All numbers will be types of good. (This apparently is thought to follow from (i), so that 'units' in (i) must cover not just mathematical units, but also numbers, thought of as unitary products of one.) So if Forms are numbers, then all Forms will be types of good. But this produces a dilemma, whichever of two views one takes about the extent of the world of Forms. If there are Forms only of types of good (presumably, items like justice, generosity, etc.), then Forms will not be self-sufficient objects, since items like generosity, etc. are dependent on independent items like men, in which they are found. On the other hand, if there *are* Forms for such objects (i.e. Forms of man, horse, etc.), then since all Forms are types of good, horse and man will be different types of good, and so will be the individual men and horses that participate in these Forms. Both alternatives are clearly absurd.

There are two points of interest about this argument.

(a) Aristotle passes without argument from, 'Forms are (after all) objects' to, 'There are Forms of objects'. Presumably he is employing the univocity principle also used in the argument at 1079ª24-ᵇ3 (see notes on that passage). (b) The last move, from 'Forms of objects are types of good' to 'Participants in those Forms are types of good', deserves notice. An obvious rejoinder would be that a predicate true of the Form does not necessarily hold of what participates in that Form; an individual man could participate in the Form of Man, which is a type of good, without therefore participating in a type of good and so being good. Aristotle is assuming that this defence is not open to a Platonist, i.e. that they do not distinguish between predicates of a Form which hold of it *qua* Form and those that hold of it *qua* the concept it represents. In this way too the present argument comes close to the argument at 1079ª24-ᵇ3.

(iii) If one is identified with good, the other principle has to be identified with evil. This move seems obvious even if the 'identification' in question is vague and metaphorical, and the Academy seem actually to have subscribed to it. According to Aristotle only Speusippus avoids it, while the others are committed to it. But if so, a whole new set of absurdities follows. No doubt the Academy would have tried to avoid them by claiming that what they said was metaphorical and not to be taken so literally. 1091ᵇ35-7 is paralleled by Λ 1075ª34-6. The remark that evil will be 'the area of the good' is puzzling and unexplained. It may have a remote connection with Aristotle's (controversial) claim (*Physics* 209ᵇ11-13) that Plato in the *Timaeus* identified matter and place. However, the word translated 'area' is also used by Aristotle himself of the good in a non-literal sense at *de Motu Animalium* 700ᵇ29 (cf. ᵇ20).

1092ª5-17: Aristotle sums up by claiming that his opponents fall into absurdities on one side or the other because their basic assumptions are at fault: the Academy's theories are fundamentally wrong, not just mistaken in details. He adds another argument against Speusippus (out of place). It is not certain whether it is Speusippus' own argument, or Aristotle's own inference, that since Speusippus' principle is incomplete, it does not exist in the primary sense: it is, in Aristotle's terms, only potentially, and not actually, what it will become. Aristotle expands elsewhere on the reply he gives here: the sperm, which is only potentially a man, is not the real origin of a man, because the actual is always prior to the potential. See Λ 1072ᵇ30–1073ª3, and Θ chapter 8, especially 1049ᵇ19-27, 1050ª4-7.

CHAPTER 5, 1092ª17–CHAPTER 6

1092ª17-ᵇ8: Some extra objections to the Academy's derivation of mathematical objects from their principles. They do not belong very well either with what precedes or with what follows—another sign that *M-N* is a collection of notes put together by an editor.

1092ª17-21: There are two distinct objections here to the Academy account of place. It is produced along with the geometrical solids in an unexplained way. In demanding more elucidation, Aristotle may be indicating that the Academy do not clearly distinguish ideal from physical space. Intermingled with this objection is a different one, which is that places can only be individuated by reference to the things whose places they are (cf. Aristotle's account in *Physics* Δ chapters 1-5), so that it is strictly wrong to give ideal objects places at all, since they are not independent objects that can be identified.

1092ᵃ21-ᵇ8: Aristotle discusses various possible interpretations of the notion that mathematical objects come from the principles, and finds them all unsatisfactory or ridiculous. His tactic of giving a precise sense to a vague assertion is particularly obvious here.

ᵃ21-4: See notes on 1079ᵇ23-4.

ᵃ24-9. The idea that numbers might be produced from elements that are mixed or juxtaposed does not seem serious, and it appears that Aristotle is making the point that the Platonist account cannot be given any reasonable interpretation as the idioms employed are normally used. Aristotle's own theory of mixture and its difference from juxtaposition is developed at *de Generatione* 327ᵃ30 ff.; he distinguishes types of mixture at *Topics* 122ᵇ25 ff., and at 150ᵇ22 and 151ᵃ20 ff. distinguishes uses of 'juxtaposition' and warns against carelessness in using the term. Here, as at 1082ᵃ20-2 (where he rejects 'mixture' as a possible description of the way a number is made up of units), he is protesting against loose and misleading employment of what are for him at least precise and technical terms.

ᵃ29-ᵇ3. Aristotle sets up a dilemma. If As 'come from' Bs then either (i) the Bs remain in the As. But this is only possible in the case of things that come into being. Aristotle is arguing that if the Bs 'remain' then this implies that at some time the As were actually produced from the Bs, which produces absurdity in the case of abstract objects like numbers.

Or (ii) As come from Bs which do not continue to form part of As, but either are used up in the process, or persist unchanged, distinct from As. Aristotle tries to find an acceptable application of this idea to the derivation of number from one and the indefinite two, and ostentatiously fails. It cannot be like generation from sperm, since one is indivisible, and cannot 'give off' anything like sperm. This looks like a joking reduction to absurdity of metaphors about generation and parenthood in connection with numbers. The only non-metaphorical alternative Aristotle considers is that the factor that does not persist when it produces numbers is a contrary. He meets this with the objection already used in chapter 1—if numbers come from one factor that persists and one that does not, then a third factor is necessary to underlie the change.

ᵇ2-8. This recalls the arguments of chapter 2, which likewise try to show that the Academy's claim that numbers are eternal cannot be reconciled with the way they use expressions of them that are only applicable to perishable things subject to change and generation and destruction. The analogy from

Empedocles is, as Aristotle rather weakly admits, very imperfect.

1092ᵇ8–1093ᵇ29: This last section of *N* is an unconnected string of arguments against the idea that numbers are 'causes', apparently in the sense of efficient causes. They are of very uneven force. Most of them present common-sense and obviously true objections to fanciful claims about the significance and explanatory power of numbers. Few people can have taken seriously the sort of idea that Aristotle attacks here (though Speusippus appears to have fallen into some kind of number-mysticism, and some Pythagorean numerology may have been fashionable in the Academy). The main substantial point that Aristotle conveys is that the Academy have been very casual about their use of the notion of 'cause', and would have benefited from an examination of the different ways in which one thing can explain another.

1092ᵇ8-25: Aristotle discusses two Pythagorean suggestions as to the way in which numbers explain things:

(i) All we know about Eurytus comes from the commentator pseudo-Alexander on this passage. According to him, Eurytus would 'posit' that the number of a man, for example, was 250, and that of plant 360. He would draw a man on a wall and fix pebbles of appropriate colours in different parts of the drawing till he had used up that number. There have been many different interpretations of what he could have been getting at in this procedure, and the general assumption is that it cannot have been as simple-minded as it appears. However, in this chapter Aristotle is out to ridicule his opponents, and it can safely be assumed that whatever Eurytus was doing with his pebbles Aristotle took it to be silly.

(ii) The Pythagoreans were impressed by the fact that the intervals of octave, fourth, and fifth are expressible as simple numerical ratios, and appear to have held the hope that all other phenomena were in principle capable of reduction to numerical ratios. In *A* chapter 5 Aristotle discusses this with some interest as a partial anticipation of the attempt to give a defining formula of a type of thing; he criticizes them, however, for superficiality. Here he stresses that even apart from the difficulty of accounting for all qualitative phenomena in terms of ratios, the Pythagorean idea does not support their thesis that 'things are numbers', since a ratio is not a number. This argument is very like the one at 991ᵇ2-21, and both express Aristotle's refusal to accept rational numbers as numbers in the proper sense (see the Introduction, p.39-40).

1092ᵇ26–1093ᵃ1: These are both fairly common-sense objections. The second point seems to be simply that if the number of fire and that of water have a common factor, then there must be something whose number that factor is, which will therefore be a constituent of both of them, although *ex hypothesi* they were both supposed to be basic elements.

1093ᵃ1-3: This argument is repeated almost at once at 9-13. It plays no part in Aristotle's serious arguments against the idea that 'Forms are numbers'.

1093ᵃ3-9: Aristotle himself does believe that there are significant cycles and periods in the life of species (cf. *de Generatione* 336ᵇ10-15); he just refuses to believe that the mathematical patterns these form are in any way decisive for our understanding of events in nature.

1093^{a}13-19: This is the only passage in Aristotle which suggests that the way we count is at all dependent on us and our interests. Presumably the answer to, 'How many stars are there in the Bear?' can only be answered by, 'It depends where you live'. But it is very doubtful whether Aristotle means us to infer that it is quite arbitrary what we count as *one constellation*. Elsewhere he tends to assume that nature provides us with our units, not that we can divide the world up into countable chunks in different ways. (No doubt this is because he does not distinguish sharply between the notion of a unit for counting and the notion of a unitary object.) In the present passage Aristotle is merely making the point that there is nothing sacred about the number of stars in any constellation, for we could find that there were more or fewer stars in what we would still call the same constellation.

1093^{a}28-1093^{b}4: Aristotle may be just criticizing a few random absurd claims; but it is possible that in this passage he is attacking a systematic parallel derivation of parts of speech and of the musical scale.

1093^{b}11-21: An interesting (because unparalleled) attempt by Aristotle to salvage something from what his opponents say. He admits that there are interesting mathematical structures reflected in nature, and that the Academy do point out formal analogies between generically different fields. But he firmly denies that this is anything more than coincidence; in particular, the numbers do not determine the natural facts. Aristotle does not give any background to these supposed analogies here, and they seem very dubious. Although Aristotle sounds less unsympathetic to them than one might expect, he cannot afford to allow that they are significant, for this would surely undermine the autonomy of different fields of inquiry, something which Aristotle is strongly committed to.

1093^{b}21-6: This is like a footnote. Even if numbers *were* causes in some ways, they would not be Form numbers, since numbers in ratios, etc. have to be repeatable, and each Form number is unique of its kind because made up of units non-combinable with units in any other number. So even if we did accept these arguments for numbers as causes, they would not lead us to accept Forms. Aristotle has stated his objection rather oddly: how could two Form numbers be 'equal' in the first place? Perhaps he means that for Plato 7 + 5 could not be equal to 12, because the units would be different. At any rate the only point he needs to make here is that Form numbers cannot be meant because they are each unique of their kind.

1093^{b}26-9: It is clear that this is meant to be a conclusion not just to this section, or to *N*, but to *M-N* as a whole.

SELECT BIBLIOGRAPHY

1. W.D. Ross's edition of the *Metaphysics* (Oxford 1953, corrected edition) is invaluable even to those without Greek for its analyses of Aristotle's argument. The whole of the *Metaphysics* is translated by Ross as vol. VIII of *The Works of Aristotle translated in English*, ed. Ross (Oxford, 1928, 2nd ed.).

2. Modern books and articles relevant to *M-N*.

Allen, R.E. 'The Generation of numbers in Plato's Parmenides', *Classical Philology* 1970.

Becker, O. (1) 'Die diairetische Erzeugung der platonischen Idealzahlen', *Quellen und Studien der Mathematik, Astronomie und Physik*, 1931.
(2) 'Versuch einer neuen Interpretation der platonischen Ideenzahlen', *Archiv für Geschichte der Philosophie* 1963.

Benacerraf, P. 'What numbers could not be', *Philosophical Review* 1965.

Benacerraf & Putnam (eds.) *Philosophy of Mathematics*, Oxford 1964.

Berti, E. *La filosofia del primo Aristotele*, Padua 1962.

Brunschwig, J. 'Ethique à Eudème 1.8 1218a15-32 et le περὶ τἀγαθοῦ' *Untersuchungen zur Eudemischen Ethik*, Berlin 1971.

Burkert, W. *Lore and Science in Ancient Pythagoreanism*, trans. Minar, Cambridge, Mass. 1972.

Cherniss, H. (1) *Aristotle's Criticism of Plato and the Academy*, Baltimore 1944.
(2) *The Riddle of the Early Academy*, Berkely 1945.
(3) Review of Saffrey, q.v.
(4) 'Plato as a mathematician', *Review of Metaphysics* 1950-1.

Cook Wilson, J. 'On the Platonist doctrine of the ἀσύμβλητοι ἀριθμοί', *Classical Review* 1904.

Crombie, I. *An Examination of Plato's Doctrines* (2 vols.), London 1962.

Ellis, B. *Basic Concepts of Measurement*, Cambridge 1968.

Findlay, J. *Plato: the Written and Unwritten Doctrines*, London 1974.

Frege, G. (1) *The Foundations of Arithmetic*, trans. J.L. Austin, Oxford 1959.
(2) *Philosophical Writings*, ed. Geach and Black, Oxford 1966.
(3) *On the Foundations of Geometry and Formal Theories of Arithmetic*, trans. E.-H. Kluge, Yale 1971.

Gadamer & Schadewaldt (eds.) *Idee und Zahl*, Heidelberg 1968.

Gaiser, K. (1) *Platons ungeschriebene Lehre*, Stuttgart 1962.
(2) 'Quellenkritische Probleme der indirekten Platonüberlieferung', in Gadamer & Schadewaldt.

Heath, T. (1) *Greek Mathematics*, vol. i, Oxford 1921.
(2) *Mathematics in Aristotle*, Oxford 1949.

Heinze, R. *Xenokrates*, Leipzig 1892.

Hintikka, J. *Time and Necessity*, Oxford 1973.

Ilting, K.-H. (1) Review of Gaiser (1), *Gnomon* 1965.

(2) 'Platons "Ungeschriebene Lehren": den Vortrag "Über das Gute"', *Phronesis* 1968.

von Ivánka, E. 'Die Polemik gegen Platon im Aufbau der aristotelischen Metaphysik', *Scholastik* 1934.

Jaeger, W. (1) *Studien zur Entstehungsgeschichte der Metaphysik des Aristoteles*, Berlin 1912.

(2) *Aristotle*, trans. R. Robinson, Oxford 1934.

(3) *Scripta Minora* II, Rome 1960.

Jevons, W.S. *The Principles of Science*, London 1913.

Kahn, C. *The Verb Be in Ancient Greek*, Dordrecht 1973.

Klein, J. *Greek Mathematical Thought and the Origin of Algebra*, trans. E. Brann, Cambridge, Mass. 1968.

Krämer, H.-J. (1) *Arete*, Heidelberg 1959.

(2) 'Retraktationen zum Problem des esoterischen Platon', *Museum Helveticum* 1964.

(3) 'Die grundsätzlichen Fragen der indirekten Platonüberlieferung' in Gadamer and Schadewaldt.

Lang, P. *De Speusippi Academici scriptis*, Bonn 1911.

Lasserre, F. *The Birth of Mathematics in the Age of Plato*, trans. Mortimer, ed. Toulmin, London 1964.

Martin, G. 'Platons Lehre von der Zahl und ihre Darstellung durch Aristoteles', *Zeitschrift für philosophische Forschung*, 1953.

Maziarz & Greenwood, *Greek Mathematical Philosophy*, New York 1968.

Merlan, P. (1) *From Platonism to Neoplatonism*, The Hague 1960.

(2) 'Aristotle, *Met*. A 6, 987b20-25, and Plotinus, *Enneads* V,4.2.8-9', *Phronesis* 1964.

(3) 'War Aristoteles je Anhänger der Ideenlehre? Jaegers letztes Wort', *Archiv für Geschichte der Philosophie* 1970.

Milhaud, G. (1) *Les Philosophes-géomètres de la Grèce*, Paris 1900.

(2) 'Aristote et les mathématiques', *Archiv für Geschichte der Philosophie* 1903.

Mueller, I. 'Aristotle on geometrical objects', *Archiv für Geschichte der Philosophie* 1970.

Owen, G.E.L. (1) 'The Platonism of Aristotle', in Strawson (ed.), *Studies in the Philosophy of Thought and Action*, Oxford 1968.

(2) 'Dialectic and Eristic in the treatment of the Forms', in Owen (ed.), *Aristotle on Dialectic*, Oxford 1970.

Philip, J. 'The "Pythagorean" theory of the derivation of magnitudes', *Phoenix* 1966.

Quine, W.V.O. (1) *From a Logical Point of View*, Harvard 1953.

(2) *Ontological Relativity*, New York 1969.

Robin, L. *La Théorie platonicienne des idées et des nombres d'après Aristote'* Paris 1908.

Ross, W.D. *Plato's Theory of Ideas*, Oxford 1951.

Russell, B. *Introduction to Mathematical Philosophy*, London 1948 (2nd ed.).

Saffrey, H.D. *Le περὶ φιλοσοφίας d'Aristote et la théorie platonicienne des idées nombres*, Leiden 1971 (2nd ed.), (containing review by Cherniss in *Gnomon* 1959).

Schofield, M. 'The dissection of unity in Plato's *Parmenides*', *Classical Philology* 1972.

Sorabji, R. 'Aristotle, Mathematics and Colour', *Classical Quarterly* 1972.

Stenzel, J. *Zahl und Gestalt*, Darmstadt 1959 (3rd ed.).

de Strycker, E. 'Trois points obscurs de terminologie mathématique chez Platon', *Revue des Études Grecques* 1950.

Taylor, A.E. 'Forms and Numbers', *Mind* 1926-7, and in *Philosophical Studies*, London 1934.

Töplitz, O. 'Das Verhältnis von Mathematik und Ideenlehre bei Platon', *Quellen und Studien zur Geschichte der Mathematik, Astronomie und Physik*, 1929.

de Vogel, C. *Philosophia*, vol. i, Assen 1969.

Wedberg, A. *Plato's Philosophy of Mathematics*, Stockholm 1955.

Whitehead, A.N. 'Mathematics and the Good', in *The Philosophy of A.N. Whitehead*, ed. P. Schilpp, Evanston 1941.

Wilpert, P. (1) 'Neue Fragmente aus περὶ τἀγαθοῦ', *Hermes* 1941.

(2) 'Platons Altersvorlesung über das Gute', *Philosophisches Jahrbuch* 1949.

(3) *Zwei aristotelische Frühschriften über die Ideenlehre*, Regensberg 1949.

Wippern, J. (ed.) *Das Problem der ungeschriebenen Lehre Platons*, Darmstadt 1972.

Addendum

A. Graeser (Ed./Hrsg.): *Mathematics and Metaphysics in Aristotle/Mathematik und Metaphysik bei Aristoteles*. Akten des X. Symposium Aristotelicum. Bern 1987. Berner Reihe philosophischer Studien 6.

GLOSSARY

ἀδιαίρετος indivisible
ἀδιάφορος undifferentiated
αἰτία cause (see p. 89-90)
ἄνισος unequal
ἀριθμός number (i.e. integer, see p. 9-11, 39-40)
ἄρτιος even
ἀρχή principle
ἀσυμβλητός uncombinable (see p. 17-19, 165-7)
ἀφαίρεσις abstraction

βάθος depth

γένεσις coming into being
γραμμή line

δεκάς dekad (i.e. the numbers 1-10)
διαίρετος divisible
διαφορά differentia
διάφορος differentiated
δυάς two; ἡ ἀόριστος δυάς, the indefinite two.
δύναμις potentiality

εἶδος form; (Platonic) Form.
ἕν one
ἐναντίον contrary
ἐνέργεια actuality
ἐπίπεδον plane
ἐπιστήμη knowledge, branch of knowledge

θέσις position

ἰδέα (Platonic) Form
ἴσος equal

καθ'αὑτό independent
καθόλου universal

λόγος argument, account

μαθηματικά mathematical objects
μέγεθος magnitude
μέτρον measure
μῆκος length
μοναδικὸς ἀριθμός number made up of abstract units (see p. 15)
μονάς unit

οὐσία real object, reality (see p. 89)

περιττός odd
πλάτος breadth
πλῆθος plurality
ποιόν quality
ποσόν quantity
πρός τι relative
πρότερον prior, before

στερεόν solid
στιγμή point
στοιχεῖον element
συμβλητός combinable (see p. 17-19, 165-7)

τόπος place

ὕλη matter
ὕστερον subsequent, after

φύσις entity (see p. 90)

χωριστός separate

223

INDEXES

I. Persons

Alexander of Aphrodisias 45, 46, 47,
  51, 52, 57, 58, 59, 60, 63, 72,
  154, 156
Allen, R.E. 48, 50
Anaxagoras 99, 125, 214
Aristoxenus 214
Asclepius 64

Becker, O. 53
Benacerraf, P. 8
Berkeley 34
Bernays, P. 3
Berti, E. 53
Bonitz, H. 80, 88, 171
Bröcker, W. 62
Brouwer, L. 43
Brunschwig, J. 152
Burkert, W. 44

Cherniss, H. 2, 10, 18, 21, 60, 68, 69,
  76, 83, 136, 152, 156, 160, 210,
  212, 214
Christ, W. 64

Democritus 97, 154
Düring, I. 88, 136

Ellis, B. 8, 14, 41
Empedocles 125, 154, 214, 218
Euclid 21, 23, 34, 47, 51, 53
Eudemus 181, 201
Eudoxus 21, 99, 138, 160
Eurytus 128, 218

Findlay, J. 2, 57
Frege, G. 1, 2, 5, 9, 10, 12, 13, 18,
  28, 31, 32, 37, 38, 41, 42, 77,
  140, 167, 173

Gaiser, K. 2, 10, 21, 40, 53, 60, 64,
  181, 210, 211, 214,
Gödel, K. 14, 209

Heath, T. 8, 47, 51, 53
Hermodorus 57, 201
Hesiod 213
Hippocrates 21
Homer 213

Iamblichus 47
Ilting, K.-H. 10, 53, 62, 214
von Ivánka, E. 88, 152

Jaeger, W. 64, 66, 75, 81-8, 142, 152,
  155, 156, 164, 187, 188, 191, 192,
  212
Jevons, W. 167

Kahn, C. 84
Kirk and Raven 213
Klein, J. 5, 6
Klibansky, R. 74
Krämer, H.-J. 2, 62, 65, 214

Labowsky, L. 74
Lasserre, F. 4
Leon 21

Melissus 86
Menaechmus 21
Merlan, P. 44, 64, 77, 155
Milhaud, G. 10
Mueller, I. 30, 34

Nehamas, A. 12
Nicomachus 47
Neoplatonists 6, 45, 51

Olympiodorus 51
Owen, G.E.L. 12, 156

Parmenides 119, 201, 202
Pascal, B. 179
Pherecydes 125, 213

INDEX

II. Subjects
(Figures in bold type refer to the translation)

INDEX